MW00786093

Harry Johnson (1923-1977)

Pioneers in Economics

Series Editor: Mark Blaug

Professor Emeritus, University of London
Consultant Professor, University of Buckingham
Visiting Professor, University of Exeter

This important series presents critical appraisals of influential economists from the 17th century to the present day. It focuses in particular on those economists who were influential in their own time and whose work has had an impact – often inadequately recognized – on the evolution and development of economic thought. The series will be indispensable for a clear understanding of the origin and development of economic ideas and the role played by the leading protagonists of the past.

A full list of published titles in this series is printed at the end of this volume.

Harry Johnson
(1923–1977)

Edited by

Mark Blaug

Professor Emeritus,
University of London

An Elgar Reference Collection

Published by
Edward Elgar Publishing Limited
Gower House
Croft Road
Aldershot
Hants GU11 3HR
England

Edward Elgar Publishing Company
Old Post Road
Brookfield
Vermont 05036
USA

A CIP catalogue record for this book is available from the British Library

A CIP catalogue record for this book is available from the US Library of Congress

ISBN 1 85278 506 3

Contents

Acknowledgements

The editor and publishers wish to thank the following who have kindly given permission for the use of copyright material.

Canadian Journal of Economics for articles: Thomas J. Courchere (1978), 'Harry G. Johnson: Macroeconomist', *Canadian Journal of Economics*, **XI** (4), Supplement, S11–S33; Richard G. Lipsey (1978), 'Harry Johnson's Contributions to the Pure Theory of International Trade', *Canadian Journal of Economics*, **XI** (4), Supplement, S34–S54; John F. Helliwell (1978), 'The Balance of Payments: A Survey of Harry Johnson's Contributions', *Canadian Journal of Economics*, **XI** (4), Supplement, S55–S86.

Elsevier Science Publishers B.V. for article: Jagdish N. Bhagwati (1977), 'Harry G. Johnson', *Journal of International Economics*, **7** (3), 221–9.

University of Chicago Press for articles: W.M. Corden (1984), 'Harry Johnson's Contributions to International Trade Theory', *Journal of Political Economy*, **92** (4), 567–91; David Laidler (1984), 'Harry Johnson as a Macroeconomist', *Journal of Political Economy*, **92** (4), 592–615; Arnold C. Harberger and David Wall (1984), 'Harry G. Johnson as a Development Economist', *Journal of Political Economy*, **92** (4), 616–41; Richard E. Caves (1984), 'Harry Johnson as a Social Scientist', *Journal of Political Economy*, **92** (4), 642–58.

Every effort has been made to trace all the copyright holders but if any have been inadvertently overlooked the publishers will be pleased to make the necessary arrangement at the first opportunity.

In addition the publishers wish to thank the library of the London School of Economics and Political Science and The Alfred Marshall Library, Cambridge University for their assistance in obtaining these articles.

Introduction

Harry Johnson was notorious in his lifetime as a living machine for producing economic literature: during a relatively short career of 27 years, he produced over 500 academic papers, 150 book reviews, 35 books and pamphlets, and hundreds of newspaper articles, many of which were written on trains and aeroplanes; so prodigious was his output that articles by him continued to appear years after his death, conveying the uncanny impression that he was still hard at it in Heaven. Moreover, almost nothing he wrote was tossed off. On the contrary, the average quality of his output was astonishingly high, synthesizing apparently unrelated contributions by others and restating previous results with a verve that made them stand out like new. But writing was only one of his many activities. He travelled ceaselessly to conferences around the world and lectured at universities up and down Europe, America, Africa and Asia. His frantic energy was fuelled by wood-carving and alcohol, producing the one while listening and consuming the other while writing.

One of his earliest contributions was a savage review of James Meade's *Theory of International Economic Policy* (1951), and international economics remained throughout his life the subject on which he was a recognized expert. But *International Trade and Economic Growth: Studies in Pure Theory* (Harvard University Press, 1958), *Money, Trade and Economic Growth: Survey Lectures in Economic Theory* (Allen & Unwin, Harvard University Press, 1962), and *Aspects of the Theory of Tariffs* (Allen & Unwin, Harvard University Press, 1971) were complemented by his work in monetary economics, as evidenced by *Essays in Monetary Economics* (Allen & Unwin, 1967), *Further Essays in Monetary Economics* (Harvard University Press, 1972), *Inflation and the Monetarist Controversy* (North-Holland, 1972), *Macroeconomics and Monetary Theory* (Gray-Mills, Aldine, 1972), and *The Theory of Income Distribution* (Gray-Mills, 1973). But he also wrote a brilliant book on *Economic Policies Toward Less Developed Countries* (Brookings Institution, Allen & Unwin, 1967) and his many sparkling essays on such wide-ranging questions as advertising, brain drain, scientific research, the Keynesian Revolution, student protest, nationalism, human capital theory, minimum wage legislation, and incomes policies are brought together in *The Canadian Quandary* (McGraw-Hill, 1973; Carleton Library, 1977), *On Economics and Society* (University of Chicago Press, 1975) and *The Shadow of Keynes* (University of Chicago Press, Basil Blackwell, 1978), written jointly with his wife, Elizabeth S. Johnson.

Johnson was born in Toronto, Canada in 1923 and graduated from the University of Toronto at the age of 20 in 1943. He began his academic career straightaway as an Acting Professor of Economics at St Francis Xavier University in Nova Scotia. After military service in the Canadian infantry, he crossed the Atlantic to take another BA at the University of Cambridge in 1946. He became an instructor at the University of Toronto in the same year, earned an MA in 1947, and then topped it by an MA at Harvard University in 1948. Returning to England, he became a Fellow at King's College, Cambridge where he taught until 1956, moving in that year to the University of Manchester as Professor of Economics. Collecting together his by now formidable list of published papers into a book, *International Trade and*

Economic Growth, he gained a doctorate with it from Harvard University in 1958. The following year he joined the University of Chicago as Professor of Economics, a post which he combined with a commuting professorship at the London School of Economics during the years 1966–74 and the Graduate Institute for International Studies in Geneva, Switzerland during the yars 1976–7. He was made a Distinguished Fellow of the American Economic Association in 1977, received honorary degrees from seven British and Canadian universities, and served as President-Elect of the Eastern Economic Association in 1975–6 and Vice-President of the American Economic Association in 1976. He was editor or co-editor of a large number of journals: *Review of Economic Studies*, *The Manchester School*, *Economica*, the *Journal of Political Economy* and the *Journal of International Economics*. He died in Geneva in 1977 at the age of 53.

His writings are characterized by the use of geometric rather than algebraic illustrations and proofs, the rigorous application of a general equilibrium framework to the analysis of economic problems, a zeal for exploring the policy implications of analytical concepts, and a general suspicion of vulgar Keynesianism, interventionism, and collectivism in all its varieties. While contributing to positive international economics, his passionate concern to provide policy-relevant economics drove him towards applied welfare economics, and most of his best work on optimum tariffs in the face of retaliation, culminating in the concept of the so-called 'scientific tariff', emphasized the welfare gains and losses of 'second-best' departures from free trade. In monetary economics, he was largely responsible for the introduction of money into the barter models of early growth theorists. In his later years he bent all his efforts towards the development of 'the monetary approach to the balance of payments', the view that balance-of-payments policies must always be accompanied by domestic credit policies designed to influence the demand for money, editing (with J.A. Frenkel) two sets of papers embodying the latest research in the field: *The Monetary Approach to the Balance of Payment* (Allen & Unwin, University of Toronto Press, 1976) and *The Economics of Exchange Rates* (Addison-Wesley, 1978). He always held a curiously ambivalent attitude to 'monetarism': in one of his most famous papers, 'The Keynesian Revolution and the Monetarist Counter-Revolution' (*American Economic Review*, May 1971), he ridiculed the scientific pretensions of monetarism and predicted its imminent decline, and yet in the field of international economic relations he was a major advocate of the view that 'money matters'.

Note

Several paragraphs in this Introduction were borrowed from my *Great Economists Since Keynes* (Wheatsheaf Books, 1985).

[1]

Journal of International Economics 7 (1977) 221–229. © North-Holland Publishing Company

HARRY G. JOHNSON

Jagdish N. BHAGWATI*

Massachusetts Institute of Technology.

Harry Johnson passed away, at the age of 53, in Geneva, Switzerland, on 9th May 1977. He had been in indifferent health since February, having suffered from a second stroke, but had seemed to be recovering with his usual tenacity so that the final coma and death came as a great shock to his many friends.

Harry Johnson's premature death merits special attention in the *Journal of International Economics*, not merely because of his lasting impact on international economics, but also because he was co-founder of the journal. When Bart van Tongeren of North-Holland, at the instance of Jan Tinbergen and Robert Solow, approached me in 1969 with the idea of starting a journal exclusively addressed to international economics, this was the very first 'specialized' economic journal that North-Holland was initiating, though there were to be many successful Schumpeterian imitators later from both North-Holland and the Academic Press. I was therefore extremely cautious and contacted Harry Johnson for cooperation. Unless he was willing to join as co-editor, along with John Chipman, I would not be willing to launch this enterprise. Harry Johnson was most enthusiastic and urged me to go ahead, offering his support as co-editor but requesting that, in view of his many other editorial responsibilities, he should be used minimally. During the formative years of the *JIE*, Johnson nonetheless provided invaluable advice on all sorts of editorial matters, including the organization of special symposia, writing invited papers and even pitching in promptly with technical reports on manuscripts that I ventured to send to him despite his *caveats* in 1969. When, finally, in 1976, the phenomenal success of the *JIE* had led to such a serious overload for the editors that it had become critical for us to have co-editors with substantial refereeing obligations, Chipman and I were loath to have Harry Johnson leave altogether and were delighted that he agreed to stay on at least as an associate editor and to continue offering to the *JIE* his support.

---

*This is a personal reminiscence, in honour of Harry Johnson. The Editors of the *JIE* are planning a special Symposium issue at a future date, as a posthumous *Festschrift*.

I first met Harry, as he was known to all, when I went to Cambridge for the Economics Tripos in 1954. Cambridge then was coming to the end of a long period of glory, the thread running from Marshall through Pigou and Keynes. Pigou was in fact still alive and could occasionally be seen if you strolled through the main court of King's College at the right time; and Lal Jayawardene from Ceylon, Harry's student and now a leading light in the deliberations of the Group of 77, had even the strange fortune of having Pigou watch over him as he took his Tripos examination in the sick room at King's! The superstars who epitomised Cambridge then and even now, especially Nicky Kaldor and Joan Robinson, were still in their full prime. Kaldor would soon be lecturing to us on his celebrated *Alternative Theories of Distribution* while Mrs. Robinson, eagerly taking on all of the bright pupils who wished special tutorials from her, would presently be plotting our conversion to her revolutionary notions on capital theory by immersing us summarily, and often with the bewilderment that spread to her readers at large, in the page proofs of her *Accumulation of Capital*. Piero Sraffa was carefully hidden through my two years and little did we know that he would be surfacing after three decades' labour with his second pearl of wisdom. [Many years later, I heard Kalecki being credited with the witticism that the only two perfect gentlemen that he had encountered in England had been Piero Sraffa, an Italian, and Maurice Dobb, a card-carrying communist. If Kalecki had been an English gentleman and had therefore the celebrated wit that goes with it, he would have probably added a third to his list: Joan Robinson!] Richard Kahn was almost equally invisible, though we caught a glimpse of him at lectures late in 1955–56: fastidious, weighing each word carefully as he slowly worked his way through the theory of interest rates, clearly an intellectual force but also suggesting a certain impatience, inherited from the wild successes of the Keynesian era, with the obtuseness of those who would not see the light. And we still had Sir Dennis Robertson, a real dividend; scarred from the battles with the Keynesians, he remained a charming, soft-spoken, distinguished figure whose lectures on *Principles* to the Tripos students were a model blend of humour, wit, irony and insights.

It would have required great gifts to capture the Cambridge undergraduate's arrogant imagination against this competition; and Harry seemed to the best and the brightest to have these in ample measure.

Harry was very much in his prime then: many of his classic papers on trade theory had already been written and had established him as a trade theorist of considerable accomplishment and importance. His *Optimum Tariffs and Retaliation* piece had qualified Tibor Scitovsky's earlier classic on the possibility of gaining with an optimum tariff despite Cournot-type retaliation. The superb *Transfer Problem and Exchange Stability* paper had brilliantly synthesised and extended the classical and Keynesian analyses of the two problems and revealed the essential link between them. And his pioneering papers on trade and growth, especially those published eventually in the *Manchester School*, were to transform the ideas of Balogh and John Williams, and Hicks' theoretical thoughts thereon in his *Inaugural* as the Drummond Professor of Political Economy at All Souls, into extremely influential theoretical constructs that would stimulate the leading trade theorists of his students' generation.

A lucky few had Harry as their College Tutor at King's. But none of us really needed to be Harry's tutees to profit from his immense presence. His lectures on the theory of international trade attracted a large audience of undergraduates, graduate students and visiting scholars – I remember being introduced, after a class, to Lorie Tarshis. Harry spoke rapidly from a text and handed out sheets of mathematical derivations and diagrams mimeographed in two tones of red and blue on a machine reputedly at the Department of Applied Economics. In virtually eight, tightly-crammed lectures, we were treated to a remarkably succinct review of the principal dimensions of trade theory. It was fascinating, and in fact seduced me into trade theory permanently, but it left us all somewhat breathless. I recall venturing up to Harry, just after he had finished stating extremely tersely the algebra on the Metzler paradox, and seeking illumination: he was kind but it did not help much. It will amuse those who knew the later Harry, who insisted on avoiding tedious mathematics and at times carried this aversion to excess, that when I ran to my own tutor, a perfectly English Cambridge don, as my lender of last resort, he took one long look at Harry's handout of tightly-packed mathematics and sighed: 'Johnson is a *glutton* for algebra, isn't he?'

We took most, however, to Harry's warmth and generosity of spirit. He read carefully, and often improved, our efforts. My piece on immiserizing growth was written, with Harry's aid and encouragement, after I took the basic ideas to him at the end of one of his lectures; and when the *Quarterly Journal of Economics* turned it down, he encouraged me to submit it to the *Review of Economic Studies* and probably helped to get it published. The theory class that he ran for the Tripos students was again a model of enlightened encouragement: Harry would reword, rephrase and make sense out of our ill-formulated remarks.

But his generosity was most evident at the Political Economy Club over which Sir Dennis Robertson presided and which was modelled after Keynes' earlier version of that Club. Here, the undergraduates who had secured Firsts and Upper Seconds in the examinations would be invited to Sir Dennis' rooms in Trinity for periodic meetings after supper. A brief paper would be read, usually by an undergraduate, and the meeting would break for tea while, in the winter sessions, Sir Dennis stoked the fire and circulated. The crunch came when lots had to be drawn and those who drew a number (up to six) had to speak their hasty thoughts when we had reassembled. It was a marvellous education, once you got over the terrors of drawing a number and performing as best you could. I recall seeing Harry often at these meetings, seeking us out for conversation during the break and generally being genial and charming. But his presence itself, we came to notice, was an act of kindness. Cambridge then was dominated by the Keynesians, who had still not forgiven Sir Dennis for his recalcitrance: one could feel the bitterness with which he was still regarded by the victors of the battles among Pigou, Robertson, and Keynes. Interestingly, in the year that I was a member of the Political Economy Club, I hardly ever saw Kaldor or Kahn or Joan Robinson, to name the most eminent, there. Harry, himself a Keynesian, deliberately exposed himself to the risk of their wrath by coming to the Political Economy Club sessions, thus lessening the intellectual and psychological isolation of Sir Dennis in his later years. This fundamental sense of decency was the essential core of Harry's personality; and it is remarkable that he was willing to stake a great deal for it.

When he left for Manchester in 1956 to take their Chair in economic theory, his reputation in international trade was unassailable. During the three years that he spent there, Harry primarily wrote, and published in the *Manchester School*, the two well-known papers on Income Distribution, both masterpieces of geometrical theorising: the demand and supply sides in the standard 2×2 model of trade theory were elegantly tied together for all future trade theorists. For some reason, these were somewhat quiet years by Harry's creative standards; and I recall, during a trip to Manchester to talk to him about my own work on the Stolper–Samuelson theorem (later published in the *Economic Journal*), Harry's being full of sparkle and enthusiasm as he had just conceived the essence of his two income-distribution papers while reading my paper. With his customary generosity, he would go on to make a gracious reference to that effect in his published papers as well: a show of hand that would help along a student! We were then also to collaborate on a long paper on historical controversies in the theory of international trade (in the 1960 *Economic Journal*) and our last joint effort was to be on the theory of tariffs (in the 1961 *Oxford Economic Papers*), this latter paper having been written mostly when I spent a term with him in Chicago (to which he had moved in 1960) and then finished when he took me with him to Queen's University at Kingston in Canada for the following summer.

Harry's transition to Chicago was to be marred by our joint paper in the 1960 *Economic Journal*. In the last section of the paper, which was almost wholly Harry's contribution, there was a rather strong footnote of the kind that Harry was so good at: it suggested that the enthusiasm for flexible exchange rates had led Egon Sohmen (whose death the *JIE* notes also in this issue) to miss a substantive point against flexible exchange rates; unfortunately for us, we had used the word 'propaganda' where we meant 'advocacy'. Sohmen, according to Roy Harrod, wished to reply; but what astonished Harry and me was that, at Chicago, Milton Friedman was up in arms. Oddly, Friedman considered the footnote to be an unprofessional piece of writing and also to constitute unwarranted bullying by Harry of a lesser economist. Unfortunately, he would not keep these notions to himself and to Harry. This style of skirmishing was entirely novel to both of us and left Harry acutely embarassed and uncomfortable;

quite conceivably, it may have added some vigour to Harry's early anti-monetarist writings at Chicaco. As it happened, Harry, who chose to stay on at Chicago, managed to survive the unpleasant situation all right. For ultimately, Harry had the intellectual strength and stamina to handle himself in such scraps; moreover, he always tried to impose on himself the admirable self-restraint and discipline to argue at a scientific rather than a debating level. Thus when Friedman proceeded to write a short comment, Harry drafted a reply: the point at issue being whether a finite equilibrium would *necessarily* exist if there was an unstable equilibrium (a point of issue in the debate, as then couched, on fixed *versus* flexible rates). We argued that we would be perfectly happy to assert the existence of a stable equilibrium if the analyst made it clear that the proposition included infinite (zero) exchange rates. Friedman presumably did not send his note to Harrod, and the exchange was not published; we took it to mean that Friedman had accepted our contention, and, to our satisfaction, John Chipman, in his later magisterial *Econometrica* survey carefully reviewed the controversy between Sohmen and us, to come out on our side.

But it was clear to me, and to Harry, that if Friedman had been right scientifically, we would have readily changed our minds. And here paradoxically may be the secret of what happened to Harry's views as he stayed on at Chicago for the rest of his magnificent career. If you are pragmatic and argue with an ideologue as bright as yourself, you will win some and lose some. Every time you lose, you will change your views because you are pragmatic. But every time the ideologue loses, he is shielded from perceiving this and will hold on to his assertions. Over time, therefore, you will move closer to the ideologue. Harry, the pragmatic scientist, who appeared to us to be mildly centrist during his years at Cambridge, moved increasingly closer therefore to a Friedmanesque world-view: this was inevitable.

Chicago, in fact, was very Friedmanesque at the time. The seminars seemed to oscillate between proving that elasticities were large with markets therefore stable, and formulating competitive hypotheses for apparently imperfectly-competitive industries and coming up with high enough R^2s. Econometrics was the handmaiden of ideology: things looked imperfect to the naked eye, especially to that of Chamberlin and Joan Robinson, but they were 'really' not so and the world was 'as if' competitive. At the same time, rather strangely, Chicago seemed to loathe mathematical economics which, everywhere else, went hand in hand with econometrics and theory. Again ideology explained this paradox: most mathematical economics seemed to undermine the case for *laissez faire* by producing esoteric constraints on existence and stability of competitive equilibrium and by facilitating the construction of the influential economic case for intervention – so it was reprehensible. Harry, in fact, had emigrated from a Cambridge which focused on the theoretical failures of the market mechanism and its apparent imperfections to the Chicago where the market imperfections were 'demonstrated' to be negligible and the imperfections rather of governmental intervention were the subject of active research. A breath of this different air would have done any English-trained economist a great deal of good; but Harry was to inhale it for nearly fifteen years. Harry's later writings on the developing countries, his impatience with UNCTAD (which he treated with undisguised and undeserved contempt), and his *Encounter* piece on Peter Bauer and his critics were the most overt indications of his shift in the political spectrum. However, Harry, who was scintillatingly successful in uncovering the political biases and value judgments in other economists' writings, especially when they were on his left, seemed strangely unaware of his own. I recall a recent letter of his to me, apropos of a piece of mine on multinationals, where he chided me for my (declared) value judgments and contrasted them with his own 'scientific' writings, and my replying to him that when we were in Cambridge we both tended to be perhaps model examples of Lionel Robbins' ideal of the 'neutral' economist but that, in the years since, the ideological company that we had kept had undoubtedly affected us both, albeit in different directions.

The other remarkable thing that was to happen to Harry on his shift to Chicago, and unrelated to it doubtless, was the extraordinary explosion of his creative and writing energies. Articles and books, edited and written, would flow from his ever-scribbling pen for the rest of his life at an accelerating pace, until he averaged at the end something like three books a year and, at the time of his death, had eighteen articles in proof! Alan Prest notes, in the *Economist*, how Harry was reputed to have finished two articles on one transatlantic flight; I myself saw him start and complete one (an algebraic note, with a Literary Appendix, on commodity schemes) on a flight back from Geneva where we had been attending an UNCTAD Expert Group session several years ago. Harry often wrote on the same topic for different journals and audiences, much like Keynes, and his papers turned up in exotic journals.

Tradition has it that an American journalist, characteristically hooked on numbers, had gone around Chicago asking the economists how many papers they had published; that, on coming to Stigler, and finding that he had only 70 to his credit, he exclaimed: 'How come? There is a much younger professor, just across the corridor, who has published 365!', to which Stigler replied: 'Ah, but mine are all different.' Funny as this story is, it misses the essence of Harry's approach to publishing. Harry rarely, if ever, published in different places without adding new insights, however small. His mind was ceaselessly active, turning things around endlessly: there was always a new wrinkle. This also reflected the seriousness with which he undertook any professional responsibilities: he was not the one to placate a request for a contribution with a xeroxed version of what he had already written. The same, fundamental sense of professional obligation underlay his willingness to write for obscure journals in the professionally peripheral areas of the world. And, paradoxically, the enormous output of papers and books was to be explained in the same way:

Harry thought it a professional obligation to publish rather than to communicate orally to the select few. Long ago, before his creative explosion, Harry explained to me that the Oxbridge tradition of communicating only to one another at High Table was elitist and wrong: that, if one had ideas, it was a professional obligation to put them down in print where the underprivileged, who were not born so well as to get to Oxbridge, would also have access. Few realised the democratic and scholarly instincts that moved Harry to his unique publishing performance.

Harry's range of contributions was equally remarkable. Within the theory of international trade, he straddled both the pure theory and international monetary economics with equal distinction. He made numerous original contributions, in which one must include the papers that he reprinted in his first major book, *International Trade and Economic Growth*, often picking up small ideas and turning them into big constructs. In fact, there was practically no important turn that international economics took in the last two decades where Harry was not in practically at the start. He had a fantastic sense of the novel and the important and rarely missed a good scent. And when he did, as with Linder and Hymer, he zeroed in very quickly afterwards with insightful extensions of his own. Thus, his classic papers on the transfer problem, on tariffs and retaliation, on the effects of tariffs on the terms of trade, on measuring the cost of protection, on customs union theory, on trade and growth, on domestic distortions and optimal policy intervention, on immiserizing growth, on smuggling and illegal trade theory, and on effective protection are on all our reading lists; one is practically embarrassed at the amount of Johnsonia to which one must treat the serious student of trade theory.

In the international monetary field, his classic paper, *Towards a General Theory of the Balance of Payments*, was a model of creative and insightful treatment of the monetary impact of payments deficits, anticipating the later focus on it by a whole generation of his and Mundell's students; he also introduced there the distinction between stock and flow deficits and between expenditure-switching and expenditure-reducing policies. And, more than in pure theory, his powers of creative synthesis were displayed to tremendous advantage in this field. In an area overcrowded with academic entrepreneurs organising conferences on the 'latest' issues in international monetary policies, Harry was to come into his own: jetsetting from one conference to another, reviewing and tying together all that he had learnt on this circuit, writing with clarity and rigour, helping the physically inactive to catch up with 'what was going on'.

His last scientific love was also in international monetary theory. He was very much taken up with what he called the monetary approach to balance of payments analysis, considering this (in a letter to Charles Furth of Allen & Unwin) to be the most important piece of work that he had been doing in the last few years. Recognizing the importance that the subject held in the eyes of perhaps the most influential international economist of his generation, John Chipman and I decided to invite a paper from Harry, addressing the issue of how the monetary approach led one to analyse important *policy* problems differently from the earlier absorption and elasticity approaches; and also to invite a major *theoretical* review article of the Frenkel–Johnson book that drew together the principal monetary contributions. The resulting papers of Harry and Frank Hahn appear, by a strange irony of fate, in this very *JIE* issue. But perhaps it is quite appropriate that these contributions on Harry's latest work should appear with this reminiscence: Harry, the professional scientist, could have himself thought of no more fitting tribute to the lasting importance of his work.

The most striking aspect of Harry's later years, however, was his remarkably successful emergence as an insightful and stimulating 'thinker', in the vein of John Williams. His Wicksell Lectures are a superb example of this transition: they are not theory in the usual, technical sense, but they are skilfully written and cry out for new ways of thinking about comparative advantage. At the Nobel Institute's Symposium on the Allocation of Economic Activity in Stockholm in June 1976, I saw Harry divesting himself on the role of technology in international trade, not as the distinguished author of the trade-theoretic papers of his youth, but in the grand manner of an intellectual, reflecting on the transition from the nomadic society to the present interdependent world where people earned income in one country, spent it in another, and retired in a third, and on what that could imply for the study of the allocation of economic activity. Harry could think big *and* well; it was not what you would have expected from an economist of his immense technical accomplishments.

In fact, it was this streak of originality and freshness that attracted many of us to him, and not merely his technical mastery. He combined it with a command of style that enabled him to write with distinction in intellectual magazines such as *Encounter* and the London *Spectator*. The blend of historical insights, political and sociological sense, total grasp of the economics of an issue, and his writing skills also made him the favourite choice of the organisers of nearly all the distinguished Lecture series in Economics: he gave, among several others, the Wicksell Lectures, the de Vries Lectures and the Stamp Lecture.

Harry's enormous interaction with the young international economists since the mid-1950s must also be recorded if one is to assess fully his unique impact on economic science. By the pedestrian criterion, sometimes fashionable among the illiterate, of how many Ph.D. students he guided during his career, Harry was a loser: one searches with difficulty for very many terribly distinguished pupils who were Harry's students in this narrow sense. Harry himself was sometimes fooled by this apparent inadequacy. I recall his theorising, at my Boston apartment, during one of his visits when Harvard was unsuccessfully trying to seduce him, that perhaps it was his tendency to work things out himself very quickly that inhibited students from pursuing leads provided by him.

Harry need not have worried. He was, in reality, a truly exciting teacher who, by his example and encouragement, stimulated your interest and raised your sights: even his terseness and rapid pace in the classroom were not a barrier to your perception that here was a uniquely gifted economist, at the frontier of his field, giving you a rare and unified view of its essential structure. But it was everyone, everywhere, who had access to his critical and creative abilities. Countless numbers of manuscripts would reach him, from aspiring students of international economics, and somehow Harry found the energy and the time to read them carefully and to write back to the authors promptly. He continued doing this long after he had started publishing furiously and the opportunity cost of his time had risen astronomically: it was again a telling example of the responsibility that invariably animated his professional behaviour. He once remarked, with dry humour, when he was staying with us and my wife asked him what he had been doing in the early hours of the morning when we had been still asleep: 'I read two manuscripts, one indifferent and the other bad; what is worse, I could have written one good paper during that time.'

The last time that I saw Harry was at a conference in Tokyo, at the Centennial of the Nihon Keizai Shimbun, in November 1976. He was to lecture in Tokyo right after the conference, fly off to Chicago where he would change planes at the airport for Martinique for another conference and then he was to fly to yet another conference on the sociological role of conferences! The next I heard of him was from T.N. Srinivasan in India who wrote about the V.K. Ramaswami Lecture that Harry had given in New Delhi in January 1977. The second stroke cut him off, not in the infirmity of a once glorious mind, but in the midst of his vital and radiant creativity. He would not have wished to settle for anything less.

[2]

Harry Johnson: macroeconomist

THOMAS J. COURCHENE / University of Western Ontario

Abstract. The first section of the paper constitutes Harry Johnson's assessment of modern macroeconomic thought and, more important, Harry's perception of how the profession at large misinterpreted the theoretical thrust of the *General Theory* and the implications that have followed in the wake of this misunderstanding. The final part of the paper focuses briefly on his contributions to understanding the functioning of macro institutions. Sandwiched between these two is a brief analysis of those of his writings which, while they deal with macro theory or policy, are as much a commentary on, or contribution to, the process by which knowledge is generated and accumulated in our discipline.

Harry Johnson: macroéconomiste. La première section de ce mémoire résume l'évaluation qu'a donnée Harry Johnson de la pensée macroéconomique moderne et élucide le diagnostic de Johnson à savoir que les économistes professionnels ont faussement interprété la portée théorique de la *Theorie générale* et que des conséquences importantes s'en sont suivies. La dernière section met l'accent sur la contribution de Johnson à une meilleure compréhension du fonctionnement des macro-institutions. Entre ces deux sections, l'auteur propose une brève analyse des travaux de Johnson qui, à l'occasion de discussions de problèmes théoriques et politiques de macroéconomie, commentent ou explicitent les vues de Johnson sur le processus d'acquisition de la connaissance en science économique.

I happen to believe that intellectual bridges are important. The world of scholarship is too small and too fragile for scholars in different countries to ignore – or worse, deliberately reject – the opportunity to learn from one another's understanding of the legacy of the long tradition of economic scholarship and attempt to apply it to the elucidation of the laws and meaning of economic reality. (7, 106)

INTRODUCTION

As the above quotation should indicate, this evaluation of Harry Johnson as a macroeconomist will not follow the traditional pattern. There is a very good

This paper was prepared for the annual meetings of the Canadian Economics Association, London, Ontario, 28–30 June 1978. I wish to thank David Laidler for our many discussions over the last few months and my colleagues Peter Howitt, Clark Leith, and Grant Reuber for comments on an earlier draft.

Canadian Journal of Economics/Revue canadienne d'Economique, XI, Supplement November/novembre 1978. Printed in Canada/Imprimé au Canada.

S12 / Thomas J. Courchene

reason for this. My colleague David Laidler has already produced a first-rate survey of Harry's money and macro contributions (Laidler, 1978). Among the questions that Laidler addresses are: What kind of macroeconomics did Harry expound? How did it evolve over the years? How much did he take from others? Why did the evolution of his thought take the path that it did? The net result of Laidler's efforts is that the profession now has an excellent chronicle of Harry Johnson's contribution to the macro and money literature. Accordingly, I have opted for a rather different perspective within which to view Harry's contributions in the general area of macro economics. Specifically, I intend to focus on some of the motivating forces behind Harry's unceasing efforts in all aspects of economics and to draw upon his work in the macro area to elaborate on them. I hope this will provide further insight into both the position that Harry carved out for himself in the profession and the nature and form of his contributions as a macroeconomist.

The above quotation from Harry's De Vries Lectures provides a personal insight into one aspect of his motivation.[1] He was indeed a builder of 'intellectual bridges' – between economists on the frontiers of the discipline and the remainder of the profession, between economists in the major centres of learning and those located in the professionally less accessible areas of the world, between the current state of the discipline and its historical antecedents, and between the economists at large and the general public. His service as one of the profession's most prolific book reviewers (over 150 book reviews) and as the profession's editor par excellence attests to the importance he attached to intellectual intermediation, as it were.

For a more comprehensive view of both the motivation behind Harry's unceasing efforts as well as his over-all approach to the subject, it is convenient to refer to the very insightful 'Memoir' in *Encounter* written by sociologist Edward Shils (1977). Consistent with the above quotation, Shils points out (1977, 85) that Harry regarded himself as a 'continuator' and an 'improver.' More important, the accumulation and dissemination of knowledge stood uppermost with him. As Shils notes:

Harry Johnson was a 'missionary' ... The goal of the progress of economics in academic study and in suppression of pride and prejudice in economic policy laid upon him the obligation to travel to innumerable conferences and to teach in many universities ... He went to learn from the best and the youngest of his colleagues, to question them about what they had written, to correct their errors and to bring them into the procession of economists who were contributing to the progress of their subject ... He wanted economics to be a science; and in order for it to become such, it was necessary to appreciate what had already been accomplished. He accepted that economics had to

1 It is of interest, perhaps, to provide the context which led to the quotation. Harry went through a rather long mathematical derivation to demonstrate the consistency between the theoretical approaches of the Dutch, the Keynesian, and the monetarist models. He was apologetic for taking his listeners through this rather tedious exercise, and the quotation provided the rationale for it. However, as I hope to demonstrate in this paper, it also provides a rationale for much if not most of Harry's activities as an economist.

progress by improving on what had been done previously. This required unremitting study of the entire literature of economics but it was not enough: it also required the study of new evidence. (ibid, 86)

As the last sentence indicates, Harry was as much interested in empirical work as in theoretical work. His aspect as an empirical economist often goes unnoticed. The impressive LSE study of the statistical foundations of the monetary approach to the balance of payments represented the last of his many excursions into the empirical side of the discipline.[2] In part, his belief in the value of empirical work was a result of his view that the ultimate goal of theory was to influence the conduct of economic affairs, i.e., to influence policy.[3] And for theory to have policy relevance it must be subjected to empirical verification.

But Harry realized that even this was not enough to ensure that new developments have an influence on decision-makers: 'The interest in monetarism and the quantity theory is to be explained more by the fact that policy based on Keynesian theory, and concentrating on fiscal policy, has been an evident failure, and that monetarism is a new idea that promises to do better, [than by a] full-scale scientific testing of the relative strength of the two approaches' (12, 84).[4] This perception led Harry to carry policy analysis much further than most of his colleagues.[5] To deduce policy implications from theoretical-cum-empirical work was not enough; that limited focus to the supply side of policy analysis. Harry went the further step of attempting to understand and appreciate the complex web of institutional fabric that im-

2 As far as Canadians are concerned, Harry's most significant venture into empirical economics was the Royal Commission monograph co-authored by John Winder (3). The level of econometric sophistication of this piece was admittedly not very high, but given the time constraint imposed on the research it was certainly adequate. The analysis addressed the full range of empirical issues associated with the impact and role of money and monetary policy. Moreover, it motivated several of Harry's later contributions and, in particular, his 'Alternative guiding principles for the use of monetary policy in Canada' (23). As a matter of fact, Harry thought quite highly of this piece. In the preface to *Further Essays in Monetary Economics* (6) he maintained that he had written only two 'real' books – one was the Brookings study (5) and the other was this monograph with Winder, which, as Harry commented, 'could find no official publication by the government that paid for it, let alone a commercial publisher' (6, 18). Although I shall not comment further in this paper on the Johnson-Winder study, it is important to recognize its existence because one of the other contributions to this volume (that by Helliwell) takes the position that Johnson was not much concerned with the empirical side of the discipline in the area of balance of payments theory and policy, and indeed may have hampered its development. I do not accept this proposition as far as the general area of macro or money is concerned, and later portions of my paper will detail some of Harry's contributions to furthering empirical work in macroeconomics.
3 As Laidler notes in his conclusion, for Harry Johnson 'the purpose of economics as a Social Science is to arrive at a set of principles for understanding and interpreting the economy that are both scientifically "robust" and sufficiently simple to be communicable to successive generations of students and policy-makers and the general public' (11, 214).
4 Equivalently: 'Public interest in and discussion of flexible rates generally appears only when the fixed rate system is obviously under serious strain, and the capacity of central bankers and others responsible to avoid a crisis is losing credibility' (28, 200).
5 It also led him to be very cynical of policy-makers and civil servants generally.

S14 / Thomas J. Courchene

pinged on the decision matrix of the policy-makers, i.e. to analyse the determinants of the *demand* for policy analysis. And he did this extremely well, as will be documented to some extent below.

A further and related facet of Johnson's approach to economics must be recognized. He was as concerned about the *process* by which knowledge is produced and eventually converted into meaningful policy application as about the resulting body of knowledge itself. As Shils notes: 'His aim was to understand and explain the zigzagging course of the growth of economic knowledge, and the significance of external social conditions and internal professional relationships on the improvement and retardation of economic analysis' (Shils, 1977, 86). While this theme is very obvious in his monetary counterrevolution article, it pervades his other writings in monetary economics as well.

Finally, Harry believed that it was of uppermost importance to preserve the integrity of economic knowledge. To misuse economics to achieve some further end, no matter how noble, was to desecrate it.[6]

This paper, then, will focus on Harry's contributions to macroeconomics both in their own right and in light of his over-all approach to economics. This dual focus will help explain why Harry's writings often took the particular slant that they did and will also facilitate the understanding of his contributions to the discipline. The first broad section of the analysis deals with his general contributions to theory and policy. The raw material for this analysis is the series of macro surveys covering the period from the mid-1950s to the mid-1970s. Essentially this section constitutes Harry Johnson's assessment of modern macroeconomic thought and, in particular, his perception of how the profession at large misinterpreted the theoretical thrust of the *General Theory* and the consequences of this misunderstanding. The final part of the paper focuses briefly on his contributions to understanding the functioning of institutions. Between these parts is a brief analysis of those writings of his which, while they deal with macro theory or policy, are as much a commentary on, or contribution to, the process by which knowledge is generated and accumulated in our discipline.

HARRY JOHNSON'S CONTRIBUTIONS TO GENERAL THEORY AND POLICY

The monetary aspects of the Keynesian Revolution

The most forceful and consistent impression made by Harry's many macro survey articles is that he had a great respect for the analytical contributions of

---

6 In the preface to his *Essays in Monetary Economics* (4), Harry acknowledges that in the last chapter of the book, dealing with the international aspect of the monetary problem of LDCs, many of his colleagues will regard him as coming down very harshly on schemes designed to solve the international monetary problem by methods that will channel resources to the less developed countries (e.g. distributing the SDRs to the Third World). His defence is

Keynes's *General Theory* and believed that these contributions had been in large measure left unrecognized by the 'Keynesians.' In terms of monetary theory, Harry's view was that Keynes's contribution was twofold: 'to break [via the demonstration that the economy could equilibrate at less than full employment] the quantity theory assumption of a direct connection between money quantity and aggregate demand' and 'to emphasize the function of money as an asset, alternative to other assets' (13, 125). More specifically, 'I have taken [Keynes's] central contribution to be his conception of money as an asset whose usefulness springs from uncertainty of future asset prices, and the chief limitation of his analysis to be his concentration on expectations of future changes in interest rates as the [only] determinant of the assets-demand for money' (14, 138). In short, 'Keynes made the analysis of the demand for money explicitly a branch of capital theory' (14, 135), although his attempt at integrating money into a full capital theoretic approach remained 'seriously incomplete' (ibid).

While Keynes's theory of liquidity preference was extended and generalized by Keynesians to comprise choices between money, bills, bonds, and equities, it nonetheless remained seriously incomplete because the influence of price level expectations on asset choices was generally neglected by Keynesian writers. Harry notes that 'for explicit analysis of it [price level expectations] one must turn to the modern quantity theory literature, where Milton Friedman's restatement of the quantity theory of money goes far towards providing a synthesis of Keynesian and classical approaches to the demand for money in capital theory terms' (14, 135).

Given the twofold nature of Keynes's contribution to monetary theory, it is easy to see why Harry hailed Friedman's work and viewed it as an extension, not an alternative, to Keynesian analysis. The Keynesian revolution left the quantity theory thoroughly discredited on the grounds that it was a mere tautology, which assumed full employment would prevail, and that implicit in the quantity theory was the assumption that velocity was infinitely malleable. Friedman revised the quantity theory by redefining it as 'a theory of the demand for money (or velocity) and not a theory of prices or output [and therefore freed it from a full-employment relationship], and made the essence of the theory the existence of a stable functional relationship between the quantity of real balances demanded and a limited number of independent variables, a relation deduced from capital theory' (15, 22). Naturally, a crucial ingredient of Friedman's restatement is that it 'introduces explicitly and emphasizes expected changes in the price level as an element in the cost of holding money and other assets fixed as to both capital value and yield in money terms, whereas Keynesian portfolio balance theory almost invariably starts from the assumption of an actual or expected stable price level' (15, 26).

---

straightforward: 'My reason for refusing to endorse such schemes is not that I am opposed to less developed countries receiving more development assistance, but that I think that no useful purpose is served by misapplying economic analysis for political ends ' (4, 8).

S16 / Thomas J. Courchene

In Harry's view, then, Friedman's application of capital theory to monetary theory was not only 'probably the most important development in monetary theory since Keynes' (16, 22)[7] but as well best interpreted as an improvement on, and derivative from, the analysis of the *General Theory*. In
light of Harry's dislike of labels (Keynesians, Monetarists, etc.) and his
passion for viewing progress in economic thought as building upon the work of
others, it must have been with a considerable degree of satisfaction that he
later noted 'in recent writings, Friedman has ceased to refer to the Chicago
Oral Tradition, and has admitted that his reformulation of the quantity theory
was "much influenced by Keynesian liquidity preference"' (15, 23).[8] Put
more directly, Harry saw Friedman as a 'true' Keynesian. In an important
sense Milton Friedman's restatement is a much clearer and more enlightening
statement of Keynes's essential contribution to the development of monetary
theory than the statements of Keynes and his followers.[9]

Dichotomy, validity, neutrality, etc.
From the standpoint of pure theory it was Harry's opinion that the 'most
fundamental issue raised by Keynes in the *General Theory* lay in his attack on
the traditional separation of monetary and value theory, the classical
dichtonomy ... according to which relative prices are determined by the
quantity of money and its velocity of circulation' (16, 17). The thrust of this
attack was that Keynes shifted the determination of the level of unemployment and the rate of interest from real theory to monetary theory. This issue
consumed a significant proportion of the profession for the better part of a
decade and culminated in Patinkin's, *Money, Interest and Prices*, the substance of which was the 'integration of money and value theory through the
explicit introduction of real balances as a determinant of behavior, and the
reconstruction of classical monetary theory' (16, 19). While Harry regarded
Money, Interest and Prices as a 'monumentally scholarly work,' he nonethe-

7 As early as 1961 Harry felt that the applicability of capital theory was likely to dominate much
   future theoretical and empirical work, so that in the fulness of time we might have to alter our
   view of Keynes's principal contribution: 'The stimulation given by the *General Theory* to the
   construction and testing of aggregative models may well prove to be Keynes's chief contribution to economics in the larger perspective of historical judgment, since the application of
   capital rather than income concepts to monetary theory may well produce better and more
   reliable results; and the present predominance of the income-expenditure approach prove to
   be a transitional stage in the analysis of economic behaviour' (14, 144). To a large degree,
   especially in the area of international money, this capital-theoretic approach has indeed
   eclipsed the income-expenditure approach. This is but one example of the great many insights
   that run through much of Harry's work in the macro area – insights that often tend to be
   overlooked in assessing Harry's contribution to the profession because they have long since
   become part of 'received theory.'
8 In turn, Friedman's comments were probably much influenced by Patinkin's demonstration
   that the 'oral tradition' stressed the quantity equation and the cumulative instability of
   velocity, so that 'what Friedman has actually presented is an elegant exposition of the modern
   portfolio approach to the demand for money which ... can only be seen as a continuation of the
   Keynesian theory of liquidity preference' (Patinkin, 1969, 47).
9 Adapted from Harry's *Inflation and the Monetarist Controversy* (7), chap. 2, n. 7.

less remained convinced that the entire debate was misdirected: 'let me say that I do not think that this particular controversy is of great relevance to practical work on monetary policy or monetary analysis, or even, I think, to monetary theory' (15, 84). In Harry's judgment Keynes, when insisting that a monetary economy is different than a barter economy, was 'trying to draw attention to the fact that in the monetary economy behavior is based on expectations about the future and that an important part of that behavior relates to the demand for money, the hoarding of money and therefore the determination of interest rates' (15, 78). The dichotomy debate went astray because at the same time it was 'concerned with a monetary economy characterized by minimal uncertainty, whereas Keynes was concerned with a highly uncertain world' (16, 17), and it was focused essentially on long-run equilibrium, whereas Keynes's focus was on short-run disequilibrium. Once again Harry was voicing his concern over the fact that able minds in the profession failed to comprehend the significance of Keynes's contribution. Basically, he felt that this was a clear case of what he referred to in his De Vries Lectures as 'intellectual backsliding': 'It is a ... characteristic reflection of the strength of orthodox tradition in economic theory that the challenge of Keynesian theory, which as mentioned was essentially concerned with changing the perspective of monetary theory from long-run equilibrium to short-run disequilibrium analysis, was met by rapidly shifting the debate back to the realm of long-run full-employment equilibrium and focusing on the questions of "neutrality" of money and the validity or otherwise of "classical dichotomy" between value theory and monetary theory, issues posed by the classical concern with money as a veil over the barter system ... and that quantity theorists have only recently turned to the central Keynesian problem of short-run monetary dynamics' (7, 44).

Macroeconomic policy
While maintaining a high regard for the analytic content of the *General Theory* and its role in the advancement of economic theory, Harry became progressively embittered with what he referred to as a 'sophisticated type of intellectual opportunism' on the part of Keynes, the result of which had dire consequences for economic policy, especially for small open economies. One aspect of this was Keynes's decision to assume the presence of a closed economy: 'Perhaps the greatest disservice that Keynes rendered the development of economics in Britain was to develop the theory of macroeconomics and money under the assumption of a closed economy' (15, 49). Combined with the assumption of fixed real wages, this led to the extension of Keynesian theory to the open economy under the manifestly unsatisfactory assumption of money illusion on the part of wage-earners, so that the determination of exchange rates came to be viewed as a relative price phenomenon rather than an absolute price phenomenon, i.e. an extension of pure trade theory rather than as an extension of monetary theory. What Harry deemed to

S18 / Thomas J. Courchene

be particularly opportunistic was that Keynes could, in succession, protest against the unemployment-creating aspect of Britain's return to the gold standard in 1925 with an overvalued pound, then oppose protection as an employment-creating policy without adequately pointing out that protection was proposed because of a political refusal to contemplate a currency devaluation, and then produce a theory of unemployment which laid the blame for it on the inherent nature of capitalism itself or, by implication, on the failure of the authorities to use domestic fiscal and monetary policy effectively rather than on the international monetary system and on Britain's relations with it.[10] The consequence for British policy-making 'has been a pronounced and persistent tendency both to regard the country's international economic relations as peripheral and to concentrate instead on domestic fiscal and monetary measures as panaceas for the country's chronic problems of international competitive weakness and slow growth' (7, 78–9).

The implications for policy analysis extended far beyond Britain. In a rather characteristic juxtaposition of external influences and the development of economic thought, Harry argues that closed-economy theoretical assumptions, despite their obvious irrelevance for most nations, were powerfully reinforced by the transfer of scientific leadership in economics from Britain to the United States, a country whose near self-sufficiency renders the closed-economy assumption more realistic. Consequently, it has been largely left to members of the economics profession from 'small open economies' to work out the theory of economic policy in an international economic context. Put somewhat differently, the monetary approach to the balance of payments which should have flowed naturally from an open-economy view of Friedman's elaborations of the monetary aspects of the *General Theory* materialized only in the late sixties and early seventies. In a rather sweeping, but certainly characteristic, generalization, Harry notes that as a result of this turn of events 'the problem that has preoccupied international monetary experts and commentators for two decades, the alleged prospect of an imminent shortage of international liquidity and need to assure a sufficiently large and rapidly growing stock of international reserves through new institutional arrangements, is an exact inversion of the real problem of the system, which is to establish international control over the magnitude and rate of growth of international reserves and to use and to restrain the rate of growth of these reserves to a non-inflationary pace' (7, 86).

However unhappy Harry may have been with the opportunism of Keynes himself, it was upon the 'Keynesians' that he came down the hardest. For it was in their hands that 'a theory in which money is important turned into a theory that money is unimportant' (14, 145). Naturally his concern with the development of economic knowledge led him to seek out the answer to this paradox. Once again he was, as Shils notes, 'trying to understand and explain

10   This is taken from chapter 3 of *Inflation and the Monetary Controversy* (7).

why distinguished talents went astray in pursuit of economic truths' (1977, 85). Part of the answer, as noted above, lay in Keynes's own assumptions of a closed economy and a failure to distinguish between nominal and real magnitudes – assumptions that the following generation of Keynesians accepted too readily. But there were other factors as well. The Keynesian model incorporated two special cases where monetary policy could not work and where fiscal policy alone could stimulate economic activity, and both these cases were generalized in the post-Keynesian era. The first was the assumption of absolute liquidity preference – a situation in which monetary policy could not reduce interest rates; the second involved the inelasticity of spending with respect to interest rates (as documented by the Oxford Institute of Statistics) through 'survey research of a kind now regarded as hopelessly superficial' (16, 17). These features, combined with the fact that Keynes 'overgeneralized a particularly bad recession' (14, 13), which Alvin Hansen converted 'into a general theory of the tendency of capitalism to wallow in secular stagnation' (16, 17), led to the demise of the role of money in the Keynesian model: 'Hence monetary policy, which Keynes had regarded as normally a powerful tool of policy, became virtually completely discredited, and fiscal policy, which he regarded as a tool that might be necessary only in a deep depression, became established as the central and only reliable tool of economic policy' (16, 17). Because this implied that interest rates had little or no influence on economic activity via aggregate demand, they may as well be kept as low as possible, and as a result central bankers were, until the Accord, relegated to the occupation of minimizing the cost of placing debt.

The post-Accord revival in monetary policy, spearheaded by the work of Robert Roosa and commonly referred to as the 'Availability Doctrine,' was the intellectual offspring of pre-Accord role of central banks as bond-supporting agencies, and therefore of 'Keynesian' interpretations of the policy content of the *General Theory*. Essentially the Availability Doctrine offered a 'solution to the conflict between the belief that a large widely held public debt obliged the central bank to confine interest rate movements to narrow limits, and the belief that large interest rate changes were necessary to obtain significant effects on spending' (16, 58). The doctrine comprised two central propositions, both of which served to alter the thrust of economic policy. The first was that widespread holding of public debt, particularly by financial institutions and corporations, facilitates monetary control by transmitting the influence of interest rate changes effected by open market operations throughout the economy. The second was that small interest rate changes could, by generating or dispelling uncertainty about future rates and by inflicting or eliminating capital losses that institutions were unwilling to realize by actual sales (i.e. the locked-in effect), achieve significant effects on spending even if the demands of spenders for credit were interest-inelastic (via influencing the availability of credit to borrowers by altering the terms of credit and the degree of credit rationing). As a result of the latter, which really

S20 / Thomas J. Courchene

focused on the imperfection of credit markets, central banks and governments across the western world were provided with a rationale for credit controls based on the availability rather than the cost of credit.

Although obviously related, the former factor probably proved to be the more significant. In the hands of the Radcliffe Committee, with its emphasis on 'liquidity' in the economy as the key variable for monetary analysis and policy, it 'represented the high tide of Keynesian disbelief in the practical relevance and theoretical importance of money as formulated in traditional monetary theory' (15, 37). With typical concern for the manner in which knowledge is generated and accumulated, Harry argues that the Yale School, under the leadership of James Tobin, 'may be interpreted as providing belatedly the intellectual foundations of the Radcliffe Committee's position on monetary theory and policy – what has come to be described in the American literature, following a phrase in Tobin's important essay on commercial banks as creators of money, as the "New View of Money"'' (15, 37–8).[11]

'The crucial distinction for the Yale School, then (as for the Radcliffe Committee), is between the financial sector and the real sector (or between stock and flow analysis) rather than between the banking system and the rest of the economy (as various versions of the contemporary quantity theory would have it) or between liquid and illiquid assets (which Leijonhufvud interprets to be the essential distinction in Keynes's own theory)' (15, 38). One of the implications of this approach where money is just one of many assets and banks are just one of many intermediaries (to paraphrase Gurley and Shaw) is the necessity to 'regard the structure of interest rates, asset yields, and credit availabilities rather than the quantity of money as the linkage between monetary and financial institutions on the one hand and the real economy on the other' (Tobin, 1967, 13) – hence the relevance to Radcliffe. While Harry readily granted that this general equilibrium portfolio analysis was 'long on elegant analysis of theoretical possibilities' (15, 41), its practical relevance was marred by the fact, noted above, that it assigned to money an absolutely certain yield of zero per cent, or, what is the same thing, assumed the prices of real goods and services to be fixed autonomously in terms of money, and therefore 'precludes consideration of many of the aspects of the problem that would naturally occur to a quantity theorist' (15, 39). Included among these is the proposition that changes in *market* interest rates may be a very poor indicator of the ease or tightness of monetary policy. Harry not only linked Radcliffe to Yale (or vice versa), but went the further step of tracing this line of analysis back to the *General Theory* itself: 'The absolute liquidity trap with bonds serving as perfect substitutes for money [is] equivalent to the Radcliffe Report/Gurley-Shaw contention that money is merely the small change of the financial system and that financial intermediation makes the elasticity of demand for money very high' (7, 48).

11 The Tobin article referred to is (Tobin, 1967).

It is probably not an overstatement to suggest that as far as most central banks were concerned the Radcliffe conception of how money interacts with the economy was the rule rather than the exception over the 1950s and 1960s. Certainly the operations of central banks of Great Britain, Canada, and the United States (as reflected, respectively, in the Radcliffe Report, the Report of the Royal Commission on Banking and Finance, and the Commission on Money and Credit) were more concerned about the cost and availability of credit than about the rate of growth of the money supply, however defined. This 'money does not matter' philosophy on the part of the central bankers was matched in popular Keynesianism by the adoption of non-monetary theories of inflation. To these, and to Johnson's assessment of them, I now turn.

Keynesian inflation theories
Keynesian theorizing about inflation, as reflected in actual policy formation, rested on much the same set of principles as underlay the rise of the availability doctrine – the possibility of a liquidity trap, the closed-economy mentality, and the lack of a distinction between monetary and real magnitudes. With characteristic generalization, Harry argued that Keynesian inflation theories rested on some rather naïve and improvised ideas:

that inflation is generally due to excess demand on production capacity, though it may on occasion be due to 'excessive' claims for real income by particular groups of workers or capitalists, implemented by wage demands (assumed to be unchecked by employer resistance) or by inflationary price increases (assumed to be unchecked by consumer resistance). This idea involves the commonplace distinction between 'demand-pull' and 'cost-push' inflation, which in technical terms attributes the inflation to the budget of value theory being irrelevant either because it exceeds the community's capacity to produce, or because it becomes inoperative in the presence of monopoly power ... In cases of 'demand-pull' inflation, the standard and obvious Keynesian policy recommendation is to cut aggregate demand down to the dimensions of aggregate supply by fiscal policy restraints ... With respect to 'cost-push' inflation, the obvious policy recommendation for people naïve enough to accept the concept in the first place is the equally naïve proposal to stop the pushing, either by appealing to the pushers' sense of decency or if necessary by subjecting them to social discipline. The intellectual flowering of this primitive appeal for flouting of economic laws by social conventions and constraints appears in the solemn recommendation by authoritative economists of the need for an incomes policy ... An incomes policy involves the self-contradicting aims of achieving an ethically-dictated alteration of the distribution of real income produced by economic forces and of achieving the economically determined distribution of real income without price inflation by piercing the veil of money (7, 55–6)

What seemed of chief concern to Harry was the virtually complete inversion of Keynes's contribution that Keynesian inflation theory embodied: 'It is an ironic paradox that Keynesian economics, having begun with a head-on attack on the alleged classical fallacy that money is merely a veil over the workings of a barter economy, should have wound up with the attempt to

S22 / Thomas J. Courchene

persuade the public that money is in fact merely a veil, and that society should not only recognize this but revert to the economics of barter – or even revert still further to the feudal notion of the 'just price' – and reduce money to the role of a pure numéraire' (7, 56–7).

As a consequence, the problem of inflation under fixed exchange rates has tended to be interpreted 'as a series or collection of individual national problems, essentially sociological in origin, rather than as an international monetary problem' (7, 9). That this should have occurred was all the more painful to Harry because the classical economists would never have taken such an insular view of inflation: 'the monetary impact of Spain's conquest of America and despoliation of its precious metals was regarded by scholars of economic history as a European (i.e. world) phenomenon and not merely as a distinguishing eccentric incident in Spanish economic history' (7, 56). With the general return to flexible exchange rates in 1973, inflation did indeed become a variable over which individual countries could, via their rates of monetary expansion, exercise control. Yet except for a few countries, exemplified by Germany and Switzerland, this went unrecognized. In one of his last substantive articles in a Canadian learned journal, Harry lashed out at this behaviour on the part of the world's policy-makers: 'Directly relevant to the current problem [i.e. inflation] is the strange, almost overnight change in world policy opinion from a fundamental misunderstanding of the fixed rate system to a fundamental misunderstanding of the floating rate system, expressed in the contention up to 1973 that inflation was not a world problem, but a national problem to be dealt with primarily by national incomes policy, and the equally convinced assertion – justified only to a small and theoretically arguable extent by 1973 escalation of oil prices – that inflation is a world problem about which national economic policy can do nothing' (17, 177).[12]

Recapitulation
In a real sense Harry was a historian of contemporary macroeconomics. He painstakingly attempted to elaborate, analyse, and integrate the many threads of the current macroeconomic fabric. There is a remarkable consistency in his many survey articles, although they cover a time span of more than two decades. Rare was the occasion when it was necessary to correct or rework some concept that he had developed in a previous commentary. It was as if he carried the collected wisdom of macroeconomics in some special corner of his mind. Whenever a new idea came to light, Harry would inevitably write a piece reviewing it, frequently correct and extend it, and always integrate it into the larger corpus of macro thought in order to highlight both its significance and position in the development of knowledge.

These surveys were full of insights that Harry seldom developed further.

12 Note that Harry is referring to the Western world in this quote, so that he uses 1973 as the break-point between fixed and flexible rates. For Canada the relevant break-point was the return to flexible rates in June 1970.

Indeed, this characteristic of Harry as a continuator and improver rather than as an innovator is probably the reason he took so long to recognize the significance of his most important original contribution to the money and macro literature, namely his conception of the balance of payments as a monetary phenomenon. This insight is embodied in two articles he wrote in 1958, 'Towards a general theory of the balance of payments' (19) and 'The balance of payments' (20). In these works Harry was interested in generalizing the 'absorption approach' to balance of payments theory. In the process, however, he provided the modern conceptual backdrop for the current monetary approach to the balance of payments:

A balance-of-payments deficit [i.e., an excess of payments by residents over receipts by residents] implies *either* dishoarding by residents *or* credit creation by the monetary authorities – either an increase in V, or a maintenance of M... Formulation of the balance of payments as the difference between aggregate payments and aggregate receipts thus illuminates the monetary aspects of balance-of-payments disequilibrium, and emphasizes its essentially monetary nature.' (19, 157).

That balance-of-payments problems are fundamentally monetary phenomena is an important proposition that must always be borne in mind; it is an obvious proposition, but one which is often overlooked.' (20, 18).

Despite the fact that Harry recognized this as an application of capital theory to monetary theory (an approach that, as noted above, he felt was the essence of Keynes's *general theory*), he himself managed to overlook this development in relation to monetary theory for the better part of a decade. Moreover, even in his important 1962 *American Economic Review* survey (16), Harry never refers to this, nor to the more basic consideration of the interaction of domestic money supply and demand with the world economy counterparts. I find this puzzling, to say the least.

Before taking leave of Harry's survey pieces, I should point out that his 1962 survey (16) was far and away the most important because in addition to synthesizing the various threads of monetary analysis it provided a most valuable blueprint for research. It was an important springboard for future work on both monetary growth models and the money supply process. A whole generation of empirical monetary economists addressed themselves to the three issues he set out: 'what specific collection of assets corresponds most closely to the theoretical concept of money ... what the variables are on which the demand for money so defined depends ... [and] whether the demand for money is sufficiently stable (16, 26).

We have seen so far a generous number of references by Harry to the manner and degree to which the profession, or a large part of it, has managed to misinterpret new developments or otherwise convert them, often at significant cost in terms of conceptual relevance, into more traditional modes of analysis. Given his concern with this it is not surprising that he should

S24 / Thomas J. Courchene

address the issue of the generation of economic knowledge more directly. The monetarist counterrevolution article is probably his best piece in this regard.

THE SOCIOLOGY AND PRODUCTION OF KNOWLEDGE

Harry's Richard T. Ely Lecture to the 1970 meetings of the American Economic Association ('The Keynesian Revolution and the Monetarist Counterrevolution') is one of his most perceptive and controversial pieces. This lecture presented his views on the determinants of the process by which knowledge is generated, the speed with which it becomes accepted, the manner in which it interacts with the existing hierarchy of personalities in the profession, and the degree to which it is likely to supersede existing knowledge.

The way he proceeds to focus on these issues is to pose a question: suppose I were Milton Friedman and wished to start a counterrevolution in monetary theory, how would I go about it? He lists five criteria that facilitated the monetarist counterrevolution (and indeed the Keynesian revolution that preceded it): 'the attack on a central and widely held theoretical proposition [money does not matter], the development of a new theory [the restatement of the quantity theory] that absorbed and rechristened the best of the old, the formulation of that theory in terms that challenged the young and enabled them to leapfrog over the old, the presentation of a new methodology [positive economics and a move away from large-scale modelling] that made more economic sense than the prevailing methodology, especially in terms of accessibility to the young and to those outside the established centres of academic excellence, and a new and presumptively crucial empirical relationship [stability of the demand for money] suitable for relatively small-scale econometric testing' (18, 63).[13]

Harry was of the opinion that the counterrevolution would not exist as orthodoxy for very long. Compared to the Keynesian revolution, it had latched on to a less important issue (inflation as against unemployment). More important, the combination of positive economics and the testing of reduced-form models would prove seriously inadequate to the prevailing intellectual standards of the discipline. Thus far, however, I think it remains entrenched partly because of the post-1970 world inflation and partly because of the sudden demise of 'disequilibrium dynamics' and the corresponding resurgence of 'rational expectations,' which refocus attention on the steady-state properties of a model. Nonetheless, I agree with Harry that 'if we are

13 In Harry's view, small-scale econometric testing was appealing to junior economists because in the prevailing Keynesian orthodoxy the tendency 'for Keynesian economics to proliferate into larger and larger models ... had the important detraction of large sums of scarce research money available only to senior economists and of turning young economists into intellectual mechanics whose function was to tighten one bolt only on a vast statistical assembly line, the end product of which would contain nothing that could visibly be identified as their own work' (18, 62).

lucky we shall be forced as a result of the counterrevolution to be more conscious of monetary influences on the economy. If we are unlucky we shall have to go through a post-counterrevolution revolution as the price of further progress on the monetary side of our science' (18, 68).

In 'Monetary theory and monetary policy' (12), written in the same year as the counterrevolution article, Harry elaborates on the interaction between the structure of the academic establishment and the diffusion of knowledge. In particular, he compares the 'highly centralized' British academic establishment with its 'extremely decentralized' American counterpart in terms of the implications of this difference for the extent of the intellectual conquest of the academic world by the Keynesian revolution:

In Britain, Keynesianism was successful in virtually sweeping the intellectual board, and becoming the dominant orthodoxy. Those of the older generation who did not accept the new Keynesian orthodoxy had either to shut up and divert their intellectual efforts to another field of economics, or become pitiful and pitied voices crying in the wilderness ... In the United States, on the other hand, the diversity and competition of the academic world meant that Keynesianism never succeeded in sweeping the academic board. It conquered Harvard and the eastern establishment, and secured its outposts in the West ... but it could not prevent the academic survival of the pre-Keynesian tradition. Moreover, in the United States, in contrast to Britain, it is possible to be both intellectually and academically respectable and, at the same time, a conservative with significant political influence. Hence an anti-Keynesian school, basing itself on a modernized quantity theory of money, could flourish; and it could be ... based on institutional and geographical rivalries between men in the same age group rather than on the mechanics of the generation gap as has been necessary in Britain. The intellectual rivalry between Paul Samuelson, as leader of the Keynesians, and Milton Friedman, as leader of the quantity theorists, is a rivalry between generational, intellectual, and institutional equals, a very different kind of rivalry than the conflict in Britain between the older generation in command of Oxford and Cambridge and the younger generation in the provincial universities (which term now includes the London School of Economics). (12, 82–4)[14]

One could continue along this vein virtually ad infinitum.[15] But I think I have already overdone the issue by treating it under a separate heading. To

14　The thrust of the above quote was really to comment on the macro policy approaches in Britain and the United States. I have tailored it to relate principally to the manner in which economic knowledge and its production and distribution interact with the structure of academia.

15　For example, this concern of Harry's that scientific advances get thwarted by professional rivalries, lost perspective, and the like, pervades a great deal of the analysis in his various surveys. Here is but a further example: 'One could add that Keynesian theory has also produced only one important contribution to general economic theory since the second world war. This was Roy Harrod's recognition (*Towards a Dynamic Economics*, London: Macmillan, 1948) that in addition to the short-run Keynesian problem of whether investment will absorb the saving that income-recipients would like to undertake at full-employment income levels, there is a long-run problem of whether the investment satisfactory to entrepreneurs will grow rapidly enough to maintain full employment of labour in the face of the natural growth of population and the presence of labour-saving technical progress. The Keynesian side of professional analysis of this question has degenerated rapidly into one of two forms,

S26 / Thomas J. Courchene

Harry, the generation of knowledge, the manner in which it is disseminated, and the external factors that influenced its acceptance were part and parcel of the integrated approach of surveying and evaluating modern macro theory and policy. However, I want to conclude this section on Harry's approach to the production of knowledge by reproducing part of Don Patinkin's tribute to Harry on the occasion of the Harry G. Johnson Memorial Service (Sjaastad, 1978):

To be concerned with the profession means to be concerned with perpetuating the profession. We are all teachers, we all have students; but not all of us have given ourselves to our students with the same concern, with the same interest in furthering their careers if they were worthy of it and discouraging them if they were not ... Harry was notorious for the fact that if a student gave him a paper, he returned it the next morning with comments. I say notorious because it put the rest of us ... to shame ... From the viewpoint of the profession, he was a citizen of the world. I don't say this in the superficial sense that he attended conferences all over the world. What I mean is that he had students all over the world, and he was concerned with their advancement, their progress, their intellectual progress, their professional progress, wherever they were. He was also concerned with the development of economics departments in different universities, not only in the United States, but in Canada as well. Thus for many years I have been a regular visitor at the University of Western Ontario, and from this I know that Harry was the guru of Western Ontario with whom they consulted on more than one occasion with reference to the development plans of the department ... He was concerned, not only with that department, but I believe with other departments in Canada ... And I suspect ... that he was concerned with the development of economics departments in other parts of the world as well.

This, of course, transcends Harry's approach to macroeconomics. But in a curious sort of way his treatment of students, compared with his treatment of

---

typified by the work of Keynes's successors at Cambridge. On the one hand there has been the effort, typified by Joan Robinson (*The Accumulation of Capital*, London: Macmillan, 1956) to show by proving fundamental logical flaws in the pure theory of capital that the capitalist system cannot possibly work, regardless of any empirical evidence to the contrary. On the other hand there has been acceptance of the fact that capitalism has in fact worked fairly well during most of its history, and especially in the postwar period, coupled with the effort to prove that the reason cannot be that traditional theories of capitalism were in fact right, but that instead the reason must be found in new and equally unorthodox extensions of Keynesian theory designed to make good the alleged inadequacy of classical theory (see Nicholas Kaldor, *Essays in Economic Stability and Growth*, Glencoe, Illinois: The Free Press, 1960; especially Part III). The orthodox conservative side of the debate, however, which has been centred in Cambridge, Massachusetts, in the persons of Paul Samuelson and Robert Solow, has been equally quick to assume away the scientific relevance of Harrod's extension of the original Keynesian question by constructing models of economic growth that simply assume the maintenance of continuous full employment by a perfectly functioning system of market competition.
  'It has been extremely unfortunate for the progress of economic science that the two Cambridges have not only neutralized each other in a sterile and essentially ideological debate – a cost characteristic of most scientific advances – but that their feuding has diverted so many young economists into the belief that heroism in this sham battle would advance the cause of economic understanding. As a result, recognizable progress in monetary theory has had to depend on scholars associated neither directly nor indirectly with these institutions of higher learning' (7, 69–70).

faculty members,[16] was very 'Keynesian.' Harry recounts that in seminars Keynes was very generous and understanding toward students but would normally pounce on faculty members (21, 31). This too was characteristic of Harry.

HARRY AS AN INSTITUTIONALIST

The last major area in this review of Harry Johnson's contributions to macroeconomics relates to his concern for the workings of institutions, and in particular the banking sector. As indicated earlier, Harry came to realize that the sheer force of analytic insight or empirical verification was in general not sufficient to alter economic policy or the policy-makers' perception of how the economy worked. Accordingly, he became increasingly aware of the necessity to probe into the preference functions of policy-makers. What follows is but a smattering of his many insights both on the operation of the major macro institutions and on the matrix of parameters that influence their decision-making.

I found some of his early writings in this area particularly fascinating, and indeed embarrassing, since they anticipated my own work on central banking by a full twenty years and I was not even aware of their existence. His 'The revival of monetary policy in Britain' presents a view of the operation of the Bank of England that can be applied with equal validity to the Bank of Canada in the latter's pre-monetarist era. For example, Harry recognized that the Bank of England's emphasis on the role of the 30 per cent liquid asset ratio for the commercial banks implied that the Bank was essentially operating under a policy of liquidity management rather than cash management: 'A more important difference from traditional techniques of monetary control is to be found in the enhanced significance of the 30 per cent liquidity rule, which can without exaggerating be said to have replaced the 8 per cent cash reserve rule as the significant ratio through which monetary policy operates, and in the use of open market operations to influence the supply of liquid assets rather than of cash alone to the banks' (22, 6). Relatedly, if the monetary authorities are attempting to control both the cost and availability of credit, for this to succeed, given any interest rate, they 'must reduce the supply of liquid assets to the banks to the point where the banks feel sufficiently illiquid to restrict the *supply* of credit to their customers' (22, 7). These are among the points made in my *Money, Inflation and the Bank of Canada* with respect to the operations of the Bank of Canada prior to its adopting a more monetarist stance.[17]

16 As Al Harberger notes, 'Harry's wrath fell mainly in some of the mighty within the profession, when he viewed them as misusing the authority they had gained on the basis of their legitimate past contributions. For Harry, an even greater burden of professional responsibility fell on an individual, once he had gained such authority' (Sjaastad, 1978).

17 It should be mentioned in passing that while Harry's analysis of the Bank of England's approach was commendable, his policy recommendations were very uncharacteristic when compared to his later policy writings. As an example, in these earlier writings Harry was a supporter of interventionist policies, such as general controls on credit.

S28 / Thomas J. Courchene

Much more insight on the operations of central banks is contained in Harry's 'Alternative guiding principles for the use of monetary policy in Canada' (23), an offshoot of his work for the Royal Commission on Banking and Finance (3). Sorting out the various alternative approaches to monetary policy, he makes some interesting comments about how central banks are likely to behave. Since central banks are in close contact with one special sector of the economy, namely the financial community, it is to be expected that their views on monetary policy will be influenced by the habits of thinking about economic affairs prevalent in the financial sector, whether or not these assessments are grounded in economic analysis. Harry pursues this line of analysis at some length. What emerges is a very clear application of what has come to be referred to as Stigler's Law – that regulation is in the interests of those being regulated or, in layman's language, that the commercial banks are likely to be the beneficiaries of central bank actions. The analysis of the institutional role of central banks also serves as a precursor for the more recent analysis by John Chant and Keith Acheson (1972), which views the Bank of Canada from the vantage point of the theory of bureaus. In addition, Harry engages in a rather extended discussion of moral suasion that anticipates the recent work by Albert Breton and Ron Wintrobe (1978), which argues that moral suasion is in the interests of the chartered banks. One sample will suffice: 'The more monopolized the sector is, the more dependent it is on government goodwill, and the more its activities are prominent in or open to public discussion, the more amenable it will be to control by moral suasion ... A directive or policy statement from the central bank makes it easier for commercial banks to refuse their customers loans while retaining their goodwill' (23, 224). In short, Harry quite clearly extended his analysis beyond the strict confines of policy and into the nature and operations of the key institutions in the macro policy area.

Harry's last piece written for a Canadian audience (*Reserve Requirements and Monetary Control*) (9) carried this theme even further. The essential message was that there was no need for reserve requirements of any kind for efficient monetary control; 'reserve requirements amount to a tax on deposit-taking institutions, proximately for the benefit of central banks and ultimately for the benefit of the government' (9, 23). This is of course an extension of his earlier *Journal of Political Economy* article on efficiency and monetary control (24). Even if banks were not subject to reserve requirements, they would develop normal patterns of reserve holding which would in principle be knowable and predictable to the central bank and its officials and which should and could be taken into account in the formulation and execution of open market policy:

That is, after all, the point of employing an extensive and presumably highly trained staff at the central bank: to understand how the financial system works and to use this knowledge in the design of central bank stabilization policy. It is, however, only too understandable, though superficially at least paradoxical, that central bank officials should seek to lighten the burden on their understanding, and reduce their responsibility for error, by pressing for restrictions on the freedom of private institutional profit-maximizing choices in order to increase the predictability of the effect of open market operations on the money supply by crude rule-of-thumb arithmetic. (9, 11–12)

Harry argues that there is a further, and institutional, rationale for the existence of reserve requirements, one concerning the revenues that accrue to the central banks and the government:

Clearly, the prestige, stature, and salary and pension entitlements of central bank employees are likely to be higher, the larger the scale of the bond, discount and other market operations the Bank has to conduct, and the larger the gross revenue against which it can charge the salaries and emoluments of the managerial and research staff employees. One need not assume that the central bank governors are overly venal, only that they share the normal belief that pay and perquisites should be proportional to portentousness of performance. The universality of this principle is attested by the contrast between the opulence of central bank establishments in new ex-colonial nations and the spartan accommodation of currency boards in the few remaining colonies lacking central banks. (9, 14)

Harry concludes the analysis by pointing out that in an open economy alternative payments arrangements (principally supplied by Americans) could become attractive if domestic banking services become relatively too expensive as a consequence of the implicit taxation through high reserve requirements, both primary and secondary:

The significant point about the availability of American-provided deposit and banking services is not, of course, that this might gradually drive the Canadian product off the market. It is the lesser, but more insidious, prospect that Canadian deposit-taking institutions will continue to provide deposit and banking services to the smaller-scale individual wealth-owners and individual firms, locked in by nationality and ignorance of alternatives to low yields from depositing and high costs of borrowing from deposit institutions, while the large-scale business of better-informed investors and borrowers passes to and through American financial intermediaries, and the profitable innovations are pioneered by foreign financial firms. (9, 72)[18]

Turning now to the interaction between institutions and macro policy, it was Harry's view that:

Central banks have a preference for a fixed exchange rate because it gives them power over governments; hence they are tempted both to manage a floating rate so as to stabilize it, and to try to steer it back towards fixity. Also, in managing monetary policy under a floating rate, their traditional objectives and methods of management – particularly with respect to interest rates – are likely to sacrifice the stabilization advantages of exchange rate flexibility to letting or making the economy fluctuate along with the outside world. (25, 19)

18 As an aside, this quotation brings out the concern for the 'average' citizen that I found characteristic of much of Harry's writings. Presumably it reflects, in part at least, his experience as a one-man department of economics at St Francis Xavier University and his brush with the Antigonish Movement.

S30 / Thomas J. Courchene

This is a remarkable statement, especially as one written in early 1971. Canada's current inflation is in large measure directly the result of our failing to pursue an independent monetary course under flexible rates or, to put it differently, our decision to 'peg' the flexible rate at or near parity over the 1971–5 period. Naturally, Harry recognized this:

The belated decision to re-float the Canadian dollar in 1970 may have been used to pursue genuine independence of Canadian action and policy. But instead, Canadian policy has, for various reasons inherent in the traditional Bank of Canada approach to monetary management, conducted monetary policy as if the economy were still on a fixed exchange rate. Indeed, Canadian monetary policy, until a fairly sharp break seems to have occurred in late 1975, went even further, into a perverse policy of permitting more inflation and using traditional monetary policy tools less effectively in fighting it, than has been true of American economic policy. (10, iv)

Harry's criticism of the Bank went further: in a one-sentence summary of my *Money, Inflation and the Bank of Canada*, Harry viewed the Bank as conveying 'the impression, even to the most timidly academic mind, of an institution trying to do a job it does not understand by using tools it does not know either how to select or how to manipulate' (10, v).

The quotation at the beginning of the previous paragraph was remarkable in another sense as well, namely that even in our 1950s float Canada did not insulate herself from the outside world. Harry elaborated on this theme in his 1975 *Canadian Public Policy/Analyse de Politique* article (17). Most observers have viewed this period of floating as evidence that exchange rate speculation was stabilizing. Harry did not see it in this light: 'In short, Canada has provided impressive evidence for floating rates on tests the successful passing of which is a consequence of the failure of Canadian policy-makers to use the floating rate as a foundation for policy independence (17, 178).

Finally, Harry also felt strongly that other instruments in the central bank arsenal, in particular the lender-of-last-resort function, had outlived their usefulness and now were a source of serious concern:

The function of lender of last resort to the private financial sector has largely ceased to be a serious problem, barring the occasional case in which mismanagement leads to the danger of bankruptcy for an established financial institution so large that the central bank, or the government, finds it preferable to treat that institution as a public corporation that cannot be allowed to fail. The really serious conflict of objectives in modern times arises instead from the assumed obligation of the central bank to act as lender of last resort to the government itself; and, governments being what they are, this is a question of lending not at penalty rates but at concessional rates of interest, and *de facto* of lending not for short periods but on a gentlemen's agreement never actually to demand repayment, only 'refinancing.' (26, 3)

Elsewhere, Harry elaborates on this in the context of providing a partial rationale for the tendency of government to assume economic obligations for political purposes without at the same time appreciating the revenue requirements: 'The ... central government, through its power to create money, has a residual and important power of taxation without representation of the citizenry. This power was constrained in earlier days by the gold standard and the absence of central banking, constraints absent from the present system of discretionary monetary management subservient to the financing needs of the state and floating exchange rates' (27, 7).

It was Harry's view that this lender-of-last-resort problem plagues the international scene as well. The Fund's 'oil facility' for concessionary borrowing by poor countries 'amounts to reversing the lender-of-last-resort function, symbolized by a penalty rate, into a lender-of-first resort function, symbolized by a concessionary rate and the concentration of lending to those least able to repay' (26, 4). More generally, the corruption of the lender-of-last-resort function and the self-interest of governments were perceived by Harry to be such that he did not hold out much hope for the emergence, through temporary attempts at international co-operation, of a 'new' IMF and therefore a return to an 'improved' fixed exchange rate system: 'A camel, so runs a familiar definition, is a horse designed by a committee. What sort of beast [refurbished IMF] is likely to result when the first aim of every committee member is to design an animal that gives himself a free ride and the others the responsibility for providing fodder and water?' (26, 3)

This rather negative view of international co-operation and of institutions generally is characteristic of Johnson to be sure. Nonetheless, Harry's purpose was not in downplaying institutions as such, but rather in exposing them for what they are – generally motivated by self-interest and likely to become the captive of interest groups. As I have attempted to argue in this section of the paper, it was natural for Harry, given his over-all approach to economics, to extend the analysis of macro policy to include the functioning of the key macro institutions. Indeed, he viewed this as a responsibility. On this (as on most other issues, since I view my role essentially as an intermediary) it is appropriate for Harry to have the last word:

One of the penalties – or privileges, as the case may be – of advancing age and professional maturation in an academic career in the social sciences is that one is forced to think in terms of progressively broadening frames of institutional and cultural reference. The young economist, whatever may have been his original motivations for becoming an academic, comes out of the graduate student well with a narrow range of specialized skills, and the stamp of his teachers' ideas heavily upon him. He makes his way initially by applying his skills ... in an institutional and social context taken as an immutable part of his environment. Only as he acquires confidence, on the one hand, and abrasive experience of the larger extra-departmental and extra-academic world, on the other, can he afford himself the liberty to question society's institutions. (8, ix)

S32 / Thomas J. Courchene

REFERENCES

Books by Harry Johnson
1 *International Trade and Economic Growth* (London: George Allen and Unwin), 1958, referred to as *ITEG*
2 *Money Trade and Economic Growth* (London: George Allen and Unwin), 1962, referred to as *MTEG*
3 *Lags in the Effects of Monetary Policy in Canada* (Working paper prepared for the Royal Commission on Banking and Finance), 1962 (co-authored by John Winder)
4 *Essays in Monetary Economics* (London: George Allen and Unwin), 1967, referred to as *EME*
5 *Economic Policies Towards Less Developed Countries* (Washington: Brookings Institution), 1967
6 *Further Essays in Monetary Economics* (London: George Allen and Unwin), 1972, referred to as *FEME*
7 *Inflation and the Monetarist Controversy*, The De Vries Lectures (Amsterdam: North Holland), 1972
8 *On Economics and Society* (Chicago: University of Chicago Press), 1975
9 *Reserve Requirements and Monetary Control*, Discussion Paper No. 66, Economic Council of Canada (October 1976)
10 *The Canadian Quandary*, Carleton Library No. 106 (Toronto: McClelland and Stewart), 1977

Articles by Harry Johnson
11 'Major issues in monetary economics.' *Oxford Economic Papers* 26 (July 1974), 212–25
12 'Monetary theory and monetary policy.' In *FEME*, 77–87
13 'Monetary theory and Keynesian economics.' In *MTEG*, 107–25
14 'The General Theory after twenty-five years.' In *MTEG*, 126–50
15 'Recent developments in monetary theory.' In *FEME*, 21–49
16 'Monetary theory and policy.' In *EME*, 15–72
17 'Inflation unemployment and the floating rate.' *Canadian Public Policy–Analyse de Politique* (Spring 1975), 176–84
18 'The Keynesian Revolution and the Monetarist Counterrevolution.' In *FEME*, 50–69
19 'Towards a general theory of the balance of payments.' In *ITEG*, 153–68
20 'The balance of payments.' In *MTEG*, 15–27
21 'Cambridge in the 1950s: memoirs of an economist.' *Encounter* 42 (January 1974), 28–39
22 'The revival of monetary policy in Britain.' *Three Banks Review* (June 1956), 3–20
23 'Alternative guiding principles for the use of monetary policy in Canada.' Reprinted in *The Canadian Quandary* (Toronto: McClelland and Stewart), 1977, 188–226
24 'Problems of efficiency in monetary management.' In *FEME*, 88–112
25 'Inflation: an international problem.' *Bankers Magazine*, 212 (July 1971), 18–20 [This is a reproduction of Harry's testimony before the Standing Senate Committee on National Finance, Senate of Canada, 26 May 1971.]
26 'International monetary reform: the 'sideways' approach.' Mimeo prepared for (and presumably published by) *Banco de Vizcaya*, Bilboa, Spain, 1976.
27 'Economic growth and the distribution of economic opportunities and benefits among men and nations: an unenthusiastic contribution toward predicting the intellectual stock market.' Mimeo prepared for the Ford Foundation
28 'The case for flexible exchange rates.' In *FEME*, 198–222

Harry Johnson: macroeconomist / S33

Other authors

Breton, A. and R. Wintrobe (1978) 'A theory of ''moral'' suasion.' This JOURNAL 11, 210–19.

Chant, J.F. and Keith Acheson (1972) 'The choice of monetary instruments and the theory of bureaucracy.' *Public Choice.* Reprinted as chapter 23 of J.P. Cairns, H.H. Binhammer, and R.W. Boadway, eds, *Canadian Banking and Monetary Policy* (Toronto, McGraw-Hill Ryerson)

Courchene, T.J. (1976) *Money, Inflation and the Bank of Canada* (Montreal: C.D. Howe Research Institute)

Laidler, D.E.W. (1978) 'Harry Johnson as a macroeconomist.' Discussion Paper 7813, Dept. of Economics, University of Western Ontario (Forthcoming in a special volume of the *Journal of Political Economy*)

Patinkin, D. (1969) 'The Chicago tradition, the quantity theory and Friedman.' *Journal of Money, Credit and Banking* 46–70

Shils, E. (1977) 'Memoir: Harry Johnson.' *Encounter*, November 1977, 85–9

Sjaastad, L., ed. (1978) 'Harry G. Johnson Memorial Service.' (Chicago, 4 Feb.) Mimeo.

Tobin, J. (1967) 'Commercial banks as creators of ''money.'' '. In D.D. Hester and J. Tobin, eds, *Financial Markets and Economic Activity*, Cowles Foundation Monograph 21 (New York: John Wiley and Sons) chap. 1

[3]

Harry Johnson's contributions to the pure theory of international trade

RICHARD G. LIPSEY / Queen's University

Abstract. This paper surveys some of the major writings of Harry Johnson on trade theory and attempts at least a partial assessment of his contribution to that field. The coverage is not exhaustive but is instead illustrative of Johnson's views on the emptiness of qualitative economics, the resulting essential part that must be played by empirical work, and the need for a revised theory of decision-making on matters of economic policy.

L'apport d'Harry Johnson à la théorie pure du commerce international. Ce mémoire passe en revue quelques-uns des travaux importants d'Harry Johnson sur la théorie du commerce international et tente de prendre une mesure partielle de son apport à ce champ d'activité. La revue ne se veut pas exhaustive : elle veut surtout illustrer les vues de Johnson sur (1) la vacuité de l'analyse économique qualitative, (2) le rôle essentiel du travail empirique, et (3) la nécessité d'une nouvelle théorie de la décision en matières de politique économique.

INTRODUCTION

In the autumn of 1953 I commenced work on a PH D in the field of international economics at the London School of Economics where two of my fellow graduate students were Ted Rybczynski and Max Corden. The three of us attended James Meade's international trade seminar, and Max went as well to the lecture course in which Meade was expounding the material that was

I am greatly indebted to Alan Berge for research assistance, comments, and suggestions. I have not tried to be exhaustive in my survey. Numerous surveys and appreciations will be published over the next few years, and, if all the authors try to do the same thing, the writings will become tedious. I have tried to argue a point of view and illustrate it from Johnson's work – although in the course of this I think I have touched on the majority of his important contributions. I do not aspire to say the last word; I only hope I say one interesting word that will be relevant to some future historian trying to put together an assessment of Johnson's contributions.

shortly to be published as *Trade and Welfare*, the second volume of his *Theory of International Economic Policy*. I first met Harry Johnson at the autumn meeting of the Oxford-Cambridge-London Joint Economics Seminar, which Harry often attended in order to meet, encourage, and exchange ideas with graduate students from the three universities.[1] I recall him intently absorbing the message, as expounded by its originator, and then encouraging the publication of what became known as the Rybczynski theorem. At other early meetings of the seminar I remember him discussing at great length the results that Max Corden was working out for his PH D. thesis on the consequences of changing factor endowments. (Max was concerned about the consequences of large-scale immigration into Australia.) Later Harry went on to become a 'major architect' of the theory of the effects of growth on trade.[2]

Harry Johnson began to make contributions to the pure theory of international trade in the early 1950s and continued to do so until his untimely death in 1977. Indeed, if one judges by publications, his contributions continued into 1978–9, because so prodigious was his output that the journals took some years to publish everything that was in his pipeline. I suppose it is not stretching things very far to say that an academic in many a less well-known university could progress from assistant to full professor on a lifetime bibliography that consisted solely of Harry's posthumously published works.

Harry was an extraordinarily productive writer, and he was proud of the fact that he had published more articles in learned journals than any other economist living or dead. Detractors pointed to the duplications in his works, and perhaps the statistics overleaf, which no doubt would have pleased Harry, give a better impression of his impact on the subject than can be gained from a mere page count.

Younger economists, especially those who have not been trained in real trade theory and who know Harry Johnson's work mainly through his later survey-style articles, sometimes ask whether he ever contributed much to the fundamental development of economics. Without for a moment suggesting that syntheses and creative surveys are *not* contributions, I would use this table to dispel any concern that Harry did nothing else. The table is not there to suggest invidious comparisons but rather to show that, on the evidence of one major text book, Harry Johnson was one of the major contributors to the currently accepted body of the real theory of international trade.

1 At that time Harry was a fellow of King's College, Cambridge. In 1956 he became professor of economic theory at the University of Manchester. In 1959 he broke his professional association with Britain and went to the University of Chicago, where he became Charles F. Grey Distinguished Service Professor. In 1966 he accepted a chair of economics at the London School of Economics, which he held jointly with his Chicago appointment. In 1974 he resigned his LSE chair, breaking his professional association with Britain for the second and last time.

2 This is the phrase used by M. Chacholiades (1978) to characterize Harry's contribution to this part of international trade theory.

S36 / Richard G. Lipsey

References to leading trade theorists in a
standard text book of international trade theory[3]

	No. of Separate page citations to this author's name in index	No. of chapters in which at least one of this author's works is cited[4]	No. of separate works by this author cited somewhere in book
Ohlin	62	6	2
Heckscher	59	3	1
Samuelson	58	10	18
Johnson	47	12	26
Bhagwati	41	11	16
Meade	36	12	6
Pareto	30	0	0
Kemp	28	11	17
Lerner	27	10	4
Vanek	27	12	12

THE EMPTINESS OF PRIVATE-SECTOR QUALITATIVE ECONOMICS

Much of Harry's work on trade theory was done in the 1950s, and this work included some of his most original contributions to any field. Harry seldom posed new problems; he seldom, if ever, wrote *the* seminal work. But like 99 per cent of those who do make some sort of contribution, he took existing problems and made advances in our understanding of them. His advances, however, were on a broader front and of deeper penetration than those made by most of his contemporaries.

Viewed in the early 1960s from my vantage point as one of the founding members of the LSE Staff Seminar on Methodology, Measurement and Testing in Economics (the then-famous M^2T Seminar), Harry's work had an obvious unity to it. Samuelson had stated in the *Foundations* (1947) the agenda for qualitative economics: from sign restrictions on the behavioural parameters we seek to determine sign restrictions on the partial derivatives of each of the endogenous variables Y with respect to each of the exogenous

---

3 The textbook is Chacholiades (1978), and the authors are those who get at least four printed lines of individual page references in the index. Authors with three printed lines of page references are Baldwin, Caves, Chipman, Corden, Edgeworth, Harberler, Ricardo, Stolper, and Viner. Altogether there are 245 names in the author's index. (I quote these additional facts only to show that the attribution of ideas to their originators is extensive in this book.)

4 Material cited within the body of each chapter is collected in that chapter's selected bibliography. In some cases, however, the selected bibliographies of two chapters are combined. For this reason, although there are twenty-three chapters, the maximum possible score on my method of counting is twenty-one.

variables Z.[5] As time went on and theoretical studies became sharper and more incisive, exceptions were found to most of the qualitative 'laws' that earlier economists had stated.

The conclusion reached by many, although by no means all, economists during the 1950s and 1960s was that, with possibly a few important exceptions, pure qualitative economics was empty.[6] Since, given the usual sign restrictions on behavioural parameters, it could tell us nothing more than that the signs of $\partial Y_j / \partial Z_i$ could be either positive or negative or zero for each and every i and j, it was consistent with any conceivable combination of real-world observations. It followed that the progress of economics required the input into theories of something more restrictive than merely the signs of behavioural parameters.[7] Seen from this point of view, Harry's work on pure trade in the 1950s, which seemed so nihilistic to many of his contemporaries,[8] consisted of a series of case studies in which an extremely ingenious and subtle mind found exceptions to virtually all of the qualitative 'laws' of international economics with which he was presented.

Harry was, for example, presented with the 'law' that the optimum tariff raised a country's welfare only if its trading partners sat passively by, whereas, if each levied the optimum tariff as seen by itself, all countries would lose as a result of the ensuing tariff war. He showed this to be wrong because the equilibrium at which further tariff changes would seem unprofitable to any country could leave the country that started the whole tariff war better off, worse off, or just as well off as it was under free trade (Johnson, 1953). Optimum tariff theory was qualitatively empty with respect to predictions regarding the outcome of a tariff war.[9]

Presented with certain propositions that seemed to follow from the Heckscher-Ohlin model of international trade, he joined the rising chorus of

5 The 'laws' of supply and demand seemed to be a great (pre-Samuelsonian) example. But even here the early discovery of the Giffen case robbed the theory of competitive markets of its qualitative content. It became necessary to appeal to empirical knowledge to suggest that the Giffen case was 'unlikely' (even if not impossible) in order to argue that the partial derivatives of price and quantity with respect to a host of exogenous variables could be signed in the 'normal' or 'usual' (non-Giffen) case.

6 Even today there is disagreement on the content of qualitative economics. I hope readers will separate their judgments on the questions: Is qualitative economics empty? and Did Harry Johnson think qualitative economics was empty? My own answer to both questions is yes, but in this paper I am only concerned to argue that yes is the correct answer to the second question.

7 See Archibald (1965) for a discussion of some of the reasons why the qualitative content of most maximizing models is so scant.

8 Whatever people now recall was their opinion of Harry then, this was a charge that I became weary of trying to refute around the senior common room of the LSE (between 1955 and 1963 when I was on the LSE staff) and elsewhere, including some of the leading US universities that I visited in 1963–4.

9 Like so many things that had to be rediscovered after the second world war, Nicholas Kaldor (1940) had got it right in an earlier era. Harry himself gives Kaldor credit for seeing the correct answer.

S38 / Richard G. Lipsey

economists who, while accepting the value of the model, dissented from the qualitative 'laws' that had at first seemed to follow from it. In this, as in many of his other major contributions, Harry was not the first dissenter; his contribution was to bring to each issue an analytical ability that often allowed him to have the last word by exhausting the set of theoretically possible cases and then presenting his analysis in a cogent manner that fully exposed the nature of the problem. In the case of 'Factor endowments, international trade and factor prices' (1957), Harry's contribution was to give a masterfull and clear presentation based on 'a diagrammatic representation of the technological side of the economy, developed from one originated by Mr R.F. Harrod' (1958b, 18).[10] This diagram is truly vintage Johnson; it allowed him to handle a large number of variables on a two-dimensional figure in such a way that relations between them that might otherwise have been obscure seemed to leap to the eye, and it was an analytical, not just an illustrative device. As many 'factor reversals' as desired could be allowed for, and the consequences of opening trade in various initial-endowment positions could then be studied. The conclusions reached were characteristic of what many fellow economists of the time regarded as Johnsonian nihilism:

First, it is not necessarily true that a country will export the commodity which uses relatively intensively the factor with which the country is relatively heavily endowed ... Second, it is not necessarily true that a country will export the commodity which uses relatively more of a factor which would be relatively cheaper in the absence of trade ... Thirdly, the proposition that trade will tend to equalize relative factor prices, and will in fact do so if both countries continue to produce both goods, is valid only on [certain conditions] ... Thus the conclusions of the Heckscher-Ohlin model depend not only on the assumption of competition, absence of trade barriers, constant returns to scale, and so forth, but also on an *empirical assumption* about the nature of technology or the degree of variation in the factor endowments of countries. (Johnson, 1958b, 28–9, italics added)

Those contemporaries who found such conclusions nihilistic were surely misguided. Whatever the psychoanalytical reasons for Harry's wanting to upset existing generalizations, the exposure of any error must be welcomed as at the very least the removal of a roadblock from the path to further knowledge.

In the early 1950s Harry was faced with the alleged phenomenon of a persistent 'dollar shortage' in Britain and Europe. The problem was one of balance-of-payments deficits for most European countries that had persisted since the establishment of the Bretton Woods system of pegged exchange rates. I often heard Harry, in referring to this system, talk of the tendency of economists to decide in each decade that there was some one price that was of such fundamental importance that it must be fixed and thus prevented from

10 The series of articles under discussion have all been reprinted in Johnson (1958b). When the title is quoted, reference is given to the original source, but page references are all to the reprints in (1958b).

doing its job! In an earlier time this was the interest rate, at the time he was writing it was the exchange rate, in the mid-1970s it was probably the domestic price of gas and oil in many of the oil-importing countries.

The dollar problem was thought to be more or less permanent, and economists sought to explain why this was so.[11] In 'Increasing productivity, income-price trends and the trade balance' (1954), Harry addressed himself to the logic of the argument that 'attributes [the] dollar shortage to the effects of the rapid increase in American productivity in lowering the money prices of American goods relative to the prices of goods produced elsewhere' [Johnson, 1958b, 114]. He reached several characteristic conclusions. First, 'increasing productivity in the United States affects the American trade balance in two ways, and not just one as this theory implies. In addition to its effect on relative prices of American and foreign goods, increasing American productivity raises American real income and therefore ... increases American demand for imports ... Consequently, in so far as proponents of this theory emphasize the high rate of increase of American productivity per se, rather than its alleged effects on relative prices, their analysis is misleading or wrong' (ibid). Once again, no unambiguous qualitative result emerges from the disturbance to be investigated given only sign constraints on behavioural parameters. 'Secondly, with regard to the effect of increasing American productivity on the relative prices of American and foreign goods, the assumption that relatively falling American prices turn the trade balance of the United States in its favour necessarily implies that elasticities of international demand are high enough.' Sign restrictions on elasticities are not sufficient. Harry then concludes: 'Nothing in the argument presented here, however, contradicts the proposition that productivity and price trends in the world economy *may* lead to a chronic dollar shortage of the type described. Indeed our analysis points to a number of factors which might contribute to this result' (ibid, 115, italics added). Clearly anything can happen, and all that theory can do at this level of abstraction is to point to those variables on which we would need *quantitative* restrictions before a clear prediction could be made.

His work on the dollar problem gave rise to a more detailed analysis of growth and trade. In 'Economic expansion and international trade' (1955), Harry probably came as close as he ever did in the real theory of trade to being seminal. The method is comparative-static. Two countries are studied: Man-

11 As Harry later came to recognize and to stress in conversation, the chronic dollar shortage was but one example in a long string of cases in which economists have thought that a problem that persisted for more than a couple of years must persist into the indefinite future. 'Permanent' secular stagnation in the 1930s, a 'permanent' dollar shortage in the 1950s, and 'permanent' structural unemployment in the United States in the early 1960s were examples.

With hindsight, some of the reasons given – a relatively high rate of productivity growth in the United States, a chronically falling US price level because money incomes rise slower than productivity, US technical progress that is biased in the direction of import substitutes, a relatively high degree of cyclical instability in the US economy – seem almost quaint and illustrate the extremely casual empiricism indulged in by many of the authors.

S40 / Richard G. Lipsey

cunia, which has a comparative advantage in relatively high-income-elastic manufactured goods, and Agraria, which has a comparative advantage in relatively low-income-elastic agricultural goods. Exogenous changes whose comparative static effects are studied one at a time are, first, technical progress in the case of both classical (only in manufacturing) and equal rates in both industries, second, capital accumulation, and, third, population growth in the face of both mildly diminishing returns and strongly diminishing returns. The effects of each of these on trade, first through production, then through consumption, and finally the net effect of both, is analysed for each country. Five possible trade effects are recognized: ultra anti-trade bias, anti-trade bias, neutral, pro-trade bias, and ultra pro-trade bias. These terms distinguish production cases in which the change under consideration reduces the supply of exportables absolutely, increases the supply of exportables less than in proportion to the increase in output, increases it in proportion to the increase in output, increases it more than in proportion to the increase in output, and reduces the domestic supply of importable goods. Parallel definitions apply on the consumption side. A remarkable table (1958b, 82) summarizes all the possible effects that can follow from each of the changes studied. This analysis, extraordinary in its richness, clearly advanced greatly the profession's understanding of the complexity of the possible impacts of growth on trade.[12]

Harry was also presented with Marshall's dictum that any position of unstable equilibrium in the foreign exchange market must be flanked by two stable positions. Many writers, including Friedman and Sohmen, had used this as a reply to the elasticity pessimists, saying in effect 'even if there is an unstable exchange equilibrium, there *must* be a stable equilibrium at both a higher and a lower exchange rate.' Harry in his joint article with Bhagwati (1960) showed that this argument depends on the two empirical assumptions: that the demand for imports is both 'terminable,' i.e. $q^d(p) = 0$ for $p \geq \bar{p}$, where $\bar{p}$ is some finite value, and 'insatiable,' i.e. $q^d \to \infty$ as $p \to 0$. The latter assumption is manifestly false for any good whose consumption requires time, while the former cannot be shown to be necessary as a matter of logic. Johnson and Bhagwati showed that many cases are possible, depending on which assumption is violated for which country. If, for example, both assumptions are violated for both countries, then there may be only one equilibrium at a finite exchange ratio, and this may be unstable. Once again, presented with a qualitative economic 'law,' Harry showed that it was wrong and that,

---

12 Harry's original contributions were to the comparative-static analysis of the effects of growth on trade. In the mid-1960s continuous growth models were applied to international economics and the effects of trade on growth were then studied. In (1971b and 1972b) Harry brought his ingenious geometric inventiveness and his masterly expository abilities to the latter type of models and helped to bring them within the reach of readers who found modern growth theory difficult to comprehend.

given only sign restrictions on parameters, virtually any result was possible. The range of possible outcomes could be narrowed, so he argued, only if quantitative restrictions could be added to some or all of the behavioural parameters.

In making the case for my interpretation of the thrust of Harry Johnson's early work on trade theory I have reviewed all but one of the articles on pure trade theory included in his first collection of essays (Johnson 1958b), as well as his 1960 article with Bhagwati.[13] Harry also maintained his sceptical approach to qualitative economic 'laws' when he came to review the works of others. Perhaps his most famous book review, and the one that in 1958 possibly cost him the chair of international economics at the London School of Economics, was his 1951 review article of James Meade's *The Balance of Payments* (Meade, 1951). Views on this article, entitled 'A taxonomic approach to economic policy,' differed enormously; some regarded it as an important methodological document, while other regarded it as unfair, unreasonable, and ungentlemanly in its content and tone.[14]

In the course of this review Harry gave some substantial, although qualified, praise to Meade's book. For example, 'even though most of Professor Meade's analytical results have been obtained by other writers employing particular models of which his is the general case, the conception of this [Meade's] model must be regarded as a notable act of creative synthesis.' The general tone of the review is, however, severely critical. Many (although not all) of Harry's criticisms have stood the test of time. For example, the profession uses the concept of balance-of-payments disequilibrium advocated by Johnson rather than the one used by Meade and severely criticized by

13 I have omitted chapter 5, which extends the Harrod-Domar growth model to a two-country world. Although the Harrod-Domar model was immensely important in pointing the way towards more interesting and elaborate growth models, it was of little use in itself for analysing observed phenomena. Hence the extension of this specific model to more than one country seems also to have been of little use in pointing the way to further useful work in trade theory.

14 All of it seems to me, on rereading it again after so many years, to come within the range of fair, although severe, comment, and I find it hard to recreate the feeling of shocked offence that it created among Professor Meade's professorial colleagues in the LSE senior common room. Indeed, some senior chair holders never forgave Johnson, and this was soon to affect the course of events. When James Meade left the LSE to take the Marshall chair at Cambridge in 1957, the LSE junior staff whom I knew had a short list containing only one name, H.G. Johnson. Apparently many of the full professors were surprised when they heard that the less-senior staff thought it a scandal that Harry was not appointed to succeed Meade. I never heard Harry say anything against the person appointed in his stead. He did, however, maintain a sense of outrage that the British academic establishment could apparently decide appointments on what seemed to him irrelevant grounds. I am sure it never occurred to him at the time that the criticisms he was making of Meade would be taken by Meade's colleagues as reprehensible behaviour relevant to subsequent academic decisions. (I hasten to add that I never heard James Meade say anything to suggest that he himself took Harry's criticisms personally or that his regard for Harry as an economist had diminished as a result of the criticisms.) See Johnson and Nobay (1975) for Johnson's subsequent evaluation of Meade's writings on trade theory.

S42 / Richard G. Lipsey

Johnson.[15] Robert Mundell takes a different view from mine, however, when he writes: 'There is no question in my mind that the reviews of this [Meade's] work published in the 1950s did not do justice to it or recognize its real significance ... This is only partly because of defects of its organization and presentation. ... I should attribute its tepid reception rather to the state of confusion of the science in the early 1950s, and the lack of sensible criteria by which merit could be separated from chaff' (Mundell, 1968, 113, n. 3). I do not myself agree with Mundell at least as far as Harry's review is concerned; nor do I know to what sensible criterion developed since the 1950s he refers. The Nobel Prize attests to the obvious fact that Meade's work has stood the test of time. Matters of tone aside, however, I feel that Harry's criticisms of Meade have also stood the test of time. One can surely make great advances in theory (which Meade no doubt did) while also being open to criticism on the way one applies one's theory to policy situations (which in my opinion Meade was). The modern example of Milton Friedman, another Nobel Prize winner, leaps to mind.

The main thrust of Harry's criticism was against Meade's willingness to draw policy conclusions from qualitative theory alone (Johnson, 1951, 826–8):

Nevertheless, Professor Meade has made an impressive attempt to develop a theory of international economic policy. The reviewer does not, however, believe that much assistance could be rendered to practical economic policy by further development along the lines he has laid down. This opinion is based on two general considerations.

The first of these is the nature of economic theory itself, which, as Professor Meade and most other economists use it, is essentially taxonomic, a method of classifying the universe of possible cases. It is possible, by pure theory, to specify the direction or sign of the influence of one variable on another in a limited number of cases; but the problems in which most theorists are interested require the specification of the direction of the net outcome of influences operating in opposite directions, and this in turn requires a specification of the magnitudes as well as the signs of the influences. For such problems, all that theory can do is to specify some (measurable) quantity on which the outcome will depend.

To determine the outcome in any particular case, however, it is necessary to measure the quantity ...

Once this is admitted, it follows immediately that the role of economic theory in the solution of practical problems is extremely limited: the important (and more difficult) part of the task becomes the problem of measurement, however it is performed. Furthermore, beyond a certain point economic theory may easily become a handicap rather than a help; this is because the taxonomic approach is subject to two distinct forms of bias. The first is that, in order to keep the number of possible classifications within manageable bounds, and their distinguishing characteristics readily understandable, the theorist is strongly tempted to simplify his problems to the point at

15 Meade defined a potential balance-of-payments deficit as 'the amount of accommodating finance which it would have been necessary to provide in any period in order to avoid any depreciation in the exchange rate without the employment of exchange controls, import restrictions, or other governmental measures specially devised to restrict the demand for foreign currencies' (Meade, 1951, 15, as quoted in Johnson, 1951, 814).

which his results cannot be applied at all easily to practical problems ... Second, in order to choose between the impossible number of alternatives with which even a relatively simple analytical problem confronts him, the theorist is strongly tempted to eliminate some of the cases by prejudging the results of measurement he does not and perhaps could not make, either by illegitimately assuming that a number of qualitative statements can be added up into a quantitative fact [which elsewhere in his review Harry accuses Meade of doing], or by postulating an ideal world in which only the cases he chooses will exist. This temptation is particularly dangerous when questions of economic policy are involved, because then the desire for simplicity may be reinforced by personal preferences in prompting the exclusion of possible cases.

Many economists misunderstood Harry's criticisms of Meade. It was, and still is, common to hear such views as 'Harry, who lives in a glass house of taxonomy, has criticized Meade for doing what he himself does all the time.' Such critics misunderstood Harry's very consistent philosophy of economics, and Harry certainly contributed to this misunderstanding by choosing an inappropriate title for his review of Meade's book. Harry was not complaining about taxonomy, since he himself had done plenty of that. He was complaining rather about how Meade went from taxonomy to policy recommendations. The sequence is in three steps: first, a taxonomic classification of all possible results; second, quantification of some or all of the parameters so as to restrict the number of possible outcomes; and, third, policy advice based on the predictions of the quantitatively restricted model. Harry's major complaint, as the above quote shows, was directed at the second stage not the first. He accused Meade of arriving at quantitative judgments (without which his theory would be empty) by a series of qualitative considerations, sometimes as crude as counting the number of arguments that a given parameter would be large and subtracting the number of arguments that the parameter would be small. In Harry's view, qualitative economics was empty, so that when it came to restricting the range of possible outcomes sufficiently to make it possible to give advice on alternative policies, there was no substitute for careful quantitative analysis – an analysis he believed Meade to have assumed but not to have made.

Let us now return to Harry's own original contributions and survey one of the topics to which he contributed most, the pure theory of tariffs. Many of his most important contributions are collected in his volume *Aspects of the Theory of Tariffs* (1971a).[16] The first article, 'International trade, income distribution, the offer curve and the effects of tariffs' (1959), is vintage Johnson. It reports on his 'efforts to construct a truly general, though simplified, model of trade and tariff theory incorporating the distribution of income' (1971a, x). The model is simplified in the sense that it deals with a world of two countries, two factors, and two commodities. It is general in the

16 When the title is given, the reference is to the original article; page references, however, are to the reprints in (1971a).

S44 / Richard G. Lipsey

sense that within its confines, it allows for all effects and repercussions of everything on everything else. Harry might have argued that further elaborations were unnecessary because if one can show that one cannot sign $\partial Y_j/\partial Z_i$ for all i and j in a simple model, one is unlikely to be able to sign them in more complex models. Since Harry was usually busy showing that as far as pure theory goes anything could happen, whereas others had thought that pure theory showed that only certain things could happen, it was clear that adding to the complexity of his models (e.g. more countries, more factors, more commodities) would not have changed his conclusions.

In this paper Johnson derives offer curves (as far as I know for the first time in the literature) not from a unique community indifference map but by using two types of factor-owners – labourers and capitalists – each with its own community indifference map. This permits him to study the effects of income distribution on trade as well as the effects of trade on income distribution. The enriched set of results obtained follows from the fact that in his model 'an increase in the relative price of the imported good has, in addition to the usual income and substitution effects, the effect of shifting domestic production towards producing more of that good and less of the export good, and redistributing income towards the factor used relatively intensively in producing that good, thus altering the weights of the preference systems of the two factors in determining aggregate demand for goods' (1971a, 11). This allows offer curves to have shapes – butterfly-like extending into two quadrants and snake-like – that, although looking pathological to someone trained in the Marshallian tradition, can be shown to follow from some quite innocent-looking sets of basic circumstances.

Harry's conclusions are, as we should by now expect, that there are very few qualitative predictions that can be made. For example: multiple and unstable equilibria are possible even when the foreign demand for imports is elastic throughout; an increase in the foreign demand for imports could lead to a *fall* in the trade of both commodities and a reversal in flow, with former exports becoming imports and former imports becoming exports; the imposition of tariffs may raise, lower, or leave unchanged both the world price and the internal price of the imports of the levying country; an increase in tariffs, as well as raising the real income of the factor used intensively in the protected industry, may also raise the real income of the second factor.

In 'A generalised theory of the effects of tariffs on the terms of trade' (with Bhagwati, 1961a), Harry relaxes four conditions usually maintained throughout previous theories: (1) the initial situation is one of free trade, (2) the pattern of consumers' expenditures is independent of the expenditure of government, (3) the private sector can be aggregated to obtain a unique set of community indifference curves or their equivalent, and (4) factor supplies are fixed. He shows that these relaxations greatly expand the set of circumstances under which a tariff can worsen the terms of trade of the levying country.

In the classic article 'Optimal trade intervention in the face of domestic distortions' (1965b), Harry discusses the second-best implications for trade of the existence of domestic distortions. Demolishing a number of false arguments that domestic distortions can best be corrected by tariffs, he shows in general that domestic distortions are best offset by further (second-best) countervailing distortions that do not discriminate between domestic and imported goods. He also shows that the use of tariffs will not only lower welfare below the second-best level that could be obtained given a set of fixed domestic distortions, but that they may lower welfare below its free-trade level. The substance of this long, carefully reasoned article deserves to be in the textbooks alongside the fallacious first-best arguments for tariffs. This would help to counter the widespread belief that tariffs are a sensible second-best reaction to a wide set of domestic distortions that cannot be removed directly.

In 'Two notes on tariffs, distortions and growth' (1967) Harry is back on his basic theme: an increase in productivity g in protected industries may lower rather than raise welfare: $\partial W/\partial g \gtreqless 0$; and the hypothesis that 'if the causes of growth were biased towards augmenting production of the commodity favoured by the distortion, the rate of growth of real output at world market prices would be less than it would be in the absence of the distortion, and conversely' is wrong. Instead, 'real growth may be *either faster* or *slower* in the presence of a distortion than it would be in the absence of any distortion' 1971a, 180–1, [italics added].

When summarized article after article, as I am doing, the repeated conclusion that anything can happen begins to seem tedious, and it is easy to see how earlier readers often felt Harry was 'too negative' or even 'nihilistic.' But many economists did believe, for example, that, except in the case of Bhagawti's immiserizing growth, an increase in productivity would make a country better off. Thus Harry's demonstration that if the productivity growth occurs in a protected industry the country could be made worse off under a wide set of conditions must be regarded as an important correction of error. It added to knowledge by making people aware of hitherto unsuspected possibilities.

THE NEED FOR QUANTITATIVE ECONOMICS

Harry held that quantitative restrictions are needed to give theories predictive power. He was no high-powered econometrician, and it can even be argued that he used too little of his enormous influence among students and researchers to encourage econometric analysis of trade problems. He did, however, do empirical work, and he did welcome and make use of empirical results whenever they were established by others. A typical piece of work in which he combined other people's econometrics with data of his own to reach quantitative conclusions was his 1966 paper on sugar protectionism. He concludes: 'replacement of the present national systems of protection by

S46 / Richard G. Lipsey

deficiency payments (scientific protection) would increase the export earnings of these [sugar-producing] countries by something in the neighbourhood of half a billion dollars (42).

There are many other examples of similar work, but in the interests of brevity I shall now confine myself to the material on this subject that is in his 1971 collection of tariff essays. In 'The gains from exploiting monopoly or monopsony power in international trade' (1968a), Harry can be seen following up the logic of his own position on the emptiness of qualitative economics. The optimum tariff argument had long been one of the few correct arguments for the proposition that tariffs could raise rather than lower the welfare of the levying country. Harry develops the usual formulas and then puts a range of numbers into them, concluding: 'the gains from an optimum tariff policy will be relatively small unless the import ratio is [very] large or the demand elasticity [very] small' (1971a, 175). (An inspection of his table leads me to add the two 'verys' which Harry did not employ.) The response of many readers to this sort of article was an accusation of 'naïve, back-of-the-envelope calculations.' But if qualitative laws are impossible, and detailed empirical measurements are not available, then this kind of calculation *is* a useful halfway house that can give some help in assessing the likelihood that certain signs and magnitudes of results will be found in real situations.

In 'The cost of protection and the scientific tariff' (1960), Harry also considers quantities. Earlier, in a path-breaking empirical article (1958a), he had estimated the comparative-static gains to Britain from entering the European Common Market to be very small – much less than 1 per cent of its GNP.[17] In the 'Cost of protection,' Harry generalized this argument showing, for example, that 'The consumption cost [of tariffs] ... involves multiplying the compensated elasticity of demand by half the product of three fractions, each of which is likely to be small. The resulting figure will be a very small fraction unless high expenditure proportions [on imports], high elasticities, and high tariff rates go together' (1971a, 202).

In 'The costs of protection and self-sufficiency' (1965d), Harry continued with this theme, calculating the changes in welfare as a result of tariffs in simple models into which a wide range of parameter values had been substi-

17 Harry's position on the common market caused some substantial uproar at the time. Almost alone, Harry insisted on the necessity of, and actually tried to do, quantitative measurement of potential gains to Britain of entry into the EEC. Harry was openly critical of the bulk of the British profession for using qualitative arguments to reach the quantitative restrictions required to give advice on the balance of advantage to Britain. Harry saw the behaviour of British economists as being in the Meade tradition that he had earlier criticized (although Meade himself was not in the 'offending camp' this time). The severe criticisms that Harry frequently made of the British profession's handling of many policy issues all stemmed from the same methodological viewpoint. He felt that at least the most visible members of the profession were still back in the 1930s, arguing qualitatively about quantitative issues. He compared them unfavourably with American economists, who, whatever their doctrinal positions, had, he felt, long ago grasped the essentially quantitative nature of the subject.

The pure theory of international trade / S47

tuted. He concluded that 'both the total gains from international trade and the
cost of protection are likely to be relatively small in the large advanced
industrial countries, owing to their relatively flexible economic structures,
probably high elasticities of substitution among goods on which this consumption is concentrated, and relatively low natural dependence on trade'
(1971a, 236).

THE CONTENT OF QUALITATIVE ECONOMICS OF THE
PUBLIC SECTOR

While holding that qualitative economics was empty with respect to such
disturbances as changes in factor supplies, changes in production functions,
and shifts in demand, Harry held that standard theory did make qualitative
predictions about the behaviour of policy-makers and that these predictions
were continually contradicted by the facts. The theory in question is based on
the two assumptions: first, that policy-makers are rational and, second, that
policy-makers seek to maximize the economic welfare of their citizens. The
standard theory has strong implications about the direction of changes in
policy (e.g. towards universal free trade). Harry came to argue in many of his
later writings that these implications were at variance with the facts because
policy could be seen to be moving in the opposite direction from that which the
theory predicted.
    Harry's answer to this problem was not to abandon the hypothesis of the
rationality of policy-makers but instead to expand their objective functions to
include variables omitted from traditional welfare economics. For example, in
the latter part of the 1960 paper on the 'Cost of protection,' he begins a rational
discussion of some non-economic motives for levying tariffs: to promote
national self-sufficiency and independence, to promote diversification, industrialization, or agriculturalization, to promote a 'way of life,' to increase
military preparedness, and to be used in subsequent international bargaining.
He analyses what policies are rational given these 'non-economic' objectives.
    In 'An economic theory of protectionism, tariff bargaining and the forma-
tion of customs unions' (1965a), Harry takes this kind of analysis much
further. The article was inspired by the questioning of the late John Knapp,
Harry's former colleague at Manchester, who with his habit of asking awkward questions kept asking Harry: 'Why, if reduction of tariffs is economically beneficial, [do] tariff negotiators always regard a tariff reduction as a
concession that must be compensated by reciprocal tariff reductions by the
other party to the bargain?' (Quoted in Johnson, 1971a, 240) As Harry himself
observes, the standard theory of tariffs leaves economics 'without a theory ...
of the nature of tariff bargaining, the commercial policies adopted by various
countries, the conditions under which countries are willing to embark on
customs unions, and the arguments and considerations that have weight in

S48 / Richard G. Lipsey

persuading countries to change their commercial policies' (1971a, 239). Seldom has an economic theorist posed a more important set of (implicit) questions.

Harry goes on to build his theory of policy decisions by adding the assumption that 'there exists a collective preference for industrial production, in the sense that the electorate is willing to spend real resources through government action in order to make the volume of industrial production and employment larger than it would be under free international competition. Industrial production, in other words, appears as a collective consumption good yielding a flow of satisfaction to the electorate independent of the satisfactions they derive directly from the consumption of industrial products' (1971a, 241–2). I doubt if this will provide the whole answer, but it does turn out to be an extraordinarily fruitful hypothesis. It helps to explain behaviour that otherwise seems perverse both when manufacturing and agricultural countries engage in tariff bargaining and when countries producing a variety of industrial products bargain with each other. It also helps to explain the circumstances under which customs unions, rather than non-preferential tariff reductions, will seem attractive. There are far too many propositions for summary, but one example may be quoted:

The standard economic analysis of customs unions stresses the gains from trade creation, against which must be weighed the losses from trade diversion ... These arguments, however, are equally arguments for unilateral tariff elimination ... The arguments usually advanced for customs unions in political discussion, however, generally ignore any possible gain from trade creation, in the sense of the replacement of domestic production by cheaper imports, and instead regard this as a price to be paid for the benefits of expanded export markets, those benefits result from both trade creation and trade diversion in favour of domestically produced products ... In these arguments, trade diversion is valued for its effects in increasing [industrial] production within the union, not for its effects in improving the terms of trade with the outside world; this is significant, because the conditions under which a customs union will divert the most trade are those under which its terms-of-trade effects will be the least ... an argument of this kind will be attractive to countries with a strong preference for industrial production that are ... at a comparative disadvantage in industrial production in relation to the world market. A customs union enables them to satisfy their preference for industrial production through trade creation and trade diversion, to an extent that would not be possible through negotiation of non-discriminatory tariff reduction.

Standard theory would suggest that ... [internal] arrangements would seek to maximize efficiency of production within the union, regardless of where production was located. The preference for industrial production hypothesis, however, would imply that any customs union arrangement would include provisions [as does the Treaty of Rome] to insure that each member obtains a 'fair-share' of industrial production. (1971a, 274–6)

If economics is to explain actual policy behaviour and give advice relevant to policy-makers, new hypotheses are needed about variables, such as Johnson's 'collective industrial good,' that occur in the policy-maker's objective function. Here again we see Harry responding to discrepancies between existing theory and actual observation and in the forefront of those attempting to reduce the discrepancy by amending theory. Clearly, as Johnson demonstrates, it is possible to be an empirical economist without always applying the latest techniques of econometric estimation.

The fourth part of the book of tariff essays concerns the theory of effective protection and includes the 1965 paper (Johnson and Kenen, 1965c) which, along with Corden's 1966 paper, are, according to Chacholiades, 'The seminal contributions to the theory of effective protection' (1978, 441).[18] The whole theory of effective protection is motivated by quantitative concerns. A qualitative economist only needs to know that tariffs do or do not exist; a quantitative economist, however, needs to know *how much* protection is conferred by particular tariff systems. The theory of effective protection is designed to help him arrive at quantitative answers to such questions.

I said above, when discussing 'The economic theory of protectionism,' that I thought Harry's insertion of industrial production as an argument into policy-makers' objective functions would not provide the whole answer. This is partly because I feel that objectives stemming from nationalistic and xenophobic motives need to be there as well. Harry and I never saw eye to eye on this. He was the supreme rationalist, who thought, for example, that Canadian nationalist policies such as high tariffs could be changed by pointing out that they would not achieve the end of raising living standards. I felt that these welfare arguments were only convenient rationalizations and that another argument would be invented as soon as one was destroyed. It seems to me that nationalism and xenophobia are very deep-seated, possibly instinctual, attitudes commonly found in territorial primates. Two bands of apes hurling abuse across the mutual border of their territories may be behaving 'irrationally,' but they are responsing to deep-seated urges, and their behaviour has survival value. Problems of terrible potential arise when behaviour patterns (inherited either genetically or culturally) through changed circumstances come to have destructive power rather than survival value. Although it is undoubtedly useful to point out that such behaviour is often irrational, this may not help to change it, since it is often not consciously adopted as part of a rational search for well-specified goals. Harry never accepted the possibility that nationalism might be deeply rooted in instinctual behaviour, and so, in my view, he partially misunderstood its sources and its power to resist rational argument. (Advances in biology promise drastically to reduce our ignorance of such matters over the next decades.)

For these reasons I feel that Harry's writings on this subject (e.g. Johnson, 1961b) were sometimes wide of the mark, although they were valuable in pointing out the errors in many of the rational arguments advanced for

18 Neither Johnson nor Corden were the originators of the idea, which, like most ideas in economics, can be traced back to the dim origins of the whole subject. One of the earliest explicit statements in modern literature, and the earliest reference given by Johnson himself, is Barber (1955).

S50 / Richard G. Lipsey

nationalistic measures. Like Harry, I would like to weaken the forces of Canadian nationalism where they lead to self-emiserizing policies. I believe, however, that we will not succeed until we have a deeper understanding of such attitudes and do not automatically assume that nationalistic policies are merely means adopted in a rational pursuit of maximum economic welfare.

JOHNSON'S WORLD VIEW

I have tried to survey Harry's technical contributions to the pure theory of international trade, most of which were advanced in the 1950s and early 1960s. As time went on he developed a world view of international economics that was broadly based and dynamic and hence could not be expressed as precisely and formally as could his earlier static and comparative-static work. This material is really beyond the scope I have given myself in this paper, but since it will not fall within the purview of any of the other authors in the symposium, I feel that I should at least mention it.

The fullest expression of this view is to be found in his 1968 Wicksell Lectures, but a useful summary, together with important critical comments by several economists, is given in Johnson (1969). This dynamic 'model' of the world economy gave Harry a coherent view of numerous policy issues. Examples are that American direct investment is not a threat to receiving countries but is a way in which knowledge is diffused to their benefit, that the alleged technological gap between the 'have' and 'have-not' countries is nothing more than a vehicle for disguised merchantilist arguments, that brain drains from poorer to richer countries should be a source of concern only in so far as the cost of educating the migrants imposes a burden on those who remain behind, and that most nationalist, protectionist policies are 'irrational.'

Most people who become involved in policy develop some such grand, world-view model. It is usually impossible to formulate the model strictly because its grand design and broad applicability defies tight rigorous specification in the present state of economics. Not too many other economists, however, have managed to be as articulate and open about their world view as Harry was.

CONCLUSIONS

I have illustrated some of Harry's strengths by going through material to be found mainly in *International Trade and Economic Growth* (1958b) and *Aspects of the Theory of Tariffs* (1971a). One of his major limitations was that he would not take the time to work his ideas into the integrated form of a monograph. This led to duplication and weakened the impact of his main theses from what they would have been if given the sustained, integrated treatment required for a monograph. For example, in the introduction to his 1971 book of tariff essays he wrote 'the latter, which contain the introduction to the original lecture series and in one sense is a summary of that series, is reprinted as Chapter 3 of Part I. Its inclusion at this point is premature and awkward' (1971a, ix). Yet he could see nothing to do except include it since he needed some of its material but was unwilling to discard what was duplicated and irrelevant and then rework what remained into a monograph. The papers in this, as in other volumes of collected essays, are insightful, penetrating, and fruitful in their ability to explain the world; but in another sense they can be regarded as a set of first drafts of chapters that were never integrated into the book that, if written, would have had a magnified impact on the development of the subject.

A friend said to me when he heard that I was undertaking this task: 'It would take a Harry Johnson to survey the works of Harry Johnson.' I am inclined to agree, and hardly need to point out that I am no Harry Johnson. I have not tried to convey the substance of Harry's contributions; their scope and variety defy summarization in a short overview. I have tried rather to persuade my readers of what I have been saying ever since 1953, when almost at the same time I first met Harry and first became acquainted with his work on trade. He was not someone who thought theory was an end in itself; he was not satisfied merely with a taxonomy of all possible cases; he did not deal unconcernedly in obviously unreal theory; he was no mere writer of footnotes on, and surveys of, other people's work. In one field at least, the field of real trade theory, he was a major contributor of original research.

Not only was Harry a major architect of modern trade theory, his work had an underlying philosophy that gave it a unity that might not be apparent to the casual observer. When I first offered to write this survey it was because I wished to say in print what I had said so often in debate, that Harry's work was not nihilistic or mindlessly taxonomic; instead it advanced knowledge by showing that a series of generalizations thought to be true were not in fact true, and that he was providing case studies on the general theme of the relative emptiness of qualitative economics. In my arrogance I had always thought that I understood the unity behind Harry's work (in this field at least) better than he did himself. When I came to reread his major trade works at one time I was surprised at how clearly he saw the philosophy behind what he was doing. His three main themes are not only clearly evident in his work, they are explicitly stated by him many times.

The first theme was to expose the comparative emptiness of qualitative economics by showing that, except in the simplest of models, it was impossible to sign $\partial Y_j / \partial Z_i$ for most, if not all, i and j. Harry continually took cases where others had come up with a sign and showed either that their logic was wrong or that, in a slightly more complex model, the signing of the result was

S52 / Richard G. Lipsey

no longer possible.[19] The second theme was the need for quantitative restrictions so that it would be possible to make predictions more restrictive than that Y_j may go up, down, or stay the same when Z_i is changed. Although he was no econometrician, he welcomed econometric work and in its absence did not hesitate to insert numbers into his theories to see what the range of parameter values would have to be for some particular result to occur. Although no substitute for sophisticated econometric work, this did allow readers to form some judgments on the likelihood of particular results actually occurring, and did show believers in those results what kinds of magnitudes they would have to show to exist if their conjectured results were in fact to occur. The third theme was that if economic theory is to explain behaviour it must be able to explain the behaviour of policy-makers better than it now does. Here the empirical economist does not need sophisticated econometric techniques to perceive that the behaviour of policy-makers is often inconsistent with the two hypotheses that policy-makers are rational and that the goal of policy-makers is to maximize economic welfare as defined by economists. Harry pioneered ideas for placing arguments into the policy-maker's objective functions other than those admitted by traditional welfare economics. Having done this he then made a new economic analysis of the relation between means and the revised set of ends. The test of the revised theory was whether or not it could explain and predict policy decisions better than did traditional welfare-maximization theory.

All these themes are natural in the work of someone who believed that economics could be a science that would explain and predict what we see in the world, and who abhorred error wherever he saw it. In espousing his third theme, Harry was in the forefront. Today a growing chorus of economists is calling for better explanations of policy decisions than just 'error' and 'perversity,' and the questions Harry posed will be in the forefront of economic studies in the 1980s. Without satisfactory answers to them we will no more understand policy decisions on inflation, unemployment, energy prices, and rent controls than decisions on tariffs, customs unions, and commercial policy.

19 To my surprise my view on this point has been challenged by more than one eminent trade theorist who has read the manuscript of this paper. Because of this I will add one further quotation that I have just come across in which Harry is very clear on this point. In a review (1972a) of my PH D thesis on customs unions (Lipsey, 1970), he writes "Lipsey ... contributed much ... to the understanding of the nature of the basic problem and of the techniques required to handle it. The general result, however, is ... that anything at all can happen and that what actually happens will depend on empirical parameters that no one can yet estimate ... This result, rather unsatisfactory from the point of view of the pure theorist who believes that an armchair is the best vehicle for arriving at truth, has been confirmed by any number of subsequent writers' (729–30).

REFERENCES

Archibald, G.C. (1965) 'The qualitative content of maximizing models.' *Journal of Political Economy* 73, 27–36

Barber, C.L. (1955) 'Canadian tariff policy.' *Canadian Journal of Economics and Political Science* 21, 513–30.

Bhagwati, J. and H.G. Johnson (1960) 'Notes on some controversies in the theory of international trade.' *Economic Journal* 70, 74–93

Chacholiades, M. (1978) *International Trade Theory and Policy* (New York: McGraw-Hill)

Corden, W.M. (1966) 'The structure of a tariff system and the effective protection rate.' *Journal of Political Economy* 74, 221–37

Johnson, H. G. (1951) 'The taxonomic approach to economic policy.' *Economic Journal* 61, 812–28

– (1953) 'Optimum tariffs and retaliation.' *Review of Economic Studies* 21, 142–53

– (1954) 'Increasing productivity, income-price trends and the trade balance.' *Economic Journal* 64, 462–85

– (1955) 'Economic expansion and international trade.' *Manchester School of Economic and Social Studies* 23, 95–112

– (1957) 'Factor endowments, international trade and factor prices.' *Manchester School of Economic and Social Studies* 25, 270–83

– (1958a) 'The gains from freer trade with Europe: an estimate.' *Manchester School of Economic and Social Studies* 26, 247–55

– (1958b) *International Trade and Economic Growth* (London: Allen and Unwin)

– (1959) 'International trade, income distribution, the offer curve, and the effects of tariffs.' *Manchester School of Economic and Social Studies* 27, 215–42

– (1960) 'The cost of protection and the scientific tariff.' *Journal of Political Economy* 67, 327–45

– (with J. Bhagwati) (1961a) 'A generalized theory of the effects of tariffs on the terms of trade. *Oxford Economic Papers* 12, 225–53

– (1961b) 'Problems of Canadian nationalism.' *International Journal* 16, 238–50

– (1962) *Money, Trade and Economic Growth* (London: Allen and Unwin)

– (1965a) 'An economic theory of protectionism, tariff bargaining and the formation of customs unions.' *Journal of Political Economy* 73, 256–83

– (1965b) 'Optimal trade interventions in the presence of domestic distortions.' In R.E. Baldwin et al., *Trade Growth and the Balance of Payments: Essays in Honour of Gottried Haberler* (Chicago: Rand McNally) 3–34

– (with P. Kenen) (1965c) *Trade and Development* (Geneva: Librairie Droz) 9–29

– (1965d) 'The costs of protectionism and self-sufficiency.' *Quarterly Journal of Economics* 72, 356–72

– (1966) 'Sugar Protection and the export earnings of less developed countries: variations on a theme by R.H. Snake.' *Economica* NS33, 34–42

– (1967) 'Two notes on tariffs, distortions and growth.' Originally published under other titles in the *Economic Journal* 77, 151–4, and 80, 990–2, reprinted as chapter 7 in Johnson (1971a)

– (1968a) 'The gains from exploiting monopoly or monopsony power in international trade.' *Economica* 35, 151–6

– (1968b) 'Comparative cost and commercial policy theory for a developing world economy.' *Wicksell Lectures* (Stockholm: Almqvist and Wicksell)

– (1969) 'The theory of international trade.' In P.A. Samuelson, ed., *International Relations* (London: Macmillan) 55–66

S54 / Richard G. Lipsey

- (1971a) *Aspects of the Theory of Tariffs* (London: Allen and Unwin)
- (1971b) 'Trade and growth: a geometrical exposition.' *Journal of International Economics* 1, 83–101
- (1972a) 'Review of Lipsey (1970)' *Economic Journal* 82, 728–30
- (1972b) 'Trade and growth: a correction.' *Journal of International Economics* 2, 87–8
- (with A.R. Nobay) (1975) 'James Edward Meade: a partial tribute.' *Manchester School of Economic and Social Studies* 43, 213–19

Kaldor, N. (1940) 'A note on tariffs and the terms of trade.' *Economica* 7, 377–80

Lipsey, R.G. (1970) *The Theory of Customs Unions: A General Equilibrium Analysis* (London: Weidenfeld & Nicolson)

Meade, J.E. (1951) *The Theory of International Economic Policy*. Vol. 1. *The Balance of Payments* (London: Oxford University Press)

Mundell, R.W. (1968) *International Economics* (New York: Macmillan)

Samuelson, P.A. (1947) *Foundations of Economic Analysis* (Cambridge, Mass.: Harvard University Press)

[4]

The balance of payments: a survey of Harry Johnson's contributions

JOHN F. HELLIWELL / University of British Columbia

Abstract. This survey is in two parts. The first part uses Johnson's own classification scheme to analyse his contributions to alternative approaches to balance-of-payments theory. Three categories are distinguished: the elasticity and absorption approaches, the Keynesian multiplier and Keynesian policy approaches, and the monetary approach. The second part of the paper deals with Johnson's contributions to six specific issues: the transfer problem, policies for internal and external balance, the role of gold, flexible exchange rates, the breakdown of the Bretton Woods system, and world liquidity and inflation. A short concluding section evaluates Johnson's influence on the direction and content of balance-of-payments analysis.

La balance des paiements: une revue de l'apport d'Harry Johnson. Cette revue se divise en deux parties. La première utilise le cadre de référence utilisé par Johnson pour analyser ses divers travaux et leur apport aux diverses approches à la théorie de la balance des paiements (les approches par l'élasticité et l'absorption, les approches keynesiennes – multiplicateur et politique – et l'approche monétaire). La seconde partie examine l'apport de Johnson au débat sur six problèmes particuliers: le problème des transferts, les politiques de maintien de l'équilibre interne et externe, le rôle de l'or, les taux de change flexibles, l'échec du système élaboré à Bretton-Woods, et la liquidité mondiale et l'inflation. En conclusion, l'auteur tente de dégager une mesure de l'influence de Johnson sur le contenu et la direction de l'analyse de la balance des paiements.

This paper, like much else that has been written about the balance of payments over the past twenty-five years, is heavily dependent on the works of Harry Johnson for its organization as well as its content. In the first main section of the paper, I shall describe Harry Johnson's main approaches to balance-of-payments theory, using his own (1976d) classification scheme for

I am grateful for comments received on earlier versions of this paper presented at seminars at McMaster University and at MIT. Special thanks, but no blame, are due for helpful comments from Rudiger Dornbusch, Stanley Fischer, Herbert Grubel, Peter Jonson, and Doug Purvis. Thanks also to Leigh Mazany and to Hilary Wilson for research and typing.

Canadian Journal of Economics/Revue canadienne d'Economique, XI, Supplement
November/novembre 1978. Printed in Canada/Imprimé au Canada.

S56 / John F. Helliwell

that purpose. He used a fivefold classification of approaches, which I have consolidated into three groups: the elasticity and absorption approaches, the Keynesian multiplier and policy approaches, and finally the monetary approach to the balance of payments. The main emphasis will be on the monetary approach, partly because there are more unsettled questions of theory and policy to be addressed in this area, but primarily because it represents what is probably the most important focus of Harry Johnson's work during the 1970s.

In the second part of the paper I shall deal with several specific problems or issues to which Harry Johnson has made important contributions. Any such selection must be arbitrary, as Harry Johnson's contributions have been vast and varied enough to embrace almost every important issue in the analysis of the balance of payments. I have selected six issues: the transfer problem, policies for internal and external balance, gold, exchange rate flexibility, the breakdown of the Bretton Woods system, and world inflation. Even with these selected issues my treatment will be uneven, sometimes being discursive and descriptive of the broad outlines of Johnson's contributions and in other places dealing with quite specific points of analysis or exposition. In this, too, I am following Harry Johnson's example, although I am much less graceful than he was in switching from detailed analysis of small points to broad perspectives on large issues.

ALTERNATIVE APPROACHES TO BALANCE-OF-PAYMENTS THEORY

Elasticity and absorption approaches

'Towards a general theory of the balance of payments'[1] contains Harry Johnson's justly celebrated explanation of the elasticity and absorption approaches within a framework of monetary analysis. Two important pairs of concepts were introduced. One pair, the 'expenditure-switching' and 'expenditure-reducing' aspects of a successful devaluation, were used to make the primary distinction between the elasticity and absorption approaches. The elasticity approach emphasizes expenditure-switching effects under alternative assumptions about the price elasticities of supply and demand for imports and exports. The absorption approach, with its view of a balance-of-payments deficit as an excess of total spending (absorption) over total receipts, involves concentration on the need to reduce total spending (to the extent that output cannot be increased) until balance between spending and output is restored.

The distinction between 'expenditure-switching' and 'expenditure-reducing' effects can be illustrated by Figure 1, which is a slight modification of the textbook 'Keynesian cross.'

---

1 First published in 1958, and since reprinted in Caves and Johnson (1968), Frenkel and Johnson (1976) and elsewhere.

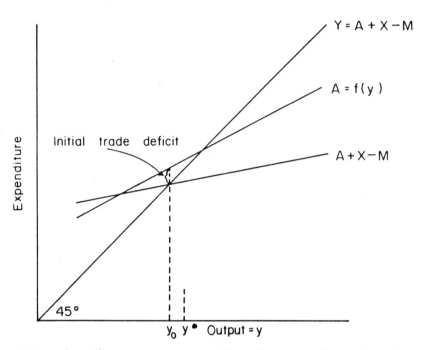

FIGURE 1 Expenditure, output, and balance of trade. Components of expenditure: A is domestic absorption, X is exports, M is imports. Real output, assumed equal to income, is Y. Initial output is Y_0, and full employment output is Y^*.

The absorption line A is steeper than the aggregate demand line $A + X - M$ because imports are a fraction of absorption. Suppose that there is an initial balance-of-trade deficit, measured by the vertical distance from A to $A + X - M$ at the level of output determined by the intersection of the $A + X - M$ and the 45° lines. The expenditure-switching effects of a devaluation are shown by a rise in the $A + X - M$ line relative to the A line. This will take place, in the simplest model with perfectly elastic supplies of imports and exports and with import prices fixed in domestic currency and export prices fixed in foreign currency, if the 'elasticities' (Marshall-Lerner) condition is met – that the sum of the price elasticities of demand for imports and for exports exceeds unity.

The 'expenditure-reducing' aspect of the devaluation is to lower the A line (and hence the $A + X - M$ line) enough that the intersection of the $A + X - M$ line with the 45° line should not be to the right of the full-employment level of output Y^*.

In his 1958 analysis Johnson noted that the pre-war 'elasticity' and 'foreign-trade multiplier theory' elements of 'traditional' theory were improved upon in two respects by the emerging 'new (though still Keynesian) theoretical approach to balance-of-payments theory ... It poses the problems of balance-of-payments adjustment in a way which highlights their policy

S58 / John F. Helliwell

implications; and it allows for conditions of full employment and inflation' (Caves and Johnson, 1968, 375).

Johnson argued that the fundamental contribution of the absorption approach was to emphasize that under conditions of full employment the success of a devaluation depends entirely on a reduction in the level of real domestic spending. Johnson's own contribution to the absorption approach lay in emphasizing the possibility of the necessary reduction in spending being achieved by policy rather than by the impact of inflation on spending.[2]

In developing the policy focus of his 1958 paper, Johnson distinguished a second pair of concepts: 'stock' deficits and 'flow' deficits: 'The importance of the distinction stems from the fact that a 'stock' deficit is inherently temporary and implies no real worsening of the country's economic position, whereas a 'flow' deficit is not inherently temporary and may imply a worsening of the country's economic position' (Caves and Johnson, 1968, 379).

The stock deficit, for which his example is a once-and-for-all alteration in portfolio preferences, provides an argument 'in favour of the use of controls on international capital movements as against the alternative methods available,' because the alternative policies (monetary contraction or exchange depreciation) set up 'unavoidable repercussions on the flow equilibrium of the economy' (ibid, 380).

By contrast, 'flow' deficits require more fundamental policy changes, with the appropriate mix of expenditure-switching and expenditure-reducing policies determined by how close the economy is to full employment. Nowadays, analysts would make Johnson's distinction in some other terms, perhaps distinguishing between 'temporary' and 'continuing' disturbances to the balance of payments. It is now more usual, and advisedly so, to use 'stocks' and 'flows' as analytical counterparts in any model or situation, and not to use them as descriptions of alternative states of affairs.

By the middle 1970s (e.g. in 1976d), Harry Johnson was defining the elasticity and absorption approaches in more stylized and restrictive terms, with the elasticity approach being identified with a propensity to hoard of 1.0 with respect to available income from export increases or import decreases brought about by relative price changes. The absorption approach was stylized (in 1976d) by a fully employed economy with all imports and exports priced at world prices and devaluation having its effects solely through income redistribution and real balance effects caused by the inflation.

Also noticeable by the 1970s was a marked lessening of Harry Johnson's emphasis on policy alternatives for dealing with the balance of payments, especially the alternative of using direct controls to deal with stock deficits. After twenty years of convertible currencies and greatly liberalized trade and

---

2 Johnson argues (Caves and Johnson, 1968, 385, fn 16) that Alexander (1952) did not adequately recognize the policy alternative, while Meade (1951) assumed the necessary expenditure-reducing policies without considering the inflation alternative.

capital flows, Harry Johnson and the world economy were both changed. In the 1970s, Harry Johnson was much less inclined to offer willingly to governments the option of treating balance-of-payments disequilibria as a series of 'stock deficits,' each justifying the use of an equally 'temporary' offsetting control.

Keynesian multiplier and Keynesian policy approaches to balance-of-payments analysis

Harry Johnson (1976e) identifies the 'Keynesian multiplier' approach with the contributions of Harberger (1950), Laursen and Metzler (1950), and Meade (1951), and attributes the origin of the Keynesian policy approach to the latter. He rightly notes the problems of thinking of the absorption, Keynesian multiplier, and Keynesian policy approaches as being successive or even competing approaches, given that the primary references were all written about the same time and were not in general regarded as competitors by their authors. There is a sense, in fact, in which 'it is all in Meade', but even readers as assiduous as Johnson (in 1951, a review article on Meade's classic book), Tsiang (in his 1961 synthesis of elasticity and absorption approaches), and Alexander (in his 1959 synthesis) had trouble with Meade's 'overcomplicated model and its formidable list of variables' (Tsiang, 1961, in Caves and Johnson, 1968, 391). There is a second problem, which Tsiang raised with Meade's analysis: even though the model itself has all the necessary channels, most of the working out is done either under the assumption of internal balance or with a 'Keynesian neutral monetary policy,' meaning that the money supply is made perfectly elastic at the rate of interest chosen as a policy variable. This latter definition of 'neutral monetary policy,' which was followed in some of the 1960s papers developing the Keynesian policy approach, suppresses the explicit treatment of monetary flows. With this definition of a neutral monetary policy, it is possible, although it is seldom done, to determine the degree of domestic credit expansion or contraction required to peg the nominal interest rate.

Some of the 1960s 'Keynesian policy' literature, and all of the 1970s textbook integration of open economy analysis into the standard Hicksian IS-LM analysis, treats 'neutral monetary policy' as an unchanged money supply. All the literature that might be called the Keynesian multiplier approach suppresses explicit treatment of money and inflation; it can alternatively be thought of as partial analysis of a more complete system, with the interest rate (which in this model provides the links between money and spending) held at some predetermined level.

Johnson (1976d, 450) describes the Keynesian multiplier approach as 'making good the deficiency of the simple "elasticity" approach by recognizing and allowing for the implications of changes in expenditure on output, income, expenditure, and again output for balance-of-payments equilibrium.'

To find the net balance-of-payments effect of a devaluation, the import-increasing effects of the multiplied increase in expenditure must be set against the 'expenditure-switching' effects of the devaluation, in increasing the level of exports and decreasing imports as a fraction of expenditure.

In the course of spelling out the necessary conditions for the devaluation to improve the balance of payments (assumed equal to the balance of trade in the non-monetary Keynesian multiplier approach), Johnson (1976d) develops a geometric exposition with some superficial similarities to the Keynesian cross so often used to explain basic non-monetary multiplier theory. Johnson's diagram, however, plots domestic output on the vertical axis and expenditure on the horizontal axis, so that the 45° line represents the equality of imports and exports (hence the equality of domestic absorption and output, $C + I + G = Y$), not the usual equality of national expenditure and output ($C + I + G + X - M = Y$). In the usual diagram the level of output is determined automatically at the intersection of the spending line and the 45° line; in Johnson's diagram there is no way of locating the (temporary) equilibrium level of either output or expenditure. I think this leads him into expositional error, and it is certainly likely to confuse others who are more used to the conventional notation. For example, Johnson starts (1976d, 450) with a situation of initial intersection of the 45° line and the line showing aggregate demand for domestic output as a function (with slope less than 1.0) of domestic absorption. He then considers a devaluation that will (if the elasticity conditions are satisfied) push up the aggregate demand curve for domestic output. Johnson shows this as producing a new level of output at the intersection of the 45° line with the aggregate demand line (at point P' of Johnson's Figure 3 in 1976d, 450) but as not telling us what happens to the balance of payments. On the contrary, the new level of output indicated by the intersection of the 45° line and the demand for output will only be achieved if the devaluation has a zero net effect on the balance of trade, so that the pre- and post-devaluation solutions lie on the 45° line, indicating a zero balance of trade. Thus the diagram either tells us about the level of income *and* the balance of trade, but only by assuming at the outset that devaluation has a zero net impact on the balance of trade, or it tells us about neither, because it does not contain enough information to identify the levels of output and expenditure.

The alternative geometric exposition of Figure 1 above can be used to make Johnson's points more clearly. It extends the usual 'Keynesian cross' by starting with the usual closed economy $C + I + G$ line, which becomes the domestic absorption line A in this open economy version. A total expenditure line $A + X$ (not shown) could be obtained by adding X (assumed independent of Y) to the absorption line. We draw the final line for aggregate net demand $(A + X - M)$ for domestic output by subtracting the volume of imports. The import 'wedge' can be made proportional to absorption A, to total final demand $A + X$, or (more realistically) to some weighted sum of final demand components.[3] The level of output (which is measured along the horizontal axis in this diagram, as in the usual Keynesian cross diagram) is determined by the intersection of the 45° line with the $A + X - M$ line, and the trade balance at that level of income is given as the vertical distance between the A line and the $A + X - M$ line. In this expository framework, a devaluation increases X and either increases or decreases the import 'wedge,' depending on whether the price elasticity of the demand for imports is less or greater than 1.0 in absolute value.[4]

Naturally, whether a devaluation improves or worsens the balance of trade depends on the extent of the shifts in the X and M components, as well as on possible shifts in the absorption curve due to real balance effects of the devaluation and peak income effects arising from any devaluation-induced changes in the terms of trade.

Viewed in this way, the Keynesian multiplier approach combines the basic elements of the absorption and elasticity approaches, except that it does not spell out the monetary linkages as clearly as would be desired by some earlier synthesizers of the two approaches, e.g. Johnson (1958) and Tsiang (1961).

The Keynesian policy approach, which Johnson (1976e) associates primarily with Meade (1951), was made best known by papers in the early 1960s by Fleming (1962) and Mundell (1962; 1968, 217–71) and has since become the primary framework for graphical textbook exposition of the macroeconomic policy choices of an open economy. Harry Johnson's own contributions following this approach are discussed in the next section, dealing with policies for internal and external balance.

The Keynesian policy approach, with its use of two policy instruments to achieve both internal and external balance, can quite properly be regarded as accommodating the key theoretical proposition of the monetary approach to the balance of payments. I shall argue in the next section that Harry Johnson would now regard the key element of the monetary approach to be the link between balance-of-payments imbalances and changes in the domestic money supply. The monetary approach asserts that there is only one money supply consistent with balance-of-payments equilibrium and concentrates on explaining how balance-of-payments disequilibria give rise to an automatic process of adjustment of the money supply. The Keynesian policy approach asserts, in its simpler versions, that there is a single pair of monetary and fiscal

---

3 Any of these ways of determining imports is preferable, as is Johnson's treatment of imports as a fraction of total final demand, to the usual textbook treatment that makes imports a function of output rather than absorption. The latter treatment does not permit proper modelling of the ballooning of imports when absorption rises and output is subject to capacity restraints. Robert Mundell has made a similar point about the problems created by defining imports as a fraction of income rather than absorption (1968, 138).

4 This assumes that all variables are measured in terms of domestic currency; one could alternatively set the framework up in terms of foreign prices, in which case the dependence of the direction of shift on the size of the price elasticity shifts from imports to exports.

S62 / John F. Helliwell

policies consistent with internal and external balance. There are two important differences between the two approaches. First, the monetary approach often assumes either continuous full employment or a relatively speedy and automatic adjustment towards full employment, and thus does not require explicit use of fiscal policy for stabilization purposes. Second, the Keynesian policy approach short-circuits the automatic process of money supply adjustment by immediately adjusting the domestic source component of the money supply so that, in conjunction with the desired stock of foreign exchange, the total money supply is what it must be to achieve external balance. Thus the issue of sterilizing the monetary effects of reserve flows never arises, because monetary policy is established as required to avoid gains or losses of foreign exchange.

As will be shown later, other points have been made about the feasibility of the Keynesian policy approach to the balance of payments. The most important of the difficulties relating to the simpler versions of the approach relate to the longer-term implications of using continuing net capital flows to offset trade imbalance. To treat these difficulties seriously, one has to specify the demands for domestic and foreign securities in terms of portfolio size and composition and to explain also the current account effects of the resulting interest and dividend payments. These points do not require consideration in this section, however, as the required amendments to theoretical and empirical models can and have been made and do not mark a necessary point of contrast between Keynesian and monetary approaches to the balance of payments.

The monetary approach to balance-of-payments theory
Harry Johnson did more than anyone else to define the boundaries and to establish the claims of the monetary approach to the balance of payments.[5] In a well-known 1971 lecture, published since in several places, Johnson described the 'new' approach as 'emerging from several sources' (1972d, 229), including, on the practical side, the failure of the 1967 UK devaluation to have the desired results, and, on the theoretical side, the contributions of Koopmans and Mundell (1972d, 229).[6] Johnson states that the main departure of the monetary approach from the Keynesian policy approach lies in rejecting the possibility of insulating the domestic money supply from the effects of balance-of-payments surpluses and deficits. 'The new approach assumes – in some cases asserts – that these monetary inflows or outflows associated with surpluses or deficits are not sterilized – or cannot be, within a period relevant

5 His major contributions include 1972a, 1972e, 1975a, 1975d, 1976b, 1976d, 1977a, 1977b, and Frenkel and Johnson 1976.
6 No specific references to Koopmans or Mundell are given by Johnson. The reference to Koopmans is apparently based on a paper by F. De Jong noted elsewhere by Johnson (1972e, 32). Mundell (1968, 150) first defined the 'monetary approach' to the balance of payments as stressing the identity linking the balance of payments to the excess of hoarding over credit creation.

to policy analysis – but instead influence the domestic money supply. Deficits and surpluses represent phases of stock adjustment in the money market and not equilibrium flows, and should not be treated within an analytical framework that treats them as equilibrium phenomena' (1972d, 235).

Johnson then went on, in the context of a rather rigidly defined system (one world price level, one world interest rate, rigidly fixed exchange rates, and instantaneously complete equilibration of money supply and demand) to show how, under these assumptions, monetary policy in a small country has no impact on the domestic money supply but only on the size of international reserves relative to the domestic credit backing of the domestic money supply. The analysis was then extended to the world system to show how the equilibrium growth rates of world prices depend on the growth rate of the world money supply, with each country having rising or falling foreign reserves according to whether its additions to domestic credit fell short of or exceeded the additions to the domestic demand for money.

The key mechanism in the monetary approach is often considered to be the price-specie flow mechanism of David Hume, because in both cases the money supply adjusts automatically to restore equilibrium in the balance of payments. However, the emphasis in the Hume mechanism is on relative price differentials triggering trade flows that in turn cause reserve flows that eventually remove the relative price differentials. In partial contrast to this, much of the monetary approach in the balance of payments emphasizes the determination of prices at the world level and treats the balance of payments solely as the device that guarantees the equilibration of money supply and demand.

One of the most interesting features of the monetary approach to the balance of payments, especially in the post-1973 development and defence of it by Harry Johnson, has been the adversarial tone of the analysis. This tone is surprising because there would appear to be little in the way of professional resistance to consideration of the consequences and difficulties inherent in sterilization policies, and hence to serious questioning of the assumption of national monetary independence commonly adopted in textbook analysis. Indeed, the matter was addressed very clearly in Johnson's own 1958 emphasis on the futility of attempting to sterilize the monetary consequences of continuing disturbances to the balance of payments, and thus postponing the inevitable adjustments required to restore equilibrium. Perhaps the stage for dispute was set by Mundell's (1962) popularization of Meade's analysis of the use of monetary and fiscal policies to achieve internal and external equilibrium. Explicit in this analysis is the possibility of using monetary policy to avoid what otherwise would be a balance-of-payments deficit by attracting foreign capital in sufficient quantities to offset a trade deficit. Not only did this analysis apparently permit a judicious choice of monetary and fiscal policies to be used to achieve internal and external balance, but it also appeared to permit (e.g. Mundell 1968, 226–7), the use, at least temporarily, of steriliza-

S64 / John F. Helliwell

tion policy to achieve a 'quasi-equilibrium' in which a balance of payments deficit coexists with an unchanging money supply. These two cases are more similar than might first appear. In the first case the continuing flow of additional credit is provided by private foreign lenders; in the second case the government runs down its net stock of official reserves or builds up its official foreign indebtedness. In a growth context this type of strategy can be feasible for extended periods, but in the absence of continuing flows of new foreign savings, it is made unsustainable by the continuing increase in debt-service costs and the ever-higher interest rates required as the foreign debts loom larger in relation to domestic income and foreign portfolios.

Even in the context of the Keynesian policy approach, these limitations had been widely recognized, and had led to portfolio-balance or stock-adjustment interpretations of capital flows for open economies (Oates, 1966) and similar treatment of the total demand for government debt in closed economies (Ott and Ott, 1965; Christ, 1967). The portfolio equilibrium conditions for a non-growing economy imply zero net saving for the government, for the private sector, and for the foreign sector. These are the same stock equilibrium conditions that are at the centre of the monetary approach to the balance of payments, although the monetary approach places primary emphasis on the stock demand for money and tends to play down the importance of bonds, real assets, and the other non-monetary components of wealth.

It must remain something of a puzzle why so much stress was placed, by Johnson and others, on the extent to which the monetary approach differs from what is described wtihout much supporting detail, as the 'traditional approach.' The puzzle becomes even deeper when one notes that the same papers and authors (e.g. Meade 1951 and Mundell 1968) that were regarded as leading exponents of the Keynesian policy approach are also seen as providing the essence of the monetary approach.[7]

Putting aside these issues of presentation and style, I shall now take up some of what seem to me to be the more interesting and still unsettled features of the monetary approach.

1 The distinction between the 'monetary approach to the balance of payments' and the 'monetarist' approach to the analysis of a closed economy.
In his 1971 presentation of the 'monetary approach,' Johnson made no attempt either to link or to separate these approaches. If anything, one is tempted to infer some linkage, as at one point Johnson describes the models

---

7 Another slightly puzzling feature of some of the papers utilising the monetary approach is the extent to which an air of controversy is built up by reference to un-named detractors who are said to have made extreme counterclaims. For example, in the introductory chapter of Frenkel and Johnson (1976), a brief account 'implicitly disposes of various, and often ill-informed, criticisms that have tended to be made of it, and which amount essentially to red herrings across the trail of scientific study and understanding.' References to the sources of the red herrings are not included; this too reflects a departure from the well-referenced and careful analytic style that is usually a hallmark of Harry Johnson's exposition of balance-of-payments issues.

he presents as 'monetarist models of balance-of-payments behaviour' (1972d, 237). Subsequently, however, a distinction was drawn primarily between the policy implications of the two approaches. For example, in Frenkel and Johnson (1976, 24) the monetary approach to the balance of payments

is described as 'monetary' instead of 'monetarist,' precisely to avoid confusion with recent domestic policy debates in which the term 'monetarist' has been used by the debaters to represent alternatively attaching 'appropriate' and 'too much' importance to money. ... The monetary approach to the balance of payments asserts neither that monetary mismanagement is the only cause, nor that monetary policy change is the only possible cure, for balance of payments problems; it does suggest, however, that monetary processes will bring about a cure of some kind – not necessarily very attractive – unless frustrated by deliberate monetary policy action, and that policies that neglect or aggravate the monetary implications of deficits and surpluses will not be successful in the declared objectives'[8]

The distinction was made again later by Johnson:

The description 'the monetary approach' has, unfortunately, given rise to a great deal of ignorant and sometimes deliberate misunderstanding. Its use was intended to put the emphasis on ... the use of the techniques of monetary theory ... [and] to stress the link with the grand long-standing, classical tradition of international monetary analysis. Instead, it led to identification of a virtually independent development in international monetary economics with the domestic monetary policy debate over 'monetarism' vs 'Keynesianism' or 'fiscalism' in the United States, and more recently in the United Kingdom, and to the injection into the field of international monetary theory of ideological and anti-scientific modes of argument, stereotyping of theories into straw men, misrepresentations of theories for the purposes of vilification, and misquotation for the purposes of academic nit-picking. (1976e, 13–14)

These quotations suggest why Johnson was increasingly keen on distinguishing the 'monetary approach to the balance of payments' from domestic 'monetarist' approaches, and on dropping some of the more extreme assumptions (one world price level, full employment of factors, one world interest rate) of his earlier work on the monetary approach. Even in 1972, when he was less concerned to differentiate monetary and monetarist approaches, he argued that the equilibrium assumptions of the monetary approach would have to be dropped:

But the real practical problem – with which theorists and empirical workers have been struggling for some years in the area of domestic monetary theory – is how to marry the

8 Frenkel and Johnson (1976, 24). This echoes very closely the point made by Johnson in his 1958 'Towards a general theory': 'balance-of-payments deficits and difficulties are essentially monetary phenomena, traceable to either of two causes: too low a ratio of international reserves relative to the domestic money supply, so that the economic policy authorities cannot rely on the natural self-correcting process; or the pursuit of governmental policies which oblige the authorities to feed the deficit by credit creation ... To conclude that balance-of-payments problems are essentially monetary is not, of course, to assert that they are attributable to monetary mismanagement – they may be, or they may be the result of "real" forces in the face of which the monetary authorities play a passive role.'

S66 / John F. Helliwell

monetarist and Keynesian analysis in a way relevant to the short-run context (albeit a run of several calendar years) with which the policy-makers are concerned, and which is characterized both by variations in production and employment as well as in money prices, and by variations in the relations among export, import, and non-traded goods prices which are assumed away in the long-run equilibrium analysis of the monetarist approach. Chapter 9 [a reprinting of Johnson's 1971 lecture] presents only the bare monetarist bones of the new approach and does not attempt to arrive at any such synthesis; but the achievement of such a synthesis is, to my mind, the really challenging task facing international monetary theory in its next stage of development. (1972d, 14)

It seems clear to me that Harry Johnson not only thought such a synthesis to be important but wished the monetary approach to the balance of payments to be defined broadly enough to include the eventual synthesis. Writing in 1976, he still believed that 'the central problem of monetary analysis that ... needs to be solved ... is the problem of the operation of, and the policies needed to control satisfactorily, an economy which responds to disturbances by adjustments of *both* the price level *and* aggregate output' (1976e, 6).

2 The distinction between the 'monetary approach' to the balance of payments and the 'world monetarist' approach to world inflation.
This distinction has been made most clearly by Whitman (1975). The prototypical 'world monetarists,' in her view, are Arthur Laffer and Robert Mundell (as represented by their contributions to Johnson and Swoboda, 1973), whose assumptions and analysis are almost identical to those used by Johnson (1972a) in his initial exposition of the monetary approach to the balance of payments: no sterilization, full employment, and one world price level.[9] Whitman argues (1975, 512), and I would agree, that the essential feature of the monetary approach to the balance of payments is the rejection of sterilization, and hence the inclusion of an endogenous money supply that reaches a stationary value only when there is a zero balance of payments. The world monetarist position, by contrast, emphasizes that national output cannot be influenced at all by domestic monetary policy, and monetary policy can influence national price levels only to the extent that the exchange rate is flexible or the world money supply is (under fixed exchange rates) affected by the domestic monetary policy. Neither the monetary approach nor the world monetarist approach attaches any great importance to the distinction between the trade and capital accounts of the balance of payments or to the determination of the economy's supply potential.

9 The 'world monetarists' are also advocates of fixed exchange rates, and this may also be a major point of distinction. Note that there are three Mundells being referred to in this survey: the Mundell who popularized the notions of assigning monetary and fiscal policies to achieve internal and external balance (as typified by chapters 15–17 of Mundell, 1968); the Mundell who originated the monetary approach to the balance of payments (chapters 10 and 18 of Mundell, 1968, and part II of Mundell, 1971); and the 'world monetarist' Mundell referred to by Whitman. The links between these strands of Mundell's work deserve a survey of their own.

3 What does the 'monetary approach' imply about money market equilibrium?
The literature, both theoretical and applied, of the monetary approach to the balance of payments is somewhat divided on the existence and importance of disequilibrium between money supply and money demand. Papers based on the assumption of full equilibrium and fast-clearing markets (e.g. Johnson, 1972a) emphasize the supposition that money demanders always have the stocks of money they wish to hold, and any excess supply of domestic credit simply leads to an immediately offsetting reduction in foreign exchange reserves caused by an inflow of either goods or securities.[10]

In contrast to this, there have been important theoretical contributions (Prais, 1961, reprinted in IMF, 1977: Jonson and Kierzkowski, 1975: and Dornbusch 1973a, 1973b) and empirical applications (Polak, 1957, and Rhomberg, 1965, both reprinted in IMF 1977; Jonson, 1976; Jonson and Rankin, 1977) that have been or would be considered by Harry Johnson to be part of the monetary approach to the balance of payments yet attach great importance to continuing disequilibrium in the money market as a central part of the balance-of-payments adjustment process. The question arises most dramatically in the empirical work of Peter Jonson (1976, Jonson, Moses, and Wymer, 1976), which was initially part of the International Monetary Research Programme directed by Harry Johnson at the London School of Economics and which makes extensive use of the discrepancy between the actual (supply-determined) stock of money and the equilibrium quantity demanded (a function of income and the interest rate) to influence absorption, prices, capital flows, and the trade balance. In a recent survey essay, Peter Jonson (1977) argues that the idea of money as a buffer stock that absorbs short-term discrepancies between money supply and demand is consistent with the grand tradition of monetary analysis, although not with the usual estimated demand for money functions.

To be more precise about the role of money disequilibrium effects, we must specify what is meant by monetary disequilibrium. If one means only that the quantity of money demanded will change, under fixed exchange rates, as the economy adjusts to a balance-of-payments disturbance, then the monetary approach requires monetary disequilibrium until balance-of-payments equilibrium is restored, and the alternative Keynesian policy approach avoids money-market disequilibrium only by an initial adjustment of the money supply to a level consistent with balance-of-payments equilibrium. In both of these cases there is no monetary disequilibrium in the sense of a discrepancy between the stock demand for and supply of money at current levels of output.

Dornbusch (1973a, 1973b; both based on a 1971 Chicago PH D thesis for which Harry Johnson was a committee member) makes extensive use of a

10 In an extensive review article of Frenkel and Johnson (1976), Hahn (1977) argues that the stability and uniqueness of the postulated equilibrium are not properly established.

flow measure of hoarding determined as some fraction of the discrepancy between the desired and actual stock of money balances. However, the model contains only nominal income as a determinant of desired money balances, and international trade in securities is not considered, so that the apparent stock disequilibrium can alternatively be interpreted as a partially reduced form of a model with money demand a function of the interest rate as well as nominal income, and with the interest rate moving sufficiently to avoid excess supply or demand in the money market.[11]

Monetary disequilibrium in a more fundamental sense is a central feature of Peter Jonson's (1976) application of a monetary approach to the United Kingdom balance of payments and the Jonson, Moses, and Wymer (1976) model of the Australian economy. In these models the demand for money is based on nominal income and the long-term rate of interest; the actual quantity held is supply-determined; and the discrepancy between the two values is used to influence expenditure, prices, and capital flows. Even in these models it is possible to think of there being some short-term interest rate that does swing enough to produce a short-term equality between money demand and supply; but this would not be true to their spirit, which involves emphasis on the buffer-stock role of money balances, and on the information costs and transactions costs that delay the conversion of unexpected income into increased nominal expenditure or purchase of longer-term portfolio assets. This branch of the monetary approach to the balance of payments thus does involve quantitative measures of monetary disequilibrium in important ways and is pushing towards what Harry Johnson (1972d, 14) regarded as the essential analysis of monetary influences in a context in which production, employment, and prices all vary during the process of adjustment.

Another branch of the monetary approach to the balance of payments, as exemplified by the empirical applications of Kouri and Porter (1974), Girton and Roper (1977), Aghevli and Khan (in IMF, 1977, 275–90), and the empirical chapters in Frenkel and Johnson (1976), assumes that the money market is in continuous equilibrium, with money demand usually (but not always) a function of income and interest rates. Harry Johnson has not passed any clear judgment, so far as I can find, between these alternative branches of the monetary approach.

4 Does the monetary approach to the balance of payments imply that monetary policy can have no lasting effect on either the balance of payments or on output?

11 A similar reworking can be done for an earlier theoretical exposition of the monetary approach by Prais (1961, reprinted in IMF, 1977, 147–61). Rhomberg (1965, reprinted in IMF, 1977, 163–84) used an empirical measure of stock excess money demand, similar to the theoretical formulations of Dornbusch and Prais, to apply the monetary approach to the balance-of-payments statistics of developing countries. It seems natural to prefer a quantitative measure of money supply less a constant-velocity demand for money in place of a market interest rate as a link between money, expenditure, and the balance of payments when securities markets are thin and interest rates often unrepresentative.

Now that a distinction has been made between the monetary approach and the domestic and world monetarist approaches, this question is simpler to handle. The monetary approach does not assume the pre-existing full employment of resources, and thus permits initial increases in output, because the changes in absorption are not fully matched by changes in net imports. The absence of sterilization implies that the money supply will adjust endogenously until the balance of payments returns to zero. This does not of itself imply that either the money supply or the level of output need eventually return to its initial level. Analysis of the possibilities lies beyond the scope of this survey paper, and beyond most of the theoretical and empirical models used so far in analysing the monetary approach to the balance of payments.

PROBLEMS OF THEORY AND POLICY

The transfer problem
The transfer problem is likely to come back into its own as a focus for macroeconomic analysis. Reparations payments were the motivation for the analysis in the 1920s, while fifty years later the macroeconomic impacts of the post-1973 increases in oil prices almost demand to be treated, at least in part, as a deferred transfer from oil consumers to oil producers. What is slightly surprising is that while there has been a substantial continuing activity, in which Harry Johnson has himself been a prominent contributor (e.g. 1973, 1974a, 1974b, 1975b, and 1976c), in the analysis of the transfer problem under the classical conditions of full employment and continued balance of trade, there has not yet been a resurgence of interest in the analysis under contemporary conditions of widespread underutilized capacity and continuing trade imbalances. I shall try to redress this imbalance slightly in this survey, in part because Harry Johnson himself has been the most longstanding (from 1956 to Frenkel and Johnson, 1976, 270–2) of the important contributors to the Keynesian analysis, and in part because there remain some puzzling features of that strand of the literature.

Following Harry Johnson's own classification of issues, the transfer problem has two parts, each of which can be analysed on either Keynesian or classical assumptions (1956, 212–13). The first part of the problem is whether the transfer is initially, at the pre-transfer prices and exchange rates, over- or under-effected.[12] The second part is whether an appropriate mechanism of adjustment is called into play if the transfer is initially over- or under-effected. As Johnson has pointed out (1956, 221–5), the second part of the problem is really the question of whether the foreign exchange market is stable when subjected to a shock equal in size to the amount by which the transfer is initially over- or under-effected.

The 'classical presumption' is that a transfer is initially under-effected, this presumption then leading to Keynes's arguments (1929) against reparations

---

12 A transfer is said to be under-effected if the trade balance of the country making the transfer payment (the transferor) does not increase by enough to match the size of the transfer.

S70 / John F. Helliwell

payments on the grounds that the total burden of the transfer might become impossibly high if it were expressed in terms of the transferor's import good. This aspect of the problem was picked up by Harry Johnson in a recent contribution (1975b) in which he used specific Cobb-Douglas utility functions to define the maximum size of transfer consistent with maintaining any specified level of utility in the transferor country.[13]

In the remainder of this section I shall follow Harry Johnson and the main body of transfer literature and deal with the first part of the transfer problem. Harry Johnson recently (1976c, 213) expressed the criterion (originally stated by Samuelson, 1952) for an under-effected transfer (in the absence of tariffs) from country A to country B as $C_A/M_A > M_B/C_B$, where C_A and M_A are country A's marginal propensities to spend on domestic and imported goods.

Harry Johnson's classic 1956 article on the transfer problem (Johnson, 1956) as Bhagwati (1977, 222) has noted, 'brilliantly synthesized and extended the classical and Keynesian analyses of the two problems (of transfers and exchange stability) and revealed the essential link between them.'

The most striking feature of the paper is the contrast between the results based on Keynesian and classical assumptions: under classical assumptions there is some ambiguity about whether the terms of trade move for or against the country making the transfer, while under Keynesian assumptions the results show that the terms of trade will definitely move against the country making the transfer (i.e. that the transfer will be initially under-effected). In the revised version of the paper reprinted in Johnson (1958) and Caves and Johnson (1968) Johnson reported that Paul Samuelson had noted this paradoxical feature of Johnson's result: 'namely, why, when the transfer is treated as an income change, the Keynesian analysis gives a definitely negative answer, whereas in the classical case the answer depends on the marginal propensities to buy foreign goods' (Caves and Johnson, 1968, 159).

In trying to unravel this puzzle, I found some difficulty with the earlier papers, which did not always make as clearly as one would wish the distinction between national income and domestic product. This distinction is naturally crucial for the analysis of transfers that are treated as transfers of income.[14] One would like to have a simple model, based on Keynesian assump-

13 In parallel series of papers (1966a, 1966b, 1973, 1974b) Johnson analysed reversed transfers, showing that the country making the initial transfer (and hence receiving the later reversal of the transfer) would gain in welfare (in the absence of time preference) if the transfer is expressed in domestic output and the classical presumption is satisfied, or if the transfer is expressed in foreign output and the classical presumption is not satisfied (1974b, 91). In either case, the total of world welfare is reduced by the reversed transfer. In (1974b), Cobb-Douglas utility functions are used to obtain hypothetical estimates of the changes in domestic, foreign, and world welfare.

14 Even in the more recent reinterpretations of the earlier discussions (e.g. Ohlin, 1974, 880) it is sometimes difficult to tell how much of the emphasis is on income-induced spending and how much is on spending-induced output. Johnson (1974b, 82) acknowledges that his own 1956 criticism of Metzler's 1942 analysis rested on a confusion between output and income effects. The matter might be allowed to rest, except that some writers (e.g. Chacholiades, 1978, 267) continue to accept Johnson's 1956 analysis of Metzler (1942).

tions about aggregation and supply conditions, that could nevertheless reveal the crucial differences between the Keynesian and classical approaches.

Country A is making a transfer of size T to country B, and, following Johnson (1956) and part 1 of Metzler's (1942) analysis, we assume that the transfer is treated as a typical change in income in both countries. Furthermore, let Y and Y^* represent domestic output and national income respectively, C_A the marginal propensity in country A to spend income on domestic goods, M_A the marginal propensity in country A to spend income on imported goods, so that $1 - C_A - M_A$ is the marginal propensity to hoard. There is no separate government sector and no international capital flow except the transfer itself. In the two-country framework typically used for analysis of the transfer problem, we therefore have:

$$dY_A = C_A dY_A{}^* + M_B dY_B{}^*, \tag{1}$$
the change in output in country A

$$dY_B = C_B dY_B{}^* + M_A dY_A{}^*, \tag{2}$$
the change in output in country B

$$dB_A = M_B dY_B{}^* - M_A dY_A{}^* - T, \tag{3}$$
the change in country A's balance of payments

$$dY_A{}^* = dY_A - T, \tag{4}$$
definition of change in A's national income

$$dY_B{}^* = dY_B + T. \tag{5}$$
definition of change in B's national income

In solving the model it is useful to separate the direct-spending effects of the transfer from the effects arising from induced changes in output. This gives the following expression for the change in A's balance of payments:

$$dB_A = (M_A + M_B - 1)T + M_B dY_B - M_A dY_A. \tag{6}$$

If there were no induced changes in output in either country (i.e. $dY_A = dY_B = 0$), this expression would reduce to the standard condition for an over- or under-effected transfer in the classical case: the transfer is initially under-effected if the sum of the two countries' marginal propensities to spend on imported goods is less than 1.

Solving the model allowing for induced output changes, we have

$$dB_A = (M_A + M_B - 1)T + (M_B H_B/G + M_A H_A/G)T, \tag{7}$$

where

$$G = (1 - C_B)(1 - C_A) - M_A M_B,$$
$$H_A = (1 - C_B)(C_A - M_B) - M_B(C_B - M_A),$$
$$H_B = (1 - C_A)(C_B - M_A) - M_A(C_A - M_B).$$

What use can be made of these expressions? First, let us consider the

S72 / John F. Helliwell

assumptions initially used by Samuelson (1952), wherein lack of any reason for relating preferences to whether a country is the transferee or the transferor suggests the assumption that $C_A = M_A = C_B = M_B$. Under these circumstances, $H_A = H_B = 0$ and $M_A + M_B < 1$ (if the models are stable in isolation, in Metzler's sense, i.e. $1 - M_A - C_A > 0$), so that the induced changes in output make no difference to the trade balance, and the transfer will be initially undereffected because $1 - M_A - M_B > 0$.

Jones (1970, 1975) has suggested that, if production functions are the same in both countries, the fact that countries do trade suggests a presumption in favour of consuming importables rather than exportables, i.e. $M_A > C_A : M_B > C_B$. The condition for the transfer to be over-effected is, from equation (7), $M_A(1 + H_A/G) + M_B(1 + H_B/G) > 1$. The paradoxical feature of the Keynesian analysis, as shown many years ago by Metzler (1942), is that this condition is never met, however large are M_A and M_B.[15] For example, if we adopt 'Jones-type' assumptions, with $M_A = M_B = 0.6$, the transfer is over-effected (120 per cent effected) under classical assumptions with $C_A = C_B = 0.4$ and no induced changes in output, but only 92 per cent effected with the Keynesian assumption that $C_A = C_B = 0.3$, and hence that $1 - M_A - C_A = 1 - M_B - C_B = 0.1$.

The central problem in reconciling the transfer analysis under Keynesian and classical assumptions is that neither can be easily seen as a special case of the other. As the sum of the Keynesian propensities to spend approaches 1.0, which is implied by the classical analysis, the multipliers become explosive and the Keynesian analysis breaks down. What is needed, in my view, is to couch the analysis within a minimally more general framework that does not have to be entirely demand-determined, as in the Keynesian analysis, or entirely supply-determined, as in the classical analysis.[16]

Harry Johnson's only return to the analysis of the transfer problem under Keynesian assumptions was in Frenkel and Johnson (1976, 270–2). By that time he was less anxious to reconcile the Keynesian and classical approaches than to point out the special monetary assumptions required in order to undertake transfer analysis using Keynesian (or indeed classical) frameworks that ignored the explicit analysis of the monetary consequences of either over- or under-effected transfers.

Policies for internal and external balance
Harry Johnson's first important contribution to what he later called the 'Keynesian policy approach' to balance-of-payments theory was his review article (1951) on *The Balance of Payments* by Meade. The review raised

15 As noted before, this result follows as long as each country is 'stable in isolation,' i.e., $1 - C_A - M_A > 0$.
16 Dornbusch has suggested that the common element of the Keynesian and classical analysis is that in neither case can there be an increase in the national income of the transferor country. In the classical analysis this is guaranteed by the fixity of output; in the Keynesian analysis it is guaranteed by the under-effected transfer.

issues that have relevance for Harry Johnson's own subsequent contributions. Johnson argues that Meade's book is a combination of a theoretical
approach that is 'taxonomic in the extreme' and 'academic proselytism for the
kind of national and international liberal economic order of which Professor
Meade approves' (1951, 812). The strongest criticism Johnson makes of the
taxonomic approach is the fact that the multiplication of possible outcomes is
reduced on the one hand by simplification 'to the point at which his results
cannot be applied at all easily to practical problems' or on the other hand by
'prejudging the results of measurements he does not or perhaps could not
make, either by illegitimately assuming that a number of qualitative statements can be added up into a quantitative fact, or by postulating an ideal world
in which only the cases he chooses will exist. This temptation is particularly
dangerous when questions of economic policy are involved, because the
desire for simplicity may be reinforced by personal preferences in prompting
the exclusion of possible cases' (1951, 827–8). These dangers of the use of
qualitative theory led Johnson to conclude that 'beyond a certain point
economic theory may become a handicap rather than a help' (1951, 827) and
that 'the important (and more difficult) part of the task becomes the problem of
measurement, however it is performed.' Some of this criticism of Meade's
approach has had an apparent effect on Johnson's own analysis of the balance
of payments. Harry Johnson always remained critical of theoretical work that
relied heavily on implicit or explicit value judgments, although, as Bhagwati
has noted (1977, 226), as time went on he became less likely to see this sort of
problem on the right and more likely to see it arising on the left. As for the need
to focus theoretical analysis on the particular circumstances of the problem at
hand, Harry Johnson became a master of simplifying and specializing a
general theoretical structure so as to make it applicable to contemporary
problems. However, this was always done in a qualitative manner and almost
never with any use of the tools or results of quantitative economics.

Harry Johnson's own papers applying and refining the Keynesian policy
approach were published between 1963 and 1968. They were mostly concerned with the joint choice of monetary and fiscal policies to achieve internal
and external balance under fixed exchange rates and relatively sticky domestic wages and prices. In a series of expository papers (1963, 1965, 1966c, and
section 1 of 1967), Johnson explained how monetary and fiscal policies can be
jointly used to achieve full employment and balance of payments. He notes
(1965, 45) that this assignment differs from that of Meade (1951), who assigned
monetary and fiscal policy (without distinguishing between the two) to
achieving internal balance, with the exchange rate being used to achieve
external balance. In the analysis described by Johnson (which he attributes
mainly to work in the early 1960s by R.A. Mundell reprinted as chapters 11
and 16 in Mundell, 1968), the use of monetary and fiscal policy as independent
instruments with separate effects on income and the balance of payments is
based on the interest-elasticity of international capital flows, which gives

S74 / John F. Helliwell

monetary policy an extra impact on the balance of payments. This permits policy-makers, by the judicious assignment and setting of monetary and fiscal policies, to deal even with the so-called 'conflict cases' where there is excess domestic demand coupled with a balance-of-payments deficit. In the former case, a tight fiscal policy is coupled with an easy monetary policy, while in the latter case an easy fiscal policy is matched with a tight monetary policy.[17] Johnson noted in each of these papers that the analysis is short-run, with 'no distinction between shifts of stocks of investment assets and alterations of flows of new savings' (1966c, 147) and with no provision for 'automatic processes that will tend gradually to correct the initial disequilibrium situation' (1966c, 148). He also noted that the achievement of target rates of growth could be accomplished by altering the type and mix of tax and spending policies to achieve the desired split between consumption and investment. In one of the later papers he raised more explicitly the 'welfare problem' (1972d, 177) arising from the use of international capital flows to achieve balance of payments rather than to equalize marginal returns on investment in different countries. He refers to his own analysis (1966a) of the welfare costs of exchange rate stabilization, but questions the welfare case against policy assignment by arguing that private after-tax returns on investment are not likely to match social returns in any case, and there is no reason to think that the unfettered private capital flows would produce a result 'superior to controlling capital movements and allowing the rates of domestic savings and investment to be determined by government policy, or by private decisions operating in the context of some agreed government policy' (1972d, 179).

In the most formal of this series of papers, Johnson (1966d) presented an explicit model of policy choice under fixed and flexible exchange rates, differentiating his product from the earlier models of Mundell (reprinted as chapters 11, 16, and 18 of Mundell, 1968) and Fleming, 1962, by making net capital inflows a positive function of the level of domestic output. The money supply is assumed exogenous, and hence sterilization is assumed to be possible on a continuing basis, in contrast to chapter 18 of Mundell (1968). Making capital inflows respond to income means that monetary expansion does not necessarily cause a deterioration in the balance of payments, if the income-induced capital inflows are more than large enough to offset the interest-induced capital outflows and the extra imports induced by the higher expenditure. The addition of income-induced capital flows increases the chances of getting favourable balance-of-payments effects from either a monetary or a

17 This is strictly true only if the 'neutral' policy is defined in terms of an unchanged interest rate or if the balance-of-payments equilibrium line is steeper than the LM curve. Johnson sometimes passed over this necessary qualification (e.g. at 171 of the 1972d reprinting of 1967 and at 147 of 1966c) and sometimes dealt with it by assuming that expansionary fiscal policy with a fixed money supply would worsen the balance of payments: e.g. 'The net effect on the balance of payments may go either way; for simplicity I shall assume that there is a net worsening of the overall balance' (1965, 47). Empirical evidence for Canada, derived from the RDX2 model, suggests that the balance-of-payments curve is slightly flatter than the I M curve, as shown by the results in Table 1b of Helliwell and McRae (1976)

fiscal policy designed to increase income, but renders indeterminate the comparative advantages that determine which instrument should be assigned to which target. Finally, Johnson notes the shortcomings of the model, in treating 'capital movements as flow variables dependent on income levels and interest rates' and in disguising 'the fact that balance-of-payments adjustment based on the inducement of capital flows is only a temporary form of adjustment. Johnson's contributions to this branch of the literature, and his qualifications about the policy implications, are representative of the bulk of the policy-oriented balance-of-payments literature of the 1960s. As the decade drew to a close, and the Bretton Woods monetary system grew increasingly unstable, the problems of static policy assignment rules under fixed exchange rates were increasingly dominated in the thought and writings of Harry Johnson by questions relating to the international monetary system as a whole.

The role of gold in the international monetary system

Harry Johnson's contributions on this topic extend over more than twenty years, starting in 1950 with a *Canadian Journal of Economics and Political Science* paper (1950) taking a contrary position on each of the main arguments then being made for an increase in the price of gold. At that stage, he argued primarily that an increase in the price of gold was unnecessary and would have undesirable distributional effects. The increase was held to be unnecessary for the United States because the liquidity of the banking system was double the minimum requirements. More generally, and in a vein more in line with his later views in the 1970s than in the 1960s, Johnson argued (1950, 204) that 'Liquidity cannot be more than a temporary palliative for a structural disequilibrium in the balance of international trade; and where there is fundamental balance in the pattern of international economic relations, liquidity adequate for short-run needs can always be provided by national or international credit operations not requiring the use of gold.'

During the 1960s Johnson's views on the role of gold developed in two consistent ways. On the one hand he refined his case against gold by basing it more fundamentally (e.g. 1969f) on the social savings resulting from the use of a credit rather than a commodity base for a monetary system. On the other hand (e.g. 1972d, 186–92), he developed with increasing precision the view that the gold exchange standard was inevitably unstable in an inflationary world, giving rise to a 'long-run confidence problem' (1972d, 187) for the reserve currency. During the 1960s, at least until SDR creation started at the end of the decade, the rate of growth of the stock of gold available for holding as monetary reserves fell short of the rate of growth of demand for new reserves outside the United States. According to Johnson's analysis:

Those countries have made up the difference by accumulating reserves of dollars, which are (this was written in 1967) convertible into gold ... An international monetary system of this kind is inherently unstable, in the sense that the passage of time inevitably erodes the foundation of the system in confidence in the convertibility of the

S76 / John F. Helliwell

dollar, by steadily reducing the ratio of US gold reserves to US dollars held as international monetary reserve assets by other countries and – at least eventually – steadily reducing the absolute amount of gold reserves held by the United States. (1972d, 186)

Thus Johnson was not at all surprised at the run on gold in early 1968 and the subsequent establishment of the two-tier gold market. At the end of 1968 he acknowledged once again that he would 'much prefer the theoretically logical solution, replacement of gold by international credit money ... with ... much more flexibility of exchange rates than the present system entails.' 'But if,' he continued, 'as I strongly suspect, the central banks are ... not willing to take that step, the international monetary system will become increasingly evidently an absurd arrangement, a charade in which gold is traded at a monetary price below the world market price among official transactors who will be aware that the official price of gold increasingly underrepresents its scarcity for monetary purposes' (1969a, 348). With characteristic prescience, he foresaw increasing pressures by other central banks on the United States to curtail its inflation and resulting deficit. He also foresaw the 'Nixon shock' of August 1971, when he went on to suggest that 'the United States might be goaded into, or might choose, to forestall these pressures by declaring the dollar inconvertible into gold by other monetary authorities, as Britain did with sterling in 1931' (ibid).

Being increasingly sceptical that central banks would readily adopt more flexible exchange rates, and forecasting a possible 'increasing restriction of trade and payments, ending in a return to fixed rates pegged on gold at a higher price' (ibid), Johnson was by late 1968 willing to regard an earlier and agreed increase in the price of gold as the lesser of the likely evils. Although still 'professionally prejudiced in favour of less irrational solutions' (ibid), he was now much more sympathetic than previously to long-standing advocates of a higher gold price, as is revealed in his festschreift chapter entitled 'Roy Harrod on the price of gold' (1970d). Johnson himself was now edging towards Harrod's view that while it was more 'rational' to get additional liquidity 'by printing bits of paper,' one had to 'face up to the difficulties of who authorizes the printing of the paper and how is it to be distributed among the nations of the world?' (quotations are from a 1964 *Optima* article by Roy Harrod, cited in 1970d, 286).

In the event the price of gold was raised twice, in 1971 and 1973, in the process of being removed from the centre position in the international monetary system. The final step came in mid-1974, when the definition of the SDR was changed from 0.889 grams of fine gold to a trade-weighted bundle of currencies, followed later by gradual restitution and auction of the IMF's gold holdings. Harry Johnson must be regarded as one of the clearest, most consistent, and important of the proponents of the dethroning of gold as part of the move to more generally flexible exchange rates. He was not only a clear-eyed analyst of the likely consequences of the gold exchange standard but also one of the most important influences, through countless lectures, articles, seminars, and discussions, on the evolution of national and international policy towards reducing the role of gold in the international monetary system.

Flexible exchange rates

Harry Johnson was among the most vigorous advocates of flexible exchange rates. His best known contribution was 'The case for flexible exchange rates 1969' (1969h), although there were two earlier papers on the welfare costs of exchange rate stabilization (1966a, 1966b), some analysis of partial moves towards exchange flexibility (e.g. 1969e, 1970c), and later analysis of the possibility of destabilizing but profitable speculation in a general equilibrium context (1976a). The 1969 case for floating exchange rates was essentially a negative one, with the following strands: (1) International mobility of goods, labour, and capital is not high enough to achieve the advantages that rigidly fixed exchange rates would in principle provide by enlarging currency areas. (2) No effective policies exist for compensating the suffering regions within any group of countries linked by fixed exchange rates. (3) Actual systems of pegged exchange rates have failed to provide the services of a single currency by, first, using barriers rather than adjustments to restore balance and, second, having no centralized arrangement for monetary control.[18] (4) The lack of a balance-of-payments adjustment mechanism within the Bretton Woods system.

The case for flexible exchange rates was based on (1) the automaticity of the adjustment mechanism and (2) freeing domestic economic management: 'flexible exchange rates would allow each country to pursue the mixture of unemployment and price trend objectives it prefers, with ... international equilibrium being secured by appreciation of the currencies of "price stability" countries relative to the currencies of "full employment" countries' (1969h, 23).

Johnson then defended flexible rates against charges that they would encourage instability and speculation and would encourage inflation by removing the 'discipline' of the balance-of-payments constraint. In response to the former point, Johnson argued that 'Abnormally rapid and erratic movements will occur only in response to sharp and unexpected changes in circumstances, and such changes in a fixed exchange rate system would produce equal or more uncertainty – creating policy changes in the form of devaluation deflation, or the imposition of new controls or trade and payments' (1969h, 26–7).

---

18 It is surprising that Johnson did not add at this point (1969h, 21) that the fixed exchange rate system had even failed to provide fixed exchange rates; having fluctuations about parity as a minor disturbance and actual and expected changes in par values as a major destroyer of full and certain substitutability between national monies. This issue was, however, taken up later (ibid, 26–8) when countering arguments about the instability of flexible rates.

The argument about the lack of 'discipline' in a flexible exchange rate context was dealt with primarily by references to the relatively undisciplined record under fixed exchange rates.

Having reported Johnson's 1969 case for flexible exchange rates rather fully, I turn now to consider his assessments (1975c, 1977b) of flexible exchange rates in action. His main verdict was that 'the standard objections to floating rates ... have not held water' (1975c, 205) and the system has 'worked very well' (1977b, 21). In response to concerns about the post-1973 variability of floating exchange rates, he reports research showing that exchange rates, like stock prices, tend to follow a 'random walk' and reminds his readers that 'foreign exchange markets, like stock markets, capitalize expected future price movements into current prices, so that prices may be expected to move more sharply in response to new information than consideration of current demands and supplies alone would lead one to expect' (1977b, 22).

Johnson, going on to consider the future of floating rates, forecasts an eventual but not early return to relatively fixed rates. He argues this on two grounds, the second more imaginative and convincing than the first. His first point is that past experiences with floating rates have tended to be short-lived. The second is that a smoothly operating system of flexible exchange rates is likely to involve stable rates, and hence 'it will seem a trivial step, well worth the additional benefits, to move from the de facto to de jure fixity of exchange rates' (ibid, 25).

When Johnson's 1969 and 1975–7 views on floating exchange rates are considered together, they do not constitute for me an entirely convincing and complete case. What would all the recent exchange rate volatility have been translated into had fixed rates continued in existence? What are all the important and widely shared pieces of new information that cause such rapid and frequently reversed changes in important exchange rates? It may be true, as Cornell and Dietrich (1978) have argued, that exchange rate movements have not been inconsistent with a random walk hypothesis, and it is certainly true that 'fundamental' determinants of exchange rates have been unusually difficult to forecast, but it is also true, as Westerfield (1977) has shown, that post-1973 exchange rate variability is significantly greater than pre-1973 variability. This also is true for the Canadian dollar, which has been more sharply variable since 1973 than during its earlier floating periods in the 1950s and 1970–73. This suggests to me that the Canadian switch from a monetary policy focused directly or indirectly on the exchange rate (as it was prior to 1975) may provide a more stable and certain basis for private expectations than independent monetary growth targets announced and applied separately by central banks in the major currency countries. Whether there is anything to this conjecture must remain to be seen; the point I wish to make in the context of this survey is that Harry Johnson's analysis of flexible exchange rates, like that of the profession at large, has still not properly come to grips with the post-1973 experience, and especially has not adequately explored the linkages between exchange rate expectations and monetary policy strategies.

The breakdown of the Bretton Woods system: the 'crises' of 1968–1973

As illustrated in the earlier section on gold, Harry Johnson emphasized the crisis potential of the gold exchange standard, so it was unsurprising that he produced a series of insightful papers (1969a, 1969b, 1969c, 1969d, 1970a, 1970b, 1971, 1972b, and 1972c) on the periodic crises that signalled the breakdown of the Bretton Woods system of pegged exchange rates. He did not adopt the term 'crisis' until the speculative attacks became focused, in 1968, on the US dollar itself. If he had had a chance to look back over the crises of 1968, 1971, and 1973 from the vantage point of 1978, he would probably have regarded them as a natural sequence of steps in dismantling the gold exchange standard in favour of a system of flexible exchange rates. While he never would have advocated national policies of high and variable inflation rates coupled with sharply uneven real growth, he might well have been agreeably surprised at the gradual conversion of official opinion that took place during the sequence of crises.

The three main steps in the dismantling of the gold exchange standard were the 1968 closing of the official gold window at the US Federal Reserve, the December 1971 'Smithsonian' realignments of par value (including devaluation of the US dollar in terms of the SDR), and the general floating of exchange rates in 1973. A fourth and final step, the redefinition of the SDR in terms of a basket of currencies instead of gold in mid-1974, can be left out of consideration here because it occasioned neither a crisis of the international financial system nor comment by Harry Johnson.

In his discussion of the 1968 gold crisis (e.g. 1969a, 1970a) Harry Johnson emphasized the crisis-prone nature of the gold exchange system, surveyed the extant plans for creating substitute credit facilities and for achieving slightly greater exchange rate flexibility, whether through wider bands, crawling pegs, or whatever. Consistent with his general views on gold, as discussed earlier, Johnson was inclined to welcome the reduction in the role of gold and to support the US position against revaluation of gold.

By the time of the 'Nixon shock' measures of August 1971, Harry Johnson was starting to elaborate 'the monetarist approach to stabilization policy in an open economy,'[19] emphasizing the links between the monetary policies of the United States and the 1971 crisis of confidence in the US dollar. Almost gone was his 1968 concern with adequate provision of new sources of liquidity to replace gold; attention was shifting from too little to too much money as the cause of the recurring crises. One can try to plead both cases at once; with the

---

19 The quote is the title of the third of the Professor Dr F. De Vries Lectures given by Johnson in Amsterdam in the fall of 1971 (published as 1972e, 75–108).

S80 / John F. Helliwell

crises being due to too little money of some sorts (gold and Deutschemarks) and too much of other sorts (sterling and $US), leading to inevitable destabilizing speculation as part of a multivariate application of Gresham's Law.

Liquidity, world money, and world inflation
In his 1970 analysis (1970a, 46) of the world monetary crises, Harry Johnson spoke of the liquidity problem as re-emerging in the late 1960s because of the inadequacy of the IMF provisions 'to provide for growth of international liquidity at a rate adequate to meet the needs of the expanding world economy.' But a year later, in late 1971, he was explaining that 'the new monetary approach suggests that the creation of new international reserves – specifically Special Drawing Rights at the International Monetary Fund – will in the longer run simply accelerate the pace of world inflation, rather than, as its proponents expect, lead countries to hold larger reserves relative to their international trade and payments and on this basis pursue more liberal international economic policies' (1972e, 87).

Even earlier in 1971, in a contribution to a panel discussion on world inflation, Harry Johnson was taking the following view of world inflation: 'world inflation is a world phenomenon to be explained by (two major) world developments. The first is the tremendous liberalization in world trade and payments that has gone on since 1959 ... [and the second has been] the escalation of the war in Viet Nam, and the failure of the Americans to finance that war by increasing taxes ... The basis of the world inflation is the expansion of the world money supply which results from the lack of any central control over that money supply' (Claassen and Salin, 1972, 310–11).

By late 1971, this view was being crystalized into the monetary approach to the balance of payments under fixed exchange rates and presented in numerous papers by Johnson and others, as described in a previous section of this paper. As I have described earlier, Harry Johnson seemed in the middle and late 1970s to dissociate himself (and with him the monetary approach to the balance of payments) from the world monetarist view of money and world inflation. In one of his most recent publications on the topic, he reiterated a view expressed earlier that 'the prime function of a world central bank should be to provide stable growth of the international money base of the world financial system' (1977b, 25). Without recommending any specific mechanisms for reconciling the existence of such a bank with the continued existence of independent national central banks, he did point out two institutional difficulties faced by the IMF in fulfilling such a role: (1) it still tends, 'because of its historical origins in 1930s depression thinking' (1977b, 25), to be too concerned with the danger of a liquidity shortage; (2) it tends to forget its money supply control role when acting as a lender of last resort, and to neglect 'Bagehot's dictum that lending of last resort should be conducted *at a penalty rate*' (ibid).

Without doubt Harry Johnson, with his long-standing aversion to linking

SDR creation to aid efforts (e.g. 1969g), would be increasingly nervous at the gradual conversion of the IMF from disciplinarian to a lender-with-a-heart, financing its activities by sales of some of its members' gold contributions. While I am much more prepared than he was to see the Fund play a dual role, I can only regret that we all are denied the access to further developments of his ever-acute and ever-responsive analysis of world monetary theory and institutions.

CONCLUSION

Instead of attempting to summarize what is already a very selective summary of a massive body of writings, I shall offer some personal impressions of Harry Johnson's influence on the direction and content of balance-of-payments analysis. I shall deal with four channels of influence: personal contacts, influence on students, research methods, and publications.

Harry Johnson's contacts with other balance-of-payments analysts were unparalleled. In a field that has for the past fifteen years been marked by a multitude of conferences in far-flung locations, Harry was the undisputed king of the conference circuit. He was always there, usually in some position of honour and responsibility, and he was always better prepared than the availability of time seemed to permit. One who arrived late could always count on Harry's summary to fill in most of the important gaps. As the most active of conference goers, he was always in touch with what was going on elsewhere, and was doubly influential as transporter and referee for new ideas and issues. Only Robert Mundell can be compared to Harry Johnson as an influence on the conference circuit, but their respective contributions can fairly easily be distinguished. In the realm of international conferences, as in the literature of international monetary economics, Mundell was more likely the bearer of original and often highly individual viewpoints, while Johnson was much more often in the role of clarifying critic, synthesizer of diverging approaches, and summarizer of conference progress.

Harry Johnson's personal influence on students probably occurred far more through his lectures than through supervision of research. Perhaps because of his peripatetic travels, he had relatively few research students; but his lectures were well prepared and highly regarded wherever they were given.

By his considerable influence and enormous output, Harry Johnson had a large impact on the research methods used in balance-of-payments analysis. He used prose, algebra, and geometry, combined with the skills of a master expositor. He did not develop or encourage the application of mathematical economics and econometrics to balance-of-payments issues. My personal view is that many of the issues of interest to Harry Johnson beg, if not demand, solid empirical research of an econometric nature. Perhaps in part because of the timing and location of his education and early career, Harry

S82 / John F. Helliwell

Johnson did not do any substantial econometric work. This is not surprising, especially in the field of balance-of-payments analysis. What is more suprising, for a man of his obvious powers, was that he never developed sufficient background to sort out good quantitative work from bad and as a consequence was somewhat sceptical of it all. This no doubt was part of the reason he had relatively few research students. More unfortunately, it is likely that Harry's enormous influence on the content and nature of balance-of-payments analysis are in some part responsible for the relatively undeveloped state of quantitative work in this field. His sponsorship of the International Monetary Research Program at the LSE showed some later interest in redressing this balance, but his own reports of this research (e.g. 1976e) suggest that he still felt uneasy about the empirical aspects of research.[20]

Finally, there is Harry's vast literary legacy. It was already during his life the most important source of his influence in the field. This legacy has been the main focus of my survey. Among the vast number of his writings, only a few can become standard references in generations hence; yet many more will be of use to later scholars trying to trace the history of economic thought during the Bretton Woods era. Harry documented his times and his own changing views more fully than any past or any likely future scholar of the balance of payments. His clarity of thought and language in preparing this legacy was such as to leave us heavily in his debt.

REFERENCES

Alexander, S.S. (1952) 'Effects of a devaluation on a trade balance.' *IMF Staff Papers* 2, 263–78. Reprinted in Caves and Johnson (1968, 359–73)
Alexander, S.S. (1959) 'Effects of a devaluation: a simplified synthesis of elasticities and absorption approaches.' *American Economic Review* 49, 23–42
Bhagwati, Jagdish (1977) 'Harry G. Johnson.' *Journal of International Economics* 7, 221–30
Caves, R.E. and H.G. Johnson, eds (1968) *Readings in International Economics* (Homewood: R.D. Irwin)
Chacholiades, Miltiades (1978) *International Monetary Theory and Policy* (New York: McGraw-Hill)
Christ, C.F. (1967) 'A short-run aggregate-demand model of the interdependence and effects of monetary and fiscal policies with Keynesian and classical interest elasticities.' *American Economic Review* 57, 434–43
Claassen, E. and P. Salin, eds (1972) *Stabilization Policies in Interdependent Economies* (Amsterdam: North-Holland) (Proceedings of a Conference held at the University of Paris-Dauphine, March 1971)

20 Another point about his choice of research method has been suggested by Peter Jonson. At some point in the early 1970s, Harry Johnson switched from the search for and exposition of more complete theoretical models to the use of a highly simplified version of the monetary approach to the balance of payments. In making this change, he could have been following his own advice (from chapter 2 of 1972d) on how to launch an academic revolution or counter-revolution. He later drew back from the less defensible parts of the simplified framework as some of the features used for distinctive exposition threatened to become hallmarks of an approach that he had wished to be of more general application.

Connolly, M.B. and A.K. Swoboda, eds (1973) *International Trade and Money* (London: Allen and Unwin)

Cornell, W.B. and J.K. Dietrich (1978) 'The efficiency of the market for foreign exchange under floating exchange rates.' *Review of Economics and Statistics* 60, 111–20

Dornbusch, R. (1973a) 'Currency depreciation, hoarding, and relative prices.' *Journal of Political Economy* 81, 893–915

Dornbusch, R. (1973b) 'Devaluation, money and nontraded goods.' *American Economic Review* 63, 871–80. Reprinted in Frenkel and Johnson (1976, 168–86)

Ellis, H.S. and L.A. Metzler, eds (1950) *Readings in the Theory of International Trade* (London: Allen and Unwin)

Fleming, J.M. (1962) 'Domestic financial policies under fixed and floating exchange rates.' *IMF Staff Papers* 9, 369–79

Frenkel, Jacob A. and H.G. Johnson, eds (1976) *The Monetary Approach to the Balance of Payments* (London: Allen and Unwin)

Girton, L. and D. Roper (1977) 'A monetary model of exchange market pressure applied to the postwar Canadian experience.' *American Economic Review* 67, 537–48

Hahn, Frank H. (1977) 'The monetary approach to the balance of payments.' *Journal of International Economics* 7, 231–50

Hargerger, Arnold C. (1950) 'Currency depreciation, income and the balance of trade.' *Journal of Political Economy* 58, 47–60

Helliwell, J.F. and R.N. McRae (1976) 'The interdependence of monetary, debt, and fiscal policies in an international setting.' In R.Z. Aliber, ed., *The Political Economy of Monetary Reform* (London: Macmillan) 157–78

International Monetary Fund (1977) *The Monetary Approach to the Balance of Payments* (Washington: IMF)

Johnson, Harry G. (1950) 'The case for increasing the price of gold in terms of all currencies: a contrary view.' *Canadian Journal of Economics and Political Science* 16, 199–209

– (1951) 'The taxonomic approach to economic policy.' *Economic Journal* 61, 812–32

– (1956) 'The transfer problem and exchange stability.' *Journal of Political Economy* 64, 212–25. Reprinted in Caves and Johnson (1968, 148–71)

– (1958) *International Trade and Economic Growth: Studies in Pure Theory* (London: Allen and Unwin)

– (1963) 'Equilibrium under fixed exchange rates.' *American Economic Review* 53, 112–19

– (1965) 'Notes on the theory of economic policy under fixed exchange rates.' *Osaka Economic Papers* 14, 45–8

– (1966a) 'Notes on the welfare cost of exchange rate stabilization.' *Philippine Economic Journal* 5, 277–80

– (1966b) 'The welfare costs of exchange-rate stabilization.' *Journal of Political Economy* 74, 512–18. Reprinted in Johnson (1972d, 250–62)

– (1966c) 'The objectives of economic policy and the mix of fiscal and monetary policy under fixed exchange rates.' In *Maintaining and Restoring Balance in International Payments* (Princeton: Princeton University Press) 145–50

– (1966d) 'Some aspects of the theory of economic policy in a world of capital mobility.' In Bagiotti, Tullio, ed., *Essays in Honour of Marco Fanno* (Padova: CEDAM) 345–59. Reprinted with corrections in Johnson (1972d, 151–66)

– (1967) 'Theoretical problems of the international monetary system.' *Journal of Economic Studies* 2, 3–33. Reprinted in Johnson (1972d, 167–97)

S84 / John F. Helliwell

- (1969a) 'The gold rush of 1968 in retrospect and prospect.' *American Economic Review* 59, 344–8
- (1969b) 'Financial and monetary problems of the United Kingdom.' *Journal of World Trade Law* 3, 364–73
- (1969c) 'The decline of the international monetary system.' *World Today* 25, 103–9
- (1969d) 'A monetary view of the international monetary problem.' *Business Economics* 4, 7–12
- (1969e) 'The international monetary problem: gold, dollars, Special Drawing Rights, wider bands and crawling pegs.' In *Linking Reserve Creation and Development Assistance* (Hearings, Joint Economic Committee, US 91st Congress, 1st Session) (Washington: Government Printing Office) 21–8
- (1969f) 'The seigniorage problem and international liquidity: appendix: a note on seigniorage and the social saving from substituting credit for commodity money.' In Robert A. Mundell and Alexander K. Swoboda, eds, *Monetary Problems of the International Economy* (Chicago: University of Chicago Press) 323–9. Reprinted in Johnson (1972d, 263–70)
- (1969g) 'Statement.' In *Linking Reserve Creation and Development Assistance* (Hearings, Joint Economic Committee, US 91st Congress, 1st Session) (Washington: Government Printing Office) 19–21
- (1969h) 'The case for flexible exchange rates 1969.' In Harry G. Johnson and John E. Nash (1969) *The U.K. and Floating Exchanges: A Debate on the Theoretical and Practical Implications* (London: Institute of Economic Affairs). Reprinted in Halm (1970, 91–111) and in Johnson (1972d, 198–228)
- (1970a) 'The world monetary crisis.' *Encounter* 35, 43–52
- (1970b) 'The international monetary crisis, 1969.' In I.A. McDougal and R.H. Snape, eds, *Studies in International Economics* (Amsterdam: North-Holland) 105–20. Reprinted in Johnson (1972d, 295–311)
- (1970c) 'A technical note on the width of the band required to accommodate parity changes of particular size.' In George N. Halm, ed., *Approaches to Greater Flexibility of Exchange Rates*: (Princeton: Princeton University Press) 280–1
- (1970d) 'Roy Harrod on the price of gold.' In W.A. Eltis, M.F. Scott, J.N. Wolfe, eds, *Induction, Growth and Trade: Essays in Honour of Sir Roy Harrod* (London: Clarendon Press) 266–93
- (1971) 'The international monetary crisis of 1971.' *Money Management* 16–18. Reprinted in Johnson (1972d, 353–61)
- (1972a) 'The monetary approach to balance of payments theory.' *Intermountain Economic Review* 3, 1–13. Reprinted in Johnson (1972d, 229–49) and in Connolly and Swoboda (1973, 206–23)
- (1972b) 'Political economy aspects of international monetary reform.' *Journal of International Economics* 2, 401–24
- (1972c) 'The Bretton Woods system, key currencies, and the "dollar crisis" of 1971.' *Three Banks Review* 94, 3–23
- (1972d) *Further Essays in Monetary Economics* (London: Allen and Unwin)
- (1972e) *Inflation and the Monetarist Controversy* (Amsterdam: North-Holland)
- (1973) 'Notes on the welfare effects of a reversed transfer.' *Osaka Economic Papers* 21, 42–52
- (1974a) 'The terms in which transfers are expressed – comment.' *Economic Journal* 84, 171
- (1974b) 'The welfare economics of reversed international transfers.' in G. Horwich and P. Samuelson, eds, *Trade, Stability, and Macroeconomics* (New York: Academic Press) 79–110
- (1975a) 'World inflation and the international monetary system.' *Three Banks Review* 107, 3–22

- (1975b) 'The classical transfer problem: an alternative formulation.' *Economica* 42, 20–31
- (1975c) ('Current problems of the international monetary system: 3 analyses') 'General Introduction'; 'The future of floating rates.' *Weltwirtschaftliches Archiv* 111, 203–9
- (1975d) 'The monetary approach to balance of payments theory: a diagrammatic analysis.' *Manchester School of Economics and Social Studies* 43, 220–74
- (1976a) 'Destabilizing speculation: a general equilibrium approach.' *Journal of Political Economy* 84, 101–8
- (1976b) 'Money and the balance of payments.' *Banca Nazionale del Lavoro – Quarterly Review* 116, 3–18
- (1976c) 'Notes on the classical transfer problem.' *Manchester School of Economics and Social Studies* 44, 211–19
- (1976d) 'Elasticity, absorption, Keynesian multiplier, Keynesian policy, and monetary approaches to devaluation theory: a simple geometric exposition.' *American Economic Review* 66, 448–52
- (1976e) 'Money in the open economy: a historical and analytical survey.' Prepared for the SSRC-Ford Foundation Conference on 'Macroeconomic policy and adjustment in open economies,' Ware, England, 28 April – 1 May 1976
- (1977a) 'The monetary approach to the balance of payments: a nontechnical guide.' *Journal of International Economics* 7, 251–68
- (1977b) 'Money, balance-of-payments theory, and the international monetary problem.' *Essays in International Finance* No. 124 (Princeton: Princeton University Press)

Johnson, Harry G. and Alexander K. Swoboda, eds (1973) *The Economics of Common Currencies* (London: Allen and Unwin)

Jones, R.W. (1970) 'The transfer problem revisited.' *Economica* 37, 178–84

Jones, R.W. (1975) 'Presumption and the transfer problem.' *Journal of International Economics* 6, 263–74

Jonson, P.D. (1976) 'Money and economic activity in the open economy: the United Kingdom, 1880–1970.' *Journal of Political Economy* 84, 979–1012

Jonson, P.D. (1977) 'Money, inflation, and the balance of payments.' Paper presented to the Third Pacific Basin Central Bank Conference, 8–11 November

Jonson, P.D. and H.I. Kierzkowski (1975) 'The balance of payments: an analytic exercise.' *Manchester School of Economics and Social Studies* 43, 105–33

Jonson, P.D., E. Moses, and C.R. Wymer (1976) *A Minimal Model of the Australian Economy* (Reserve Bank of Australia Discussion Paper 7601, Sydney)

Jonson, P.D. and R.W. Rankin (1977) 'Money and the balance of payments.' Paper presented at the 48th ANZAAS conference, Melbourne

Keynes, J.M. (1929) 'The German transfer problem.' *Economic Journal* 39, 1–7. Reprinted in Ellis and Metzler (1950, 161–9)

Kouri, Pentti J.K. and Michael G. Porter (1974) 'International capital flows and portfolio equilibrium.' *Journal of Political Economy* 82, 443–68

Laffer, Arthur B. (1973) 'Two arguments for fixed rates.' In Johnson and Swoboda (1973, 25–39)

Laursen, S. and L.A. Metzler (1950) 'Flexible exchange rates and the theory of employment.' *Review of Economics and Statistics* 32, 281–99

Meade, J.E. (1951) *The Balance of Payments* (London: Oxford University Press)

Metzler, L.A. (1942) 'The transfer problem reconsidered.' *Journal of Political Economy* 50, 397–414. Reprinted in Ellis and Metzler (1950, 179–97)

Mundell, R.A. (1962) 'The appropriate use of monetary and fiscal policy for internal and external stability.' *IMF Staff Papers* 9, 70–9

Mundell, R.A. (1968) *International Economics* (New York: Macmillan)

S86 / John F. Helliwell

Mundell, R.A. (1971) *Monetary Theory* (Pacific Palisades: Goodyear)
Mundell, R.A. (1973) 'A plan for a European currency.' In Johnson and Sweboda (1973, 143–77)
Oates, W.E. (1966) 'Budget balance and equilibrium income: a comment on the efficiency of fiscal and monetary policy in an open economy.' *Journal of Finance* 21, 489–98
Ohlin, Bertil (1929) 'The reparations problem: a discussion.' *Economic Journal* 39, 172–8. Reprinted in Ellis and Metzler (1950, 170–8)
Ohlin, Bertil (1974) 'On the slow development of the "total demand" idea in economic theory: reflections in connection with Dr Oppenheimer's note.' *Journal of Economic Literature* 12, 888–95
Ott, D.J. and A. Ott (1965) 'Budget balance and equilibrium income.' *Journal of Finance* 20, 71–7
Samuelson, P.A. (1952) 'The transfer problem and transport costs: the terms of trade when impediments are absent.' *Economic Journal* 62, 278–304. Reprinted in Caves and Johnson (1968, 115–47), consolidated with Samuelson (1954)
Samuelson, P.A. (1954) 'The transfer problem and transport costs: analysis of effects of trade impediments.' *Economic Journal* 64, 264–89
Samuelson, P.A. (1971) 'On the trail of conventional beliefs about the transfer problem.' In Bhagwati, Jones, Mundell, and Vanek, eds, (1971) *Trade, Balance of Payments, and Growth* (Amsterdam: North-Holland) 327–51
Tsiang, S.C. (1961) 'The role of money in trade-balance stability: synthesis of the elasticity and absorption approaches.' *American Economic Review* 51, 912–36
Westerfield, J.M. (1977) 'An examination of foreign exchange risk under fixed and floating rate regimes.' *Journal of International Economics* 7, 181–200
Whitman, M.V.N. (1975) 'Global monetarism and the monetary approach to the balance of payments.' *Brookings Papers on Economic Activity* 3, 491–536

[5]

Harry Johnson's Contributions to International Trade Theory

W. M. Corden

Australian National University

The object of this survey is to provide a thorough guide to Harry Johnson's work in the field of nonmonetary international economics—to "do a Harry Johnson" on that part of his work which includes many of his most influential contributions. He would certainly have wanted this particular survey to be thorough, as so many of his more original insights are to be found in this field. It is a field which he dominated over 2 decades, and not only through his writings.

The organization of the survey is by topics, with some attention to chronology and with inevitable overlap problems. Section I covers trade and growth, dominated by a trilogy of articles of the early 1950s, of which the third, published in 1955, is perhaps his single most significant contribution to trade theory. Section II covers static positive Heckscher-Ohlin-Samuelson (H-O-S) theory, where all his main contributions were the fruits of the 1950s, published in the *Manchester School*. Section III deals with normative protection theory—the theory of the optimal tariff, the cost of protection, and the theory of domestic distortions. His contributions here cover the whole period of his working life up to the early 1970s. This section is defined to exclude the contents of Section IV, which covers customs union theory and the theory of tariff bargaining. Section V deals with effective protection, in which his principal contributions stretched from 1965 to 1971. Section VI is entitled "Wicksell Lecture and After" and deals with his writings from 1968 on the new theories of

I am indebted to comments on earlier drafts from Kym Anderson, Heinz Arndt, Stanley Engerman, Ronald Findlay, Ross Garnaut, Melvyn Krauss, John Martin, and Jonathan Pincus.

[*Journal of Political Economy*, 1984, vol. 92, no. 4]

trade, the role of technology, human capital, and knowledge diffusion in relation to trade, international corporations, and the infant industry argument. In fact, it is a bit of a potpourri, like his famous Wicksell Lecture, but deals with some of his most stimulating work, about which he was actively thinking in his last years. Section VII tidies up, dealing with the large volume of writings not covered to this point, notably several surveys, his work on (nontrade) two-sector theory—where he used the techniques of trade theory for income distribution and other issues—his writings on international trade negotiations, and on policies toward less developed countries. The last includes what is probably his most widely read book, *Economic Policies toward Less Developed Countries* (1967a). Finally, Section VIII discusses his attitude to theory and his contribution to the work of others in the field.

Before launching into details, we must say something about the essential nature of Harry's achievements and especially the matter of his "originality." His brilliance was as a synthesizer and a user of theory to probe "real world" policy issues. As a contributor to pure theory, he must be regarded as having had an important place in the ongoing stream: he said neither the first nor the last word in the many branches of trade theory in which he wrote, but he played a big role in the collective process of building up the relevant analytical framework. In total, his contribution to pure trade theory was immense, but his originality in this field was not of the order of Ohlin's, Samuelson's, or Meade's.

As we read his many papers, one characteristic stands out: he did his best to *appear* unoriginal. His style of writing and care in acknowledgments tended to give the impression that he had not had an original idea in his life but that everything was consolidation and building on bricks laid by others. He tended not to highlight what was new in his work but rather to stress continuity in the development of economic theory. He was not a deliberate maximizer of his reputation. He made no claims for original "theorems" and usually went out of his way to give credit to others. In the preface to *International Trade and Economic Growth* (1958b)—in which he collected some of those papers that have turned out to be his most important—he wrote about his work: "In addition, they are linked by a common purpose—the consolidation of the work of previous theorists and its extension to new problems—and by a common method—the application of mathematically-based logical analysis to theoretical problems thrown up by discussion of current topics among economists, generally those relating to economic policy. The motivation, explicit and implicit, has usually been to see what could be made of the tools available, in analysing the problem that suggested itself as an interesting one" (p. 9).

This impression of unoriginality was fostered not only by the many surveys he wrote but also by the substantial element of surveying in almost every article. It was fostered by his search for simplicity in theoretical argument. It is not always realized how difficult it is to be simple.

Because of this characteristic, I have made a special point here of noting the degree of originality of various papers and of digging the nuggets of originality from what appear to be expositional or survey articles. This seems to be a necessary role for a survey of this kind. But it should not obscure the point that the Great Synthesizer should not be judged solely by the criterion of theoretical originality.

I. Growth and Trade

It is appropriate to begin with the Johnson article that has had the biggest impact on trade theory, namely, "Economic Expansion and International Trade" (1955). This article has provided the basis for one or more chapters in every trade-theory textbook and has practically founded a subbranch of the subject. It took growth in two countries through factor accumulation and technical progress as given and spelled out the effects on the volume, pattern, and terms of trade in a two-good, two-country model. It introduced the concepts of protrade, antitrade, and ultra pro- (and ultra anti-) trade biases. The article itself is extremely rich and dense in one of the characteristic Johnson styles, so that it is hardly possible to summarize it here. It explores some cases and problems that have been lost in the subsequent literature. It was inspired by Hicks (1953) and also made use of Rybczynski (1955), but there can be no doubt about its fundamental originality. It has provided the framework for analyzing a range of practical problems, notably the effects of growth on the terms of trade of developing relative to developed countries. It founded a whole literature of which the most important subsequent contribution was Findlay and Grubert (1959), which explored the effects of factor-biased technical progress in the model, a matter only hinted at in Harry's own article.

This major work was closely followed by two other articles in the same field. "Effects of Changes in Comparative Costs as Influenced by Technical Change" (1961) analyzed the effects of technical change on trade in detail. This article deserves to be more widely known. It expounded the Findlay-Grubert analysis verbally with great clarity and in addition expanded this model: a nontraded good was introduced, linking the analysis with Hicks (1953), and perfectly elastic supplies of one of the two factors were allowed for. The question was then posed whether technical change is likely to inhibit or encourage international trade. Are government and private research likely to be import or export biased? The transmission of knowledge between countries was discussed. It is interesting to read this article now; it turns out to be the link between his early growth-and-trade work and the later themes of the Wicksell Lecture.

In "Economic Development and International Trade" (1959*a*) he "packaged" the whole growth-and-trade subject very neatly. This is the article on biases now read and referred to. In it he expounded the essence of his 1955 article with the aid of some neat diagrams, leaving behind the verbal density and excessive taxonomy of the earlier article; he incorporated the Rybczynski and the Findlay-Grubert analyses; and he gave the profession (as he would put it) a simple article embodying all the main ideas in a way that a reasonably attentive undergraduate could understand.

The classic 1955 article was the third of a trilogy of articles on growth and trade published in the 3 years 1953–55. The first, "Equilibrium Growth in an International Economy" (1953), extended the Harrod-Domar analysis to the open economy. But Harry recognized subsequently that "the crux of the Harrod-Domar analysis, the knife-edge requirements of self-justifying growth, has, however, ceased to interest economic theorists, in consequence of the recognition that the savings ratio and the capital-output ratio are not parameters but variables amenable to economic policy or subject to equilibrating forces" (1958*b*, p. 10).

The second article, "Increasing Productivity, Income-Price Trends and the Trade Balance" (1954*a*), was very influential in Britain at the time. It had been commonly argued that faster productivity growth in the United States than in European countries would tend to improve the U.S. balance of payments (the "dollar problem"). He subjected this to rigorous, indeed elegant, analysis, introducing income as well as price effects—showing that income effects were likely to worsen the balance of payments of the faster-growing country. His monetary assumptions in this article were rather simple—he made various explicit money-income assumptions, with the required monetary policy implicit. While they were not unreasonable for the purpose of the exercise, I doubt that he would have approved of this approach in his later "monetary theory of the balance of payments" days. Furthermore, a complete analysis would really have had to introduce the complications of the 1955 article, allowance being made for more than one good produced in each country.

Something must be said about the quality of the exposition in these two articles. In both cases Harry expounded difficult arguments superbly. He used simple mathematics, avoided excessively complicated geometry, and clearly explained all steps verbally. Young theorists who wish to be understood by their readers, encouraged by editors who wish their journals to be read, would benefit from following the

expository techniques of these articles, especially the "Increasing Productivity" article.

The 1953 article contained a rigorous statement, with appropriate
formulae, of the concept now known as "immiserizing growth"—the
case where factor accumulation or technical progress can lower a
country's aggregate real income because of a sufficiently adverse effect of growth on its terms of trade. Awareness of the possibility goes
back to Mill and Edgeworth, but Harry was the first to revive the case
and explore it in rigorous modern terms. He did not give it a name or
a diagram, however, and he did not highlight it. In this case he left an
adequate exposition to his pupil, Jagdish N. Bhagwati, whose article is
now rightly the standard reference on the subject (Bhagwati 1958).
Furthermore, the Edgeworth-Nicholson controversy on the subject
was sorted out neatly in Bhagwati and Johnson (1960).

Harry later came back to immiserizing growth in two short notes. In
"The Possibility of Income Losses from Increased Efficiency or Factor
Accumulation in the Presence of Tariffs" (1967d), he showed in the
usual two-sector general equilibrium model that technical progress or
capital accumulation could bring about a fall in real income even
when the terms of trade do not change—that is, in a small country
model. This becomes a possibility when technical progress is concentrated in the protected industry, or the importable is relatively capital
intensive and capital accumulates, the cost of protection rising so
much as to outweigh the income gains obtainable in free trade. This
possibility was actually first uncovered by Dales (1966), who expounded it in partial equilibrium terms and whom Harry acknowledged. In "A Note on Distortions and the Rate of Growth of an Open
Economy" (1970c), the problem is to consider the effects of a tariff on
the rate of growth when there is given capital accumulation or technical progress, with the import-competing industry capital intensive or
the technical progress biased toward the import-competing industry.
His "The Possibility of Income Losses" (1967d) suggests that a tariff
would lower the rate of growth in this case because of the adverse
effect of the growing cost of protection. On the other hand, one
might expect that the more production is shifted toward the industries intensive in the faster-growing factor, the greater the weight of
that factor's growth rate in the total growth rate and hence the greater
the rate of growth. Harry found that the growth result could go either
way, though he did not succeed in obtaining any simple results. This
issue deserves further study.

In 1971 Harry published two further substantial, though overlapping, articles on trade and growth, one in the Kindleberger festschrift
(1971c) and the other in the *Journal of International Economics* (1971d).
His aim was to extend the static H-O-S model to include endogenous

capital accumulation with a constant savings ratio and constant population growth. He built on the work of a group of "more mathematically-inclined theorists," notably Oniki and Uzawa (1965), though he certainly brought out effects that are not clear in their articles. On the other hand, he limited himself to the small country case in order to make the problem tractable with his verbal and geometric methods. His explicit aim was to make this broad type of analysis more widely accessible—"to alleviate this undesirable situation of mathematicians' monopoly."

As usual with Harry's articles, one has to dig out the elements of originality (apart from the basic geometric exposition): these were his analysis of the effects of a tariff on long-run growth equilibrium (in the small country case) and the incorporation of increasing returns to scale into the comparative static analysis of the effects of growth on trade, an extension of his 1955 article. One can have reservations about the exposition in these two articles. A less busy writer would have gone on to produce the equivalent of "Economic Development and International Trade," in which the diagrams become simple and the main points emerge clearly without tiresome taxonomy. One also wonders why he wrote these papers, since he did not believe in the value of this (Oniki and Uzawa) body of mathematical trade theory. In the Wicksell Lecture (1968a) he wrote about it: "The kinds of problems suggested for theoretical analysis by this procedure, however, are too remote from the real world to be very interesting" (p. 7). I suspect he could not resist the temptation to clarify an intricate body of theory, if only to show that he had mastered it.

II. Positive Static Trade Theory

During his years at Manchester University from 1956 to 1959, Harry produced three articles that represent his principal contributions to mainstream H-O-S theory (other than the growth-and-trade work discussed above) and that have become standard references, as innumerable citations to them testify.

He consolidated the two-country, two-factor Heckscher-Ohlin model in "Factor Endowments, International Trade and Factor Prices" (1957), bringing out clearly the possibility of factor reversals. It was inspired by Harrod (1958) and built around a diagram originating in Samuelson (1949). This is one of his most widely read and cited articles in pure trade theory. In his own words, its function was "to review the existing literature with the double object of verifying the accuracy of accepted conclusions and synthesizing the methods and results of previous writers into simpler, more readily usable analysis" (preface, *International Trade and Economic Growth* [1958b, p. 9]). The possibility of factor reversals had been uncovered by Pearce (1951–52) and further explored by Jones (1956). In a sense, this paper was no more than an improvement on Harrod (1958), and he acknowledged this. What he did was to package the whole subject so neatly and tidily, with such economy of words and utter clarity, that his article, rather than the various earlier papers, is still read and has provided the basis for textbook writers.

"International Trade, Income Distribution, and the Offer Curve" (1959*b*) and "Income Distribution, the Offer Curve, and the Effects of Tariffs" (1960*c*) introduced into the standard H-O-S model the effects of income distribution changes, through resulting changes in the aggregate pattern of demand, on the offer curve. Although H-O-S theory had brought out the effects of trade and tariffs on factor income distribution, it had not allowed for the further repercussions of changes in income distribution on demand owing to differences in the spending patterns of factor owners. This introduced new possibilities of instability and multiple equilibria. These two articles— which were later republished as one in *Aspects of the Theory of Tariffs* (1971*a*)—filled an important gap in H-O-S theory. They were tightly argued, a feast of verbal mathematics and intricate theory. The second article incorporated the Lerner (1936), Metzler (1949), and Bhagwati (1959) cases concerning unexpected effects of tariffs on the terms of trade, on domestic prices, and on factor incomes; hence it was also a work of consolidation.

In a joint article with Bhagwati, "A Generalized Theory of the Effects of Tariffs on the Terms of Trade" (1961), he followed up this theme. The two authors showed that tariffs may worsen the terms of trade by reducing the demand for imports through a variety of unexpected spending effects, the government and private sectors being separated. The various cases are carefully worked out and expounded with great clarity, though most are, perhaps, of doubtful relevance to any practical issue. But this article, together with the 1959 and 1960 articles, tidied up this whole body of theory in which income distribution is affected by changes in relative prices and, in turn, through effects on demand, influences the final equilibrium.

Harry believed in the two-sector model because he believed in simplicity in theory and because he was, above all, a teacher. He learned to manipulate it for numerous purposes. The two articles on income distribution and the offer curve (1959*b*, 1960*c*) provided the foundation for much of his later two-sector work, discussed further in Section VII below.

Harry's only other contribution to H-O-S theory was in two short notes on factor-price equalization when commodities outnumber factors (1967*c*, 1970*d*). The contribution of these notes was not just to reaffirm the proposition of Samuelson (1949) that the introduction of extra commodities relative to factors strengthens the likelihood of factor-price equalization—and certainly that factor prices cannot actually diverge because of this—but to bring out the role of demand conditions for this problem: "demand conditions may make factor prices under trade converge less in the three-good than in the two-good case. . . ."

III. Normative Theory of Protection

In this field Harry wrote six substantial theoretical articles, including a trilogy on the optimum tariff and two of his most important articles—on the cost of protection and on domestic distortions. In addition, there is a pioneering empirical piece estimating ex ante the gains to the United Kingdom from freer trade with Europe.

His first contribution to the theory of protection was "Optimum Welfare and Maximum Revenue Tariffs" (1951–52), where he showed that the maximum revenue tariff must always be higher than the optimum tariff and also produced a neat consolidation of various optimum tariff formulae. The latter part was reprinted in *International Trade and Economic Growth* as "Alternative Optimum Tariff Formulae" and is a standard reference. The theory of the optimum tariff from a national point of view (taking into account the terms of trade effects of a tariff) was already fully developed by the time Harry moved into the field. His article helped to tidy it up.

"Optimum Tariffs and Retaliation" (1954*b*) was more significant and ambitious. He set out to "reassert the proposition that a country *may* gain by imposing a tariff even if other countries retaliate; and to determine the conditions under which it *will* gain in a special group of cases." This was done, typically, with great thoroughness. His starting point was the classic article by Scitovsky (1942) where the framework of the approach had been set out, and Harry was really concerned to expose an error in this article (that, once retaliation occurs, *all* parties are bound to lose). He clearly succeeded in doing so, but the real question must be about the way in which the retaliation process was conceived. Once country A imposes an optimum tariff (assuming no tariff by B), B then retaliates with an optimum tariff (assuming no change in A's tariff). Country B's retaliation consists of imposing an optimum tariff, not a bargaining tariff; and neither country takes into account the possibility that its own tariff will lead the other country to change *its* tariff. In a footnote Harry showed he was aware of this difficulty, but while a case can perhaps be made for this type of model in a multicountry model and when certain types of lag are allowed for, one must doubt whether so elaborate an analysis was worthwhile.

Harry's third contribution to optimum tariff theory came much later, with "The Gain from Exploiting Monopoly or Monopsony

Power in International Trade" (1968*b*). He showed that the national gain from an optimum tariff (without retaliation) would be higher the greater the domestic elasticities of substitution on the supply-and-demand side and the higher the ratio of imports to national income. On plausible figures he showed the likely gain to be small.

"The Cost of Protection and the Scientific Tariff" (1960*a*) was among Harry's most important articles. It marked a break with the general lines of the "orthodox" trade theory and was the first of a number of contributions from him that have helped to make the theory of trade policy much more relevant. The first part of the article, influenced by Corden (1957), developed a rigorous cost-of-protection theory in a multigood general equilibrium framework. His improvement on my work was to go beyond two goods and to spell out clearly the general equilibrium implications. The second part, on the "scientific tariff," was influenced by Young (1957). He worked out the minimum-cost tariff structures required to achieve various non-economic objectives, his aim being to formalize the logic of actual tariff policies. A development of this article was "The Costs of Protection and Self-Sufficiency" (1965*a*) in which he attached magnitudes to the consumption cost and the production cost of protection (compared with free trade) on the basis of plausible social utility functions and transformation curves. He granted that "the model . . . is far too simplified to permit the drawing of any very firm conclusions about reality, . . ." but concluded, among other things, "that the costs of protectionist policies are unlikely to be large enough, relative to potential maximum national income, to account for much of the existing major differences between the real per capita national incomes of various countries" (p. 371).

"Optimal Trade Intervention in the Presence of Domestic Distortion" (1965*c*) has proved to be one of Harry's major works—even more so, possibly, than his 1960 "Cost of Protection" paper. As it greatly influenced my own work, I can hardly be detached about it. He showed that in the presence of domestic distortions trade taxes are never first best, and that if trade taxes are used to eliminate the original distortions a net loss may ensue. He worked systematically and brilliantly through the principal arguments for protection, notably arguments resting on factor immobility or factor-price rigidity and the infant industry argument. It is true that the basic idea could be found earlier, in Meade (1955), Hagen (1958), and Bhagwati and Ramaswami (1963). Harry acknowledged as his principal inspiration the last article ("to these two authors belongs the credit for reducing a mass of ad hoc arguments concerning tariffs to a simple application of second-best welfare theory"), but any comparison with this paper, the article by Hagen, and the book by Meade must show how much of an advance Harry's article made on its predecessors. Apart from the beautifully expounded details, he provided the correct focus. Naturally, the subject has advanced since then, partly through rediscovery of themes in Meade (1955) and clarification of various implicit assumptions of "domestic distortions" theory. Harry himself later looked again at the infant industry argument.

Finally, mention must be made of his one empirical article in this field, "The Gains from Freer Trade with Europe: An Estimate" (1958a). Here he applied simple Marshallian (partial equilibrium cost of protection) analysis to a current problem, using ex ante data produced by Britain's Economist Intelligence Unit. The approach was bold and quite simple in a way that has subsequently become fashionable, but the fact is that it was one of the first calculations of this type, an advance on the "cash cost of protection" calculations previously made in Australia and Canada. Hence it is an important, much-cited article.

IV. Customs Union and Tariff-bargaining Theory

Harry's principal contribution to orthodox (Vinerian) customs union theory was an apparently expository article, "The Economic Theory of Customs Union" (1960b), which has been widely read and cited mainly because of the simplicity of its exposition compared with other papers available at the time. But it contained two novel features. First, he briefly worked out a case with economies of scale (foreshadowed, but not fully developed, in Viner [1950]). Second, he redefined trade creation to consist of a production *and a consumption* effect—instead of adhering to the Meade-Lipsey usage, in which trade creation referred only to a shift in the pattern of production leading to extra trade, while consumption shifts yielding extra trade were regarded as additional. The Meade-Lipsey approach meant that there could be a welfare gain from a trade-diverting customs union, the gain resulting from an offsetting consumption effect. It seemed much more sensible to Harry to combine all the effects that create trade—and thus yield welfare gains in the simple models used—and he set these off against the welfare-reducing effects of trade diversion. It is surprising that such a simple insight has not been more widely accepted. Harry came back to this point later, in "Trade-diverting Customs Unions: A Comment" (1974b), when he felt that unnecessary complications were being created through an inelegant definition based (probably) on a misinterpretation of Viner. In "A Note on Welfare-increasing Trade Diversion" (1975, p. 117) he argued that "this possibility is a needless analytical complication, since any such gain [i.e., gain from a union that was 'trade diverting'] must involve an increase in the volume of trade." Nevertheless, in the latter article he went on to work out the empirical possibility of such a case (on the basis of plausible utility and production function figures and an initial 25 percent tariff) and concluded that it was "probably an empty theoretical box."

"An Economic Theory of Protectionism, Tariff Bargaining, and the Formation of Customs Unions" (1965*b*) was one of Harry's most ambitious articles, and he regarded it as one of his most significant. His aim was to explain the logic of tariff bargaining and of the formation of customs unions, using the idea that "industrial production . . . appears as a collective consumption good yielding a flow of satisfaction to the electorate independent of the satisfaction they derive directly from the consumption of industrial products" (p. 258). Industrial production is a public good, and tariffs are used to foster industrial production because of a convention against export subsidization. On this basis he built an extremely elaborate theory designed to explain tariff bargaining, including tariff structures—notably, the potential benefits from discriminatory reciprocal tariff reductions. With regard to the formation of customs unions among developing countries, the approach seems useful and was developed at the same time more thoroughly in Cooper and Massell (1965). But with regard to the part of the article that was more original to Harry—the part that was concerned with the explanation of tariff bargaining among industrial countries—the hypothesis of "industrial production as a collective consumption good" has always seemed implausible to me.

The logic of tariff negotiations and tariff bargaining interested Harry over many years, and in various articles he explored different approaches. In "Optimum Tariffs and Retaliation" (1954*b*) he built on the optimum tariff approach. In "The Cost of Protection and the Scientific Tariff" (1960*a*) he briefly analyzed the implications of a "bargaining tariff" "aimed at inflicting economic damage upon another country or countries in order to obtain advantageous tariff concessions" (p. 344). Then there was the approach of the article under discussion, where industrial production is a collective consumption good, and a country's aim in bargaining is to swap extra exports of industrial products for extra imports. Finally, he came back to the logic of reciprocity in "Trade Negotiations and the New International Monetary System" (1976*b*), where he favored an explanation of bargaining policies in terms of a balancing of domestic effects within each country—damaging effects of extra imports on particular import-competing sectors being set against expected gains for exporters and consumers. "Further, what is influential politically is not the change in the volume of production, but the number of people and managers sufficiently affected either adversely or favourably by that change to motivate them to try to influence government policy" (p. 21). This is by far the most plausible framework and gives an appropriate weight to the reluctance of governments to take explicit action that will damage particular sections of the community. Clearly, had Harry lived he would have developed this line of thought further and might neatly have consolidated the various possible approaches to explaining negotiating processes.

Another article that might be noted at this point is "The Implications of Free or Freer Trade for the Harmonization of Other Policies" (1968c). This dealt exhaustively with an issue then and now relevant in the European Economic Community (and also in Canada, with regard to a possible free-trade area with the United States). It must now be the standard reference on the subject. His conclusion was that "a free trade area does not in and of itself require extensive harmonization of other policies. . . ." ". . . such harmonization is more a matter of choosing to augment the benefits of free trade than of being required to harmonize as a result of free trade."

V. Effective Protection

Harry will always be known as a pioneer, as well as popularizer, of effective protection theory. He wrote five articles in this field. His pioneering contribution was based on a lecture delivered in Geneva, "The Theory of Tariff Structure, with Special Reference to World Trade and Development" (1965d), in which he explored many aspects, characteristically correcting an error or imprecision in Barber (1955) concerned with the vertical escalation of tariff rates. This Geneva lecture was the first really theoretical article on the subject, closely followed by my own (Corden 1966). Apart from a late article, his writings on this subject were always rather piecemeal, and in this case he left the consolidation to me.

"A Model of Protection and the Exchange Rate" (1966b) brought out rigorously a paradoxical general equilibrium implication of an effective protection model—"the possibility that tariff structures may bring about a situation in which appreciation rather than depreciation would be necessary to preserve equilibrium under trade liberalization." "Nominal Tariffs, Indirect Taxes and Effective Rates of Protection: The Common Market Countries 1959" (1967), written with Herbert G. Grubel, was an important contribution, extending effective protection theory and making calculations to include excise taxes. The actual method used was subject to some valid criticisms from Gamir (1971), but this does not detract from the general significance of this article. "The Theory of Effective Protection and Preferences" (1969b) was, to some extent, an act of popularization and drew extensively and explicitly on my work; its particular contribution was to integrate effective protection theory with the theory of preferences, an interest that came out of his work on economic policies toward less developed countries. Finally, "Effective Protection and General Equilibrium Theory" (1971*b*) is a broad, very condensed survey of all the main general equilibrium issues raised by effective protection and is much influenced by my own work. Harry's own contribution—introduced characteristically without warning—is concerned with the pure trade theory case where there are more commodities than factors. He has difficulty reconciling this with the usual effective protection approach. He struggles with it, looking for simplicity with the aid of his favorite "Lerner-Pearce" diagram, and almost gives up, concluding realistically "that the prevailing mixture of general and partial equilibrium analysis is the most reasonable approach for practical economists interested in commercial policy questions, in spite of its rather shaky foundations in pure international trade theory."

Harry always acknowledged the Harvard doctoral thesis of William Travis as the source of his inspiration in this field, though he must have been influenced by Barber's (1955) article—"Canadian Tariff Policy"!—which developed the effective protection concept. One of the earliest empirical works—calculating "effective protection for labor" for the United States—came from his Chicago student Giorgio Basevi (1966). Harry's contribution was to show early awareness of the importance of the concept, to spread the simple idea and this awareness in the way he knew so well, with an emphasis on the idea's relevance for international trade negotiations, and to sort out some particular theoretical points.

VI. Wicksell Lecture and After

In his Wicksell Lecture, "Comparative Cost and Commercial Policy Theory for a Developing World Economy" (1968*a*), Harry sought to break away from orthodox international trade theorizing. For a man who had been accustomed to tying up every end and listing every assumption, this lecture was a departure. He wanted to integrate the neofactor proportions and the neotechnology theories of trade, to take into account international movements of skilled labor (the brain drain), the international corporation, and the much-discussed (at the time) technological gap between the United States and Western Europe. His purpose was "to attempt to synthesize the recent developments in the theory of international trade . . . in a broader approach to a dynamic theory of comparative cost—and of commercial policy—in a developing world" (p. 8).

The result was a stimulating *tour d'horizon* of trade theories—an attempt to spell out the logic of (and develop further) the Posner-Hufbauer-Vernon theories of technological gap trade and of the

product cycle, and much else. Apart from a superb survey and sys-
tematization of the new theories of trade, he developed his basic
theme—the application of a generalized approach to capital accumulation whereby not only the accumulation of physical and human
capital but also the growth of technology and knowledge in all forms
are parts of a capital accumulation process. This takes place unevenly
among countries—for reasons he discussed in detail—and then leads
to a number of different processes of knowledge diffusion or transfer
of production from the country of innovation to foreign locations. A
subsidiary theme—which formed the basis for two important articles
later—was that the extent of investment in knowledge and its diffusion would be socially suboptimal because of its well-known nonap-
propriability and public good characteristics.

There is no doubt that Harry valued this lecture highly, as
evidenced by the references he made to its main arguments on many
occasions later. In terms of its breadth, the issues it touches on or
opens up, the sense of relevance that pervades it, and the stimulus it
should provide for theorists and empirical workers in the future, it is
a major work.

Admittedly, it is not rigorous. Too much is left loose. Harry's aim
was to produce a grand, dynamic Heckscher-Ohlin model with the
original factors—labor and nature—combined with capital in all its
forms. Yet it seems unsatisfactory to treat all forms of capital accumulation—including investment in R & D—as in some sense similar. It is
important for the pattern of trade what sort of capital is being accumulated. It has been shown that human and physical capital must
be kept separate if the U.S. pattern of trade is to be explained (Branson 1977). Of course, Harry was aware of this, as of almost anything
in this field that other scholars might think of. But this lecture cries
out for more theoretical work, and the fact that so much insight and
potential for the development of international economics had to be
left loose is itself one component of the tragedy of Harry's early
death. The reader is also distracted by a whole range of side issues
relevant but not central to the main theme. One feels that Harry's
mind was filled with thoughts in this field and, breathlessly, he had to
spill them all out. Nevertheless, the Wicksell Lecture is a classic in
international economics—an imaginative paper that showed Harry at
his best as a man of broad vision, able to extract order out of somewhat chaotic theoretical developments and piecemeal empirical work.
It is a paper that should inspire all laborers in this vineyard, especially
graduate students in danger of getting the impression that trade
theory consists mainly of arid model building.

Three substantial articles form part of Harry's "Wicksell period,"
namely, "Some Economic Aspects of Brain Drain" (1967e), "The

Efficiency and Welfare Implications of the International Corporation" (1970*a*), and "A New View of the Infant Industry Argument" (1970*b*). In addition, he really let himself go in one of his last papers, a contribution to the Nobel Symposium on the International Allocation of Economic Activity, "Technology, Technical Progress and the International Allocation of Economic Activity" (1977*b*).

The brain drain article is a brilliant, comprehensive, compact survey of all the issues: Canadian, British, and developing country aspects are covered; taxation, income controls, and externalities are allowed for; and unsound arguments are demolished. No stone is left unturned. This must be a standard reference in the economics of migration. His main conclusion is that the brain drain need not be harmful (though it *might* be). The paper is notable for a personal testament: "I adopt a cosmopolitan liberal position, and regard nationalism as one of the less pleasant mental vices in which mankind indulges itself, or as one of the characteristics of childish immaturity out of which I hope the people of the world will ultimately grow" (1967*e*, p. 379).

The much-cited "International Corporations" paper is built around the idea that the primary function of the multinational enterprise is the generation and international transfer of productive knowledge, and that "it does not necessarily follow that recompense through monopoly profits on the use of the knowledge is the ideal arrangement for the host country" (pp. 40–41). He was seeking a rationale for the various dissatisfactions of host countries with foreign multinationals. As a Canadian, he had long thought about these dissatisfactions. The paper also contains a detailed analysis of various arguments for restricting inward foreign investment, though it probably undervalues various popular considerations that he would have described as "noneconomic."

"A New View of the Infant Industry Argument" was built around the same theme: ". . . the essential nature of the infant industry argument is now clear. What is involved is an investment in a process of acquisition of knowledge which is socially profitable but privately unprofitable because the private investor cannot appropriate the whole of the social return from his investment" (p. 60). When knowledge is a private good, there is no infant industry argument. The protection issue arises when "the relevant learning process has the inherent character of a public good" (p. 67). Traditionally, the infant industry argument has been defined as an argument for temporary intervention to protect a new venture, irrespective of the source of the conditions which justify intervention, as in his "Domestic Distortions" paper. But here he sought to narrow the definition—the essential feature of infancy being ignorance, and the argument being confined to grounds which relate to the creation and diffusion of knowledge. Harry explored here only one aspect of the traditional infant industry argument (as was pointed out in comments on this paper by Snape [1970]). But, within these limits, it is an important paper.

Finally, the Nobel Symposium paper really defies summary. He sketched out imaginatively a stylized historical process designed to explain the location of economic activity and its changes over time. Labor, capital, and technology are all mobile in varying degrees. He came back to the technological gap issue and why it is sometimes uneconomic to apply the "best" technology, and he stressed again the Wicksell point that "technology is a form of capital, and its availability alterable by investment." This must be regarded as a most stimulating, but incomplete, paper, and I hope it will be taken up and developed further by international trade theorists.

VII. Other Writings

We have now surveyed Harry Johnson's major contributions to nonmonetary international trade theory, yet an incredible number of publications remain to be noted—some of extremely high quality, including several surveys and his most widely read book.

Surveys

Harry was, of course, the surveyor general of the subject. In almost every article he surveyed the relevant literature before launching into his own contributions. Sections of the Wicksell Lecture stand out as a survey of the new theories of trade. Apart from this, his three most notable surveys are "International Trade Theory and Monopolistic Competition Theory" (1967*b*), the survey of international trade theory in the *Encyclopedia of the Social Sciences* (1968*d*), and "The Standard Theory of Tariffs" (1969*a*).

The "Monopolistic Competition" survey was a conscientious attempt to dig up everything that had ever been written on monopolistic competition and international trade—and he uncovered a surprising number of articles. But his main conclusion was that the theory of monopolistic competition had made virtually no impact on the theory of international trade, mainly because it was partial equilibrium and "appears to have no macroeconomic implications essentially different from those inherent in the assumption of pure competition habitually employed in international trade theory" (p. 204). However, he repeatedly came back to this issue, notably in the Wicksell Lecture and related writings, and stressed the relevance of monopolistic competition and product differentiation to the Wicksell issues.

The encyclopedia article is a superb piece of writing, showing Harry's ability to verbalize complex theoretical ideas, his historical perspective, and his sense of proportion. In spite of subsequent developments in the field—some of which he foreshadowed in brief remarks—it still repays reading and ought to have been reprinted in one of his collections.

"The Standard Theory of Tariffs" is a concise, very carefully written survey of the theory of tariffs as it was before the new ideas of the 1960s—effective protection, domestic distortions, and so on. It contains some new geometric devices. Harry said in the preface to *Aspects of the Theory of Tariffs* that the standard theory "struck me on reconsideration for this book as less scientifically valuable than the prior work on which it had been founded," but it is a pity he did not reprint it. Another well-known survey is "Tariffs and Economic Development" (1964b), which was updated somewhat in another survey, "Commercial Policy and Industrialization" (1972a), a lecture delivered in Panama and particularly directed to small countries. Finally, "Direct Foreign Investment: Survey of the Issues" (1972b) is a tight and comprehensive survey of the foreign investment issues from both a host and a home country point of view, much influenced by his lifelong involvement in the Canadian debate and also by Caves (1971). An original section deals with the effects of capital inflow on real wages, showing that these *might* fall. There is no better concise survey of the subject.

Two-Sector Model

International trade theorists pioneered the detailed exploration of two-sector general equilibrium models, and it had been realized for some time that their techniques could be applied usefully outside trade theory—as evidenced by Meade (1965) and various contributions to two-sector growth models. Harry really threw himself into this, with one short book, *The Two-Sector Model of General Equilibrium* (1971e), his joint text with Melvyn Krauss, *General Equilibrium Analysis: A Microeconomic Text* (1974), and, in addition, a number of sorting-out articles on "Factor Market Distortions and the Shape of the Transformation Curve" (1966a), "On the Shape and Location of the Production Possibility Curve" (1973) with Krauss and Skouras, "A Note on Factor-Income Distribution and the Factor-Owner Production Block" (1976a), "A Note on the Geometry of the Two-by-Two General Equilibrium Model" (1977a), and "Factor Intensities and the Shape of the Production Possibility Curve" (written with Lizondo and Yeh in 1977 and published in 1981). The 1966 article generated a considerable, if rather esoteric, literature. It really belongs to the *positive* theory of domestic distortions and hence has been rather hard to place in this survey. A common feature of much of this work involved the use of the Lerner-Pearce diagram and the development of some complicated geometry around it. Harry believed in the value of geometry as an expository device to spread economic literacy. He put this case strongly in his *The Two-Sector Model of General Equilibrium.* "Second, and more important, geometry lends itself far more readily than mathematical analysis to the communication of economic analysis to masses of students (though this advantage may be eroding as students in general become more numerate)."

A central theme of Harry's "two-sector" writings was a concern with income-distribution effects. His work in the field of income distribution falls outside the scope of this survey, but it was a valuable by-product of his facility with general equilibrium two-sector models derived from trade theory. His most influential article here is "The Effects of Unionization on the Distribution of Income: A General Equilibrium Approach" (1970), written with Peter Mieszkowski. As mentioned earlier, much of this work might be regarded as a continuation of his two classic articles on income distribution and the offer curve (1959*b*, 1960*c*).

International Economic Relations

Harry's most widely read book is probably *Economic Policies toward Less Developed Countries,* written at the Brookings Institution in 3 months. It is a tour de force. Magpie-like, he picked up bits and pieces of the latest relevant research and adapted and fitted them all into a coherent framework. Utterly rigorous, clear, and balanced, the book covers numerous aspects, including the political, of the subject. It was his most successful venture in "spreading economic literacy." He did not avoid complex arguments and exhaustive analysis, but, aside from some footnotes, the exposition is all verbal. Spread through this book are many insights, but perhaps the principal contribution is the analysis of the UN Conference on Trade and Development (UNCTAD) scheme for temporary trade preferences for manufactures, which he showed to be a version of an infant industry argument for protection and also related to the theory of effective protection. The book is sympathetic to the UNCTAD ideas and motivations. In later years, Harry lost patience with the rather woolly and extravagant proposals described as "The New International Economic Order" and wrote several critical, even fierce, papers on the subject, reflecting particularly on the class interests of international bureaucrats.

In addition, Harry wrote numerous papers, overlapping with each other in content, on international trade negotiations, "alternative trade strategies for the seventies," the trend to protectionism, and so on. For a short time he became an advocate (rather than an analyst) of

HARRY G. JOHNSON   585

a particular scheme, namely, the proposals for a multilateral free-trade area. *The World Economy at the Crossroads* (1965*e*) brought together much of his thinking in this and related fields at an early stage. It went into three impressions. Always in these writings he maintained high standards of rigor and clarity. His last paper in this area, "Trade Negotiations and the New International Monetary System" (1976*b*), reflected on the effects of flexible exchange rates on trade negotiations.

VIII. Some General Reflections

What did Harry believe about the role of theory and about the state of international trade theory in particular? Did his own work conform to his stated beliefs? These are interesting issues in themselves, but they have been highlighted recently by the view expressed in Lipsey's (1978) survey of Harry's contributions to trade theory, namely, that Harry believed in "the emptiness of qualitative economics."

There is really not much difficulty in determining what Harry believed—he expressed his views clearly and forcefully in print on many occasions. The best statement can be found in "The State of Theory in Relation to the Empirical Analysis" (1970*e*). The relevant passages are too long to quote fully here, but he distinguished between (1) the role of theory in the context of empirical research and (2) the broad role of theory "as a systematic approach to the understanding of economic phenomena and as the organization of disciplined thinking about these phenomena and about policies relating to them." In the first role its function is "to cast up empirically testable and refutable explanatory hypotheses, and the value of a theory is to be judged by its explanatory power in comparison with its rivals." In the second role, the purpose is "to abstract from the complexity of the real world a simplified model of the key relationships between dependent and independent variables, and to explore the positive and normative implications of changes in the 'givens' of this hypothetical system." He pointed out that "the theory of international trade has always been primarily theory in the second sense" (p. 10).

Harry's view of the role of models was well stated in his last year: ". . . the purpose of models, and of teachers in general, is to instruct students in the simplest elements of a problem. Once they have that basic understanding of interconnections, the next stage is to look at the real world and try to see the simple interconnections operating" (Ohlin, Hesselborn, and Wijkman 1977, p. 99). At the same time, he was well aware of the need to adjust models in the light of new empirical evidence. This comes through strongly in "The State of Theory in Relation to the Empirical Analysis" and, above all, in the Wicksell Lecture.

In his later years, Harry became impatient with the "pursuit of arcane analytical problems." He felt that the trend to mathematical theorizing was discrediting trade theory among the general body of economists and preventing its wider application to economic policy. One of his earliest references to this view was in his review of Staffan B. Linder's *Essay on Trade and Transformation* (1964a): "This shift of emphasis is overdue, as is a recasting of the mathematically over-elaborated present framework of trade theory" (p. 86). The theme ran through various papers in his Wicksell period. He stressed the need for some understanding of history and of the history of political economy. (On his views, see esp. his contributions to Samuelson [1969c]; "The State of Theory in Relation to the Empirical Analysis" [1970e]; and "The State of Theory" [1974a].)

Of course, he might be accused of not having followed his own precepts. Some of his early writings were not only mathematical by the standards of those days but also overelaborate, and other articles were substantially verbal or geometric mathematics of which the same criticisms could be made. Nevertheless, he always showed an awareness of the need for relevance. This is clear from the preface to *International Trade and Economic Growth* and runs through many (though not all!) of the papers collected in *Aspects of the Theory of Tariffs*. But relevance and simplicity were not his only concerns. In his early days, he had an iconoclastic desire to show that nothing simple said by a British (or other) economist could possibly be true. At times he enjoyed the pleasures of mental gymnastics. In addition, he wanted to show that he could understand and practice complex theory if he really chose.

Finally, something must be said about Harry's broader role in the development of international economics. While this survey has been devoted to Harry's own writings, his contributions to the field go well beyond the work published under his name. His interaction with a vast number of economists is well known. I think he must be given some part of the credit for numerous important articles published by others over a period of more than 20 years. If the list of acknowledgments in a paper contains his name, it can safely be assumed that he made a difference to the paper. Perhaps he encouraged the author initially, perhaps he directed the author's attention to some other work not yet published of which the author should have been aware, or perhaps he suggested redrafting, following up new lines, and so on. Above all, he had the remarkable ability to guide numerous authors in fruitful directions. He was able to see a contribution—however apparently narrow—in the perspective of the whole field and in the light of the scientific development (as he would put it) of the subject.

HARRY G. JOHNSON   587

It can be assumed that he had a significant role in most or all articles in international economics published in the *Review of Economic Studies* and in the *Journal of Political Economy* while he was an editor. He had a flair for seeing which articles were likely to become important in the field. A list of some articles in international trade theory published in the *Review of Economic Studies* or the *Journal of Political Economy* under the Johnson regimes will perhaps make the point: Jones on factor proportions theory (1956), Lipsey and Lancaster on second best (1956–57), Bhagwati on immiserizing growth (1958), Kemp and Jones on variable labor supply (1962), Bhagwati and Ramaswami on domestic distortions (1963), Balassa (1965) and Corden (1966) on effective protection, Cooper and Massell on customs union theory (1965), Kenen on nature, capital, and trade (1965), and Jones on the general equilibrium two-sector model (1965).

His interaction was certainly a two-way process. He kept his eyes and ears open for the latest idea, whether at a seminar or in a draft paper, and if it fitted into his own framework of thinking, he would not hesitate to use it and publish it even before the original author had published it—but always with full acknowledgments, and in fact providing advance publicity for the other's forthcoming paper. He played a key communication role in the field, ensuring that the paper that X was drafting took into account the unpublished ideas of Y in some faraway place. The greatest crime in his eyes was to fail to acknowledge adequately. He could forgive a lack of adequate credits to Samuelson or Hicks but not to the seminal writings of an obscure economist in Australia, Burma, or Canada.

Harry was thus "a builder of intellectual bridges," as Courchene (1978) has correctly stressed. He was a broker of ideas, contributing some of the middleman's value added. His worldwide interaction was striking. It is usual for great economists at a major center—such as Chicago or the two Cambridges—to interact with and influence local students, colleagues, or visitors, whether present or former, and to build up "schools." But Harry's circle was worldwide and in no sense institution bound. In this respect, as in so many others, he was the complete internationalist. He was the enemy of academic as of other forms of provincialism.

References

Balassa, Bela. "Tariff Protection in Industrial Countries: An Evaluation." *J.P.E.* 78 (December 1965): 573–94.
Barber, Clarence L. "Canadian Tariff Policy." *Canadian J. Econ. and Polit. Sci.* 21 (November 1955): 513–30.
Basevi, Giorgio. "The United States Tariff Structure: Estimates of Effective Rates of Protection of United States Industries and Industrial Labor." *Rev. Econ. and Statis.* 48 (May 1966): 147–60.

JOURNAL OF POLITICAL ECONOMY

Bhagwati, Jagdish N. "Immiserizing Growth: A Geometrical Note." *Rev. Econ. Studies* 25 (June 1958): 201–5.

———. "Protection, Real Wages and Real Incomes." *Econ. J.* 69 (December 1959): 733–48.

Bhagwati, Jagdish N., and Johnson, Harry G. "Notes on Some Controversies in the Theory of International Trade." *Econ. J.* 70 (March 1960): 74–93.

Bhagwati, Jagdish N., and Ramaswami, Vangal K. "Domestic Distortions, Tariffs and the Theory of Optimum Subsidy." *J.P.E.* 71 (February 1963): 44–50.

Branson, William H. "Comment." In Ohlin et al., eds., 1977.

Caves, Richard E. "International Corporations: The Industrial Economics of Foreign Investment." *Economica* 38 (February 1971): 1–27.

Cooper, C. A., and Massell, B. F. "Toward a General Theory of Customs Unions for Developing Countries." *J.P.E.* 73 (October 1965): 461–76.

Corden, W. M. "The Calculation of the Cost of Protection." *Econ. Rec.* 33 (April 1957): 29–51.

———. "The Structure of a Tariff System and the Effective Protective Rate." *J.P.E.* 74 (June 1966): 221–37.

Courchene, Thomas J. "Harry Johnson: Macroeconomist." *Canadian J. Econ.* 11 (suppl.; November 1978): S11–S33.

Dales, J. H. *The Protective Tariff in Canada's Economic Development.* Toronto: Univ. Toronto Press, 1966.

Findlay, Ronald, and Grubert, Herbert G. "Factor Intensities, Technological Progress and the Terms of Trade." *Oxford Econ. Papers* 11 (February 1959): 111–21.

Gamir, Luis. "The Calculation of Effective Rates of Protection in Spain." In *Effective Tariff Protection*, edited by Herbert G. Grubel and Harry G. Johnson. Geneva: General Agreement on Tariffs and Trade, 1971.

Hagen, Everett E. "An Economic Justification of Protectionism." *Q.J.E.* 72 (November 1958): 496–514.

Harrod, Roy F. "Factor-Price Relations under Free Trade." *Econ. J.* 68 (June 1958): 245–55.

Hicks, John R. "An Inaugural Lecture." *Oxford Econ. Papers* 5 (June 1953): 117–35.

Johnson, Harry G. "Optimum Welfare and Maximum Revenue Tariffs." *Rev. Econ. Studies* 19, no. 1 (1951–52): 28–35. Renamed "Alternative Optimum Tariff Formulae." In Johnson 1958*b*.

———. "Equilibrium Growth in an International Economy." *Canadian J. Econ. and Polit. Sci.* 19 (November 1953): 478–500.

———. "Increasing Productivity, Income-Price Trends and the Trade Balance." *Econ. J.* 64 (September 1954): 462–85. (*a*)

———. "Optimum Tariffs and Retaliation." *Rev. Econ. Studies* 21, no. 2 (1954): 142–53. (*b*)

———. "Economic Expansion and International Trade." *Manchester School Econ. and Soc. Studies* 23 (May 1955): 95–112.

———. "Factor Endowments, International Trade and Factor Prices." *Manchester School Econ. and Soc. Studies* 25 (September 1957): 270–83.

———. "The Gains from Freer Trade with Europe: An Estimate." *Manchester School Econ. and Soc. Studies* 26 (September 1958): 247–55. (*a*)

———. *International Trade and Economic Growth: Studies in Pure Theory.* London: Allen & Unwin, 1958. (*b*)

———. "Economic Development and International Trade." *Pakistan Econ. J.* 9 (December 1959): 47–71. (*a*)

———. "International Trade, Income Distribution, and the Offer Curve." *Manchester School Econ. and Soc. Studies* 27 (September 1959): 241–60. (*b*)

———. "The Cost of Protection and the Scientific Tariff." *J.P.E.* 68 (August 1960): 327–45. (*a*)

———. "The Economic Theory of Customs Union." *Pakistan Econ. J.* 10 (March 1960): 14–32. (*b*)

———. "Income Distribution, the Offer Curve, and the Effects of Tariffs." *Manchester School Econ. and Soc. Studies* 28 (September 1960): 215–42. (*c*)

———. "Effects of Changes in Comparative Costs as Influenced by Technical Change." *Malayan Econ. Rev.* 6 (October 1961): 1–13.

———. Review of *An Essay on Trade and Transformation* by Staffan B. Linder. *Economica* 31 (February 1964): 86–90. (*a*)

———. "Tariffs and Economic Development: Some Theoretical Issues." *J. Development Studies* 1 (October 1964): 3–30. (*b*)

———. "The Costs of Protection and Self-Sufficiency." *Q.J.E.* 79 (August 1965): 356–72. (*a*)

———. "An Economic Theory of Protectionism, Tariff Bargaining, and the Formation of Customs Unions." *J.P.E.* 73 (June 1965): 256–83. (*b*)

———. "Optimal Trade Intervention in the Presence of Domestic Distortion." In *Trade, Growth and the Balance of Payments: Essays in Honor of Gottfried Haberler,* by Robert E. Baldwin et al. Amsterdam: North-Holland, 1965. (*c*)

———. "The Theory of Tariff Structure, with Special Reference to World Trade and Development." In *Trade and Development,* by Harry G. Johnson and Peter B. Kenen. Geneva: Librairie Droz, 1965. (*d*)

———. *The World Economy at the Crossroads.* Oxford: Clarendon, 1965. (*e*)

———. "Factor Market Distortions and the Shape of the Transformation Curve." *Econometrica* 34 (July 1966): 696–98. (*a*)

———. "A Model of Protection and the Exchange Rate." *Rev. Econ. Studies* 33 (April 1966): 159–63. (*b*)

———. *Economic Policies toward Less Developed Countries.* Washington: Brookings Inst., 1967. (*a*)

———. "International Trade Theory and Monopolistic Competition Theory." In *Monopolistic Competition Theory: Studies in Impact,* edited by Robert E. Kuenne. New York: Wiley, 1967. (*b*)

———. "The Possibility of Factor Price Equalization When Commodities Outnumber Factors." *Econ. J.* 34 (August 1967): 282–88. (*c*)

———. "The Possibility of Income Losses from Increased Efficiency or Factor Accumulation in the Presence of Tariffs." *Econ. J.* 77 (March 1967): 151–54. (*d*)

———. "Some Economic Aspects of Brain Drain." *Pakistan Development Rev.* 7 (Autumn 1967): 379–411. (*e*)

———. "Comparative Cost and Commercial Policy Theory for a Developing World Economy." Wicksell Lecture. Stockholm: Almqvist & Wiksell, 1968. (*a*)

———. "The Gain from Exploiting Monopoly or Monopsony Power in International Trade." *Economica* 35 (May 1968): 151–56. (*b*)

———. "The Implications of Free or Freer Trade for the Harmonization of Other Policies." In *Harmonization of National Economic Policies under Free Trade,* by Harry G. Johnson, Paul Wonnacott, and Hirofumi Shibata. Toronto: Univ. Toronto Press, 1968. (*c*)

———. "International Trade: Theory." In *International Encyclopedia of the Social Sciences,* vol. 8, edited by David L. Sills. New York: Macmillan, 1968. (*d*)

———. "The Standard Theory of Tariffs." *Canadian J. Econ.* 2 (August 1969): 333–52. (*a*)

————. "The Theory of Effective Protection and Preferences." *Economica* 36 (May 1969): 119–38. (*b*)

————. "The Theory of International Trade." In *International Economic Relations: Proceedings of the Third Congress of the International Economic Association,* edited by Paul A. Samuelson. New York: Macmillan, 1969. (*c*)

————. "The Efficiency and Welfare Implications of the International Corporation." In *The International Corporation: A Symposium,* edited by Charles P. Kindleberger. Cambridge, Mass.: MIT Press, 1970. (*a*)

————. "A New View of the Infant Industry Argument." In *Studies in International Economics: Monash Conference Papers,* edited by I. A. McDougall and Richard H. Snape. Amsterdam: North-Holland, 1970. (*b*)

————. "A Note on Distortions and the Rate of Growth of an Open Economy." *Econ. J.* 80 (December 1970): 990–92. (*c*)

————. "On Factor Price Equalization When Commodities Outnumber Factors: A Comment." *Economica* 37 (February 1970): 89–90. (*d*)

————. "The State of Theory in Relation to the Empirical Analysis." In *The Technological Factor in International Trade,* edited by Raymond Vernon. New York: Columbia Univ. Press (for N.B.E.R.), 1970. (*e*)

————. *Aspects of the Theory of Tariffs.* London: Allen & Unwin, 1971. (*a*)

————. "Effective Protection and General Equilibrium Theory." In Johnson 1971a. (*b*)

————. "The Theory of Trade and Growth: A Diagrammatic Analysis." In *Trade, Balance of Payments, and Growth: Papers in International Economics in Honor of Charles P. Kindleberger,* edited by Jagdish N. Bhagwati et al. Amsterdam: North-Holland, 1971. (*c*).

————. "Trade and Growth: A Geometrical Exposition." *J. Internat. Econ.* 1 (January/March 1971): 83–101. (*d*)

————. *The Two-Sector Model of General Equilibrium.* London: Allen & Unwin, 1971. (*e*)

————. "Commercial Policy and Industrialization." *Economica* 39 (August 1972): 264–75. (*a*)

————. "Direct Foreign Investment: Survey of the Issues." In *Direct Foreign Investment in Asia and the Pacific,* edited by Peter Drysdale. Canberra: Australian National Univ. Press, 1972. (*b*)

————. "The State of Theory." *A.E.R. Papers and Proc.* 64 (May 1974): 323–24. (*a*)

————. "Trade-diverting Customs Unions: A Comment." *Econ. J.* 84 (September 1974): 618–21. (*b*)

————. "A Note on Welfare-increasing Trade Diversion." *Canadian J. Econ.* 8 (February 1975): 117–23.

————. "A Note on Factor-Income Distribution and the Factor-Owner Production Block." *Manchester School Econ. and Soc. Studies* 44 (December 1976): 303–8. (*a*)

————. "Trade Negotiations and the New International Monetary System." Commercial Policies Issues no. 1, Trade Policy Res. Centre. Leiden: Sijthoff, 1976. (*b*)

————. "A Note on the Geometry of the Two-by-Two General Equilibrium Model." *Economica* 44 (February 1977): 71–75. (*a*)

————. "Technology, Technical Progress and the International Allocation of Economic Activity." In Ohlin et al., eds., 1977. (*b*)

Johnson, Harry G., and Bhagwati, Jagdish N. "A Generalized Theory of the Effects of Tariffs on the Terms of Trade." *Oxford Econ. Papers,* n.s. 13 (October 1961): 225–53.

Johnson, Harry G., and Grubel, Herbert G. "Nominal Tariffs, Indirect Taxes and Effective Rates of Protection: The Common Market Countries 1959." *Econ. J.* 77 (December 1967): 761–76.

Johnson, Harry G., and Krauss, Melvyn B. *General Equilibrium Analysis: A Microeconomic Text.* London: Allen & Unwin, 1974.

Johnson, Harry G.; Krauss, Melvyn B.; and Skouras, Thanos. "On the Shape and Location of the Production Possibility Curve." *Economica* 40 (August 1973): 305–10.

Johnson, Harry G., and Mieszkowski, Peter. "The Effects of Unionization on the Distribution of Income: A General Equilibrium Approach." *Q.J.E.* 84 (November 1970): 539–61.

Jones, Ronald W. "Factor Proportions and the Heckscher-Ohlin Theorem." *Rev. Econ. Studies* 24 (October 1956): 1–10.

———. "The Structure of Simple General Equilibrium Models." *J.P.E.* 73 (December 1965): 557–72.

Kemp, Murray C., and Jones, Ronald W. "Variable Labor Supply and the Theory of International Trade." *J.P.E.* 70 (February 1962): 30–36.

Kenen, Peter B. "Nature, Capital, and Trade." *J.P.E.* 73 (October 1965): 437–60.

Lerner, Abba P. "The Symmetry between Import and Export Taxes." *Economica* 3 (August 1936): 306–13.

Lipsey, Richard G. "Harry Johnson's Contributions to the Pure Theory of International Trade." *Canadian J. Econ.* 11 (suppl.; November 1978): S34–S54.

Lipsey, Richard G., and Lancaster, Kelvin. "The General Theory of Second Best." *Rev. Econ. Studies* 24, no. 1 (1956–57): 11–32.

Lizondo, José S.; Johnson, Harry G.; and Yeh, Yeong-Her. "Factor Intensities and the Shape of the Production Possibility Curve." *Economica* 48 (May 1981): 199–202.

Meade, James E. *Trade and Welfare.* Oxford: Oxford Univ. Press, 1955.

———. *The Stationary Economy.* London: Allen & Unwin, 1965.

Metzler, Lloyd A. "Tariffs, the Terms of Trade, and the Distribution of National Income." *J.P.E.* 57 (February 1949): 1–29.

Ohlin, Bertil; Hesselborn, Per-Ove; and Wijkman, Per Magnus, eds. *The International Allocation of Economic Activity: Proceedings of a Nobel Symposium.* London: Macmillan, 1977.

Oniki, Hajime, and Uzawa, Hirofumi. "Patterns of Trade and Investment in a Dynamic Model of International Trade." *Rev. Econ. Studies* 32 (January 1965): 15–38.

Pearce, I. F. "The Factor Price Equalisation Myth." *Rev. Econ. Studies* 19, no. 2 (1951–52): 111–20.

Rybczynski, T. M. "Factor Endowment and Relative Commodity Prices." *Economica* 22 (November 1955): 336–41.

Samuelson, Paul A. "International Factor-Price Equalisation Once Again." *Econ. J.* 59 (June 1949): 181–97.

Scitovsky, Tibor. "A Reconsideration of the Theory of Tariffs." *Rev. Econ. Studies* 9, no. 2 (1942): 89–110.

Snape, Richard H. "A New View of the Infant Industry Argument: Comment." In *Studies in International Economics*, edited by I. A. McDougall and Richard H. Snape. Amsterdam: North-Holland, 1970.

Viner, Jacob. *The Customs Union Issue.* New York: Carnegie Endowment Internat. Peace, 1950.

Young, J. H. *Canadian Commercial Policy.* Ottawa: Royal Commission Canada's Econ. Prospects, 1957.

[6]

Harry Johnson as a Macroeconomist

David Laidler

University of Western Ontario

I. Introduction

Harry Johnson's reputation as a macroeconomist rests at least as
much on his contributions to policy debates and on his widely read
survey articles as on his original research. If one looks at his written
work from the narrow vantage point of North America, it is easy to
underestimate its importance. Much of what his later writings contain
was without a doubt "well known at Chicago" when it was published.
However, Harry's capacity for absorbing "oral tradition" was matched
by a considerable ability to contribute to it, and it is dangerous to infer
a lack of originality from this fact. In any event, in macroeconomics,
his chosen audience more often than not consisted of research workers, teachers, and students outside the major centers, not to mention
policymakers and "interested laymen." His ability to synthesize and
expound the issues being tackled and the results being attained in all
areas of the field ensured that their significance was grasped by the
profession at large far more rapidly and effectively than otherwise
would have been the case. For this reason alone he is a figure of
considerable importance in the recent history of macroeconomics.

A number of questions naturally arise. What kind of macroeconomics did he expound? How did it evolve over the years? How
much did he himself contribute to the body of knowledge that he
expounded? How much did he take from others? And why did the
evolution of his thought take the path that it did? Virtually every

I am grateful to Victoria Chick, Dennis Coppock, Tom Courchene, Clark Leith,
Marcus Miller, Michael Parkin, Don Patinkin, Franco Spinelli, and George Zis for
comments on an earlier draft which was presented at the Money Study Group University of Manchester Conference, held in memory of Harry G. Johnson, April 10–11,
1978.

[*Journal of Political Economy*, 1984, vol. 92, no. 4]

reader of this paper will already have his own views on the answers to the foregoing questions, and it would be as well to outline mine at the outset. Harry's macroeconomics evolved in a direction that led him to pay increasing attention to monetary factors, but he never became a "monetarist" as the term is understood in North America.[1] His originality in this area was not of the very highest order, but by any reasonable standard it was considerable: none of his papers makes a first approach to a new problem, but a number of them represent important contributions to bodies of literature opened up by others. Moreover, his survey papers and policy writings show frequent and highly original insights which he did not always systematically follow up himself. Finally the evolution of Harry Johnson's macroeconomics had very little indeed to do with the fact that he held a chair at the University of Chicago. The evidence of his published work shows that his views stemmed naturally from his perceptions of what the important issues of macroeconomic policy were and from his bringing to bear upon those issues the body of theory and empirical evidence that the published macroeconomic literature provided—including, of course, contributions originating in Chicago.

II. The Cambridge Keynesian

Harry began as what he himself termed a "Cambridge Keynesian" (see McKinnon, ed., 1976, p. 298). In the early 1950s, like many people working on macro and monetary problems in British universities, he subscribed to two only loosely connected bodies of macroeconomics, rather than one: pure monetary theory and knowledge about monetary policy as it was actually conducted and as it actually worked. The former cast only a limited light on the latter. Harry's commentary on Sir Dennis Robertson in the *Review of Economic Studies* (1951–52) is purely about the logic of an economic model. Despite any clear-cut reference, it is obvious that the basis of his analysis is largely Modigliani's (1944) *Econometrica* paper. One cannot deduce

---

[1] The evolution of Harry's macroeconomics was of course but one aspect of his evolution as a political economist. Over the years he undoubtedly moved from "left" to "right." This was not because he became increasingly confident in the powers of market forces to solve social problems, but rather because he became increasingly pessimistic about the willingness and ability of governments and bureaucracies to solve those same problems. He said as much in the closing passages of the preface to the 1977 edition of his *Canadian Quandary* (1963b). It is far beyond the scope of this essay to go into all of these matters. However, let me assert that just as his macroeconomics evolved as he subjected economic analysis to empirical evidence, so I am sure that similar forces governed his broader development. The contrary view, proposed by Bhagwati (1977), that Harry's views changed as a result of "arguing with an ideologue," will no doubt appeal to anyone too lazy to engage in a similar exercise on his own account.

from this essay whether, for example, he believed the fixed or flexible price version of the IS-LM model to be the more relevant, or whether he believed the liquidity trap doctrine to be important or unimportant as a practical matter. To Harry in the early 1950s it was the job of economic theory to derive the different implications of different factual assumptions, and that was all. Having just lambasted James Meade (Johnson 1951*b*) for pretending that theory could do more than that, and for slipping his own liberal (in the old-fashioned sense) ideology into what purported to be a theoretical discussion, Harry was understandably careful indeed about maintaining the purity of his own theoretical writing.[2] We have to turn to his articles on policy issues to find out what he thought was of practical significance, as opposed to what he knew to be logically true, in macroeconomics.

The 1950s in Britain saw the revival of monetary policy after a long period of pegged interest rates and direct government control over all aspects of credit allocation. They were also years of creeping inflation. Both circumstances led to substantial academic discussion—and Harry was deeply involved in British debates. His contributions display a considerable uniformity of view until 1956. In 1951, on the very eve of the revival of monetary policy, he published, in the *Economic Journal*, "Some Implications of Secular Changes in Bank Assets and Liabilities in Great Britain" (1951*a*). He noted the immense growth in the money supply and the public debt since the 1930s, and because "overcoming inflationary pressure" rather than "chronic defective demand" was likely to be the major policy problem for the future, he expected those "secular banking trends . . . to complicate rather than to ease the problems of economic policy." Although he also looked for "greater cyclical stability of the money supply" to ease "the problem of contra-cyclical policy," he hastened to note, "Neither of the effects just discussed is one to which any great quantitative significance can reasonably be attached" (1951*a*, p. 556). On the contrary, the significant implication of the facts he described was that "overall economic policy will rely on budgetary measures, buttressed with some degree of direct controls, rather than on monetary measures" (p. 555). This was partly because the use of interest rate variations "to control private borrowing would have significant repercussions on the cost of the public debt" but also because of "the decline which has occurred in the economic significance of the rates of interest which the joint-stock banks directly control," not to mention "the

[2] In later years, Harry was the first to admit that the review in question was unfair. Nevertheless it illustrates an important trait in his work. Though usually the most generous of critics, generosity vanished immediately when, rightly or wrongly, he thought that economics was being pressed into the service of either ideology or personal ambition.

generally accepted view . . . that the interest-elasticity of investment is rather low" (p. 554).

Experience during the early years of the "revival" of monetary policy did not change Harry's view about how policy in fact worked, but he did become more forthcoming about how he thought it ought to work. "The revival of quantitative credit control [i.e., a variable interest rate policy] [has] prepared the way for a genuine return to quantitative [i.e., market-oriented] methods, should the government in future desire it," but the large volume of floating debt and the "British philosophy of government intervention" (1953, p. 26) made that unlikely. Presumably he was not unhappy about that, for he had earlier argued that "the case for the rationing of credit by price . . . is largely irrelevant . . . and open to the objection that the ability to pay high interest rates is not necessarily a proof of the superior social desirability of the project to be financed." He viewed credit rationing by the banks as opposed to government with suspicion on the grounds "that there is no guarantee that the banks will ration out a limited amount of credit in accordance with the national interest" (1952, p. 129).[3]

As late as 1956, to judge from his policy writings, Harry's opinions were still much the same. In a major *Three Banks Review* article, widely read at the time (1956*b*), he identified the view that the quantity of money is a key policy variable with the view that the total volume of bank credit, as opposed to advances, is the central factor. Having thus misunderstood the position, he dismissed it on the grounds that there were many substitute sources of credit for the types of expenditure financed by bank purchases of securities, but not for the inventory investment financed by advances. Hence the cost and volume of bank advances were the important policy variables (see 1956*b*, pp. 16–17). "The influence of monetary policy, and the argument for using it, seem to rest chiefly on its effectiveness as a means of controlling stock-holding, and possibly also on its influence over short-term capital movements; its long-run influence on fixed investment is doubtful." Given these views, it is hardly surprising that he concluded that "monetary policy is unlikely to be able to do much towards solving the major long-run monetary problem of the British economy, the tendency for British wages and prices to increase more rapidly than those of Britain's international competitors. The most that monetary policy could hope to do would be to prevent the problem from being

---

[3] The reader should note that the comment on the "ability to pay high interest" comes from a footnote. In Hutchison (1968) there is a useful account of the contents of the entire symposium, in which Harry (who gives the impression of having been a very serious young man indeed—not yet 30) came in for more than a little leg-pulling from Sir Dennis Robertson and Victor Morgan.

periodically aggravated from over-full employment arising from inventory booms" (1956*b*, pp. 18–19).

It was not just because monetary policy was not of any importance in determining aggregate demand that it could not be deployed against inflation. "Substantial unemployment would be required to prevent wages from increasing at an inflationary rate," so neither monetary policy nor "alternative methods of controlling aggregate demand offer much prospect of a solution." Wage-price controls and moral suasion would do no good either: "Such methods attempt to solve the economic problem [of inflation] by ignoring the economic forces which produce it." And what were those forces? "A great deal of the inflationary problem of the post-war years can be attributed to the fact that the increase in productivity since the war has been largely absorbed by increased defence expenditure and the adverse shift in the terms of trade. . . . In future, increasing productivity should permit a steady and substantial growth of real income." This would go far toward creating "the necessary condition for a workable 'national wage-policy'—the possibility of substantial non-inflationary wage increases" (1956*b*, pp. 19–20). In 1956, then, Harry was a proponent of a rather ill-defined cost-push explanation of inflation based on the failure of real income to rise and looked to the future feasibility of an even more ill-defined national wages policy to deal with the problem.

By 1959 Harry's views had changed markedly. Though he still regarded inflation as a "minor evil" that promised to bring no "major economic catastrophe" (hyperinflation or mass unemployment caused by balance of payments crisis as, e.g., Lionel Robbins and Frank Paish tended to argue), Harry nevertheless recognized that it causes "a host of unfairnesses—some cumulative and some temporary, but all irritating—between different members of the community, and makes more complicated and frustrating the tasks of economic calculation for all concerned, including the Government itself."[1] He therefore believed that "the country can probably now afford to trade some loss of output and employment for greater stability of prices" (1958*c*, p. 151). Because he was "inclined to agree . . . that the predominant factor [causing inflation] has been high demand" (p. 149), he also agreed that ". . . demand restriction offers a more effective method of stopping wage inflation than national wages policy. But I would prefer to put the point another way: that a national wages policy is unlikely to be either acceptable or workable unless backed up by adequate control of effective demand" (p. 152).

---

[1] Harry's views concerning mild inflation in developed countries never changed from those expressed here. Indeed, he presented empirical evidence (1963*c*) that, if anything, mild inflation was conducive to economic growth.

Now this shift to a "demand pull" view of inflation is only one aspect of a change in view that becomes evident in Harry's published work after 1956. He also began to put much more emphasis on the quantity of money when discussing policy problems. In 1957 he still believed in the efficacy of direct credit controls. "The real bite of the credit squeeze has been achieved . . . through directives relating to bank advances . . . [and] through hire purchase controls," and he urged the Radcliffe Committee to consider whether such "methods could usefully be extended to include a closer supervision over building society lending policies" (1957a, pp. 342–43). However, the main burden of the note from which this quotation is taken was to draw attention to the "damning fact" that "no consolidated money supply statement is published in this country" (p. 343). The need to improve published statistics was the theme of Harry's advice to the Radcliffe Committee (1960), and by the end of 1958 he had constructed his own annual series for five monetary aggregates for the period 1930–57 (see 1959); the fact that he was willing to engage in that kind of labor, even with the aid of a research assistant, is evidence enough of the importance that he by then attached to the quantity of money. He saw the explanation for the "shortcomings of existing monetary statistics" as lying "partly in the fact that . . . though lip-service is often paid to the idea that monetary policy seeks to control the quantity of money, such control is actually conceived of in terms of its effects on the availability of money, as reflected particularly in conditions in the discount market and the lending activities of the Clearing Banks; partly in the fact that the quantity theory of money, which would provide the maximum incentive for the perfection of monetary statistics, has been so completely discredited, in the eyes of most economists, by its Keynesian rival" (1959, pp. 1–2).

The Keynesian rival in question was of course the Hicks-Modigliani-Hansen IS-LM model that had underpinned his commentary on Robertson and to the exposition of which his survey "Monetary Theory and Keynesian Economics" (1958a) was mainly devoted—and the exogenous money wage version of the IS-LM model at that. However, by 1958 the Pigou effect, which in 1952 had been dealt with in one cryptic parenthetical sentence (see 1951–52, p. 103), was presented as reducing that Keynesian theory to "a special case of . . . the neoclassical theory," albeit one that "started from an empirically relevant special assumption, derived some important meaningful results from it, and provided an approach which has since proved its usefulness for a wide range of problems" (1958a, p. 240).

For Harry to criticize received Keynesian doctrine in these purely theoretical terms was not new in 1958. He had presented much the same argument at a 1954 conference (see 1957b). However, by 1958 he was expressing doubts about that doctrine's practical relevance too. He was now arguing that the Keynesian model "has shown definite weaknesses as a theory of prices." Inflation models based on it "while they describe the inflationary process . . . do not explain it very well. The problem of explaining the differing price histories of different countries during and since the war has led to a certain tendency to return to the quantity theory of money. . . . It is clear that the accumulation of money during the war has had an important effect; but I would myself prefer to employ a neo-Keynesian explanation, based on the accumulation of assets relative to income (these assets including both money and government debt) rather than one which stressed the quantity of money *per se*" (1958a, pp. 243–44).

Thus, by 1958, before going to Chicago, Harry had become a very different kind of macroeconomist from the Cambridge Keynesian of the early 1950s. He had of course visited the United States in 1955 and had attended workshops in Chicago, but I can find no evidence of a Chicago influence on his views at this stage, at least on issues of money and inflation. Friedman appeared in his writings at this time as a contributor to the literature on the consumption function, not to that on monetary theory or inflation. The quantity theory–inspired work which he cites is A. J. Brown's *Great Inflation* (1955), not the Chicago *Studies* (Friedman 1957), and the historical experience to which he refers in the passage just quoted is also that dealt with by Brown. His argument for the importance of carrying out statistical studies of transactions velocity (1957b) sets him firmly apart from the Chicago School, with its emphasis on income velocity, but also suggests the influence of Brown and his associates, particularly in the light of work later carried out under Brown's supervision on transactions velocity (see Welham 1969). Moreover, in emphasizing the potential importance of money and government debt he looked back to matters which he himself had analyzed 7 years earlier (i.e., 1951a), though he now assessed the significance of the relevant data very differently. In short, Harry Johnson's first large step away from orthodox Cambridge Keynesianism was taken at Manchester, not at Chicago, as a response to what he perceived to be the inability of received theory to deal with an important body of evidence.[5]

[5] Two points need to be made about the foregoing paragraphs. First, the *Pakistan Economic Journal* article, though published in 1958, has its origins in a lecture delivered in the summer of 1956. I am unable to comment on how close the final published text of the article is to that of the original lecture. Also, it should be noted that there was in no sense a "sudden conversion" of Harry Johnson to the quantity theory of money as a result of reading Brown's *Great Inflation* (1955). He reviewed the book without any great enthusiasm in the *Economic Journal* (1956a). Finally, note that the absence of any reference to the Chicago *Studies* in Harry's work up to 1959 may simply reflect the fact that the book was not available in England. Reviews of it did not appear, as far as I have been able to discover, in any British journal before 1959.

HARRY G. JOHNSON   599

III. The Chicago Years

The years 1959–66, when Harry was full-time at Chicago, saw the
writing of his best-known and most highly regarded contributions to
the macroeconomics literature. The first of these, written during his
first year there, was his lecture (1961) on the twenty-fifth anniversary
of the publication of the *General Theory*. This completed the break
with Cambridge Keynesianism that had begun at Manchester.

The contribution of the *General Theory* as presented in that lecture
was only loosely related to the IS-LM model which Harry had hitherto
referred to as "Keynesian." Keynes's "central theoretical contribution
[was] that in a monetary economy the stability of employment in the
face of changes in aggregate demand for output depends on the
uncertain monetary effects of changes in money wage levels, which
changes may themselves be slow" (1961, p. 3). " 'Unemployment equilibrium' has to be reinterpreted as a disequilibrium situation in which
the dynamic adjustment is proceeding very slowly. . . . [This is] a fair
modern translation of Keynes's [Marshallian] short-period equilibrium technique" (p. 13).[6] There were weaknesses in the *General
Theory*: Keynes "overgeneralized a particularly bad depression" to
give the impression that "large-scale unemployment is the typical situation of an advanced capitalist economy," and this was important,
given his view that "traditional quantity theory becomes relevant
under full employment conditions" (p. 13). The lack of attention to
"the influence of price expectations on the assets demand for money,
and the associated necessity of distinguishing between real and
nominal interest and between fixed-interest-bearing securities and
equities" (p. 9) and the neglect of the influence of wealth on consumption were both special cases of the generally "inadequate attention
paid in the *General Theory* to problems of capital theory" (p. 6).[7] However, much harsher criticism was reserved for the Keynesians. In their
hands "a theory in which money is important [has] turned into the
theory that money is unimportant" (p. 15). Their approaches to the
problem of inflation "concentrate on the mechanism rather than the
causation of inflation; and . . . virtually assume away the possibility
of controlling inflation by monetary means" (p. 16). Their bias against
according an important role to money had caused the Keynesian
approach to inflation "to degenerate into a confused and often ob-
structive eclecticism" (p. 14).

---

[6] Harry acknowledges the work of Clower, Leontief, and Patinkin in developing this
idea. He does not give references to specific papers.

[7] The reader will note that Leijonhufvud was later to disagree with this judgment.
Note though that there is no disagreement between Johnson's 1961 lecture and Leijonhufvud's (1968) book on the importance of capital theory for Keynesian economics.
Their sole disagreement concerned the extent to which Keynes had recognized and
coped with this problem himself.

In short, his rereading of the *General Theory* caused Harry to make his own distinction between "Keynesian economics" and the "economics of Keynes" and to take the latter as the basis of his own further work in macroeconomics. In the light of this, it is hardly surprising that, though nobody understood the debates about the classical dichotomy and the neutrality of money better than Harry—for which several generations of graduate student readers of his (1962) survey have reason to be grateful—and though nobody more enjoyed wrestling with logical intricacies (Harry always liked puzzles), he recognized from the outset that the debate had little to do with Keynes's attack on the separation of monetary theory and value theory. "The argument . . . has been concerned throughout with a monetary economy characterized by minimal uncertainty, whereas Keynes was concerned with a highly uncertain world . . ." (1962, p. 17). He reiterated this view in a 1963 survey, concluding, "I do not think that this particular controversy is of great relevance to practical work on monetary policy or monetary analysis, or even I think to monetary theory" (1963*d*, p. 84), although he explicitly linked this conclusion to the absence of economic growth from the models in question rather than to the absence of an analysis of uncertainty and expectations on which he based the opening of his critique.[8]

We have already noted that, much as he admired the book, for Harry the great weakness in the *General Theory* was a neglect of capital theory, which resulted from Keynes's use of Marshallian short-period equilibrium to deal with problems of dynamic disequilibrium. Consequently, he valued highly work directed toward making good this deficiency. "Friedman's application to monetary theory of the basic principle of capital theory—that income is the yield on capital, and capital the present value of income—is probably the most important development in monetary theory since Keynes . . ." (1962, p. 33). He praised the contributions of Friedman, Spiro, and Modigliani, Ando, and Brumberg to the consumption function literature for the same reasons, as he praised the contributions to the analysis of what we would now term the "transmission mechanism" that "has been emerging in the past few years, from both 'Keynesian' and 'quantity' theorists, as an outgrowth of the formulation of monetary theory as part of a general theory of asset holding" (1962, p. 50). Again Friedman

[8] Harry did qualify the foregoing judgment in one respect: He thought the Gurley-Shaw inside money concept (1960) was important as a theoretical matter because of its implications for the Pigou effect. In the light of the outcome of the Pesek-Saving debate, his judgment here was of course erroneous. If we have interest-bearing money, it is not net wealth, but the LM curve is going to be vertical (or at least steep) so there is no need for a Pigou effect. If there is room for substantial variation in the opportunity cost of holding money, on the other hand, it must be because money does not bear a competitively determined rate of return and hence is, on the margin, net wealth.

was cited, this time in company with Tobin, Cagan, and particularly Karl Brunner, from whose work there was a lengthy quotation, as from one who had made an important contribution. But Friedman's contribution in all these cases was seen as being to a theoretical tradition started by Keynes. From the outset Harry was more critical of Friedman's empirical work, particularly of his attempts there to differentiate his approach from the Keynesian tradition as Harry by that time had come to conceive of it.

When he wrote his 1962 survey, Harry had not grasped the interrelationship between Friedman's views on the complexity of the transmission mechanism, the methodology of the famous Friedman-Meiselman study (1963), and the significance of Friedman's (1959) inability to find any well-determined or quantitatively significant relationship between the demand for money and the rate of interest.[9] In 1963, however, Harry pointed to "a certain suspicious appropriateness in the Friedman treatment of the cyclical behaviour of velocity" (1963d, p. 102). He returned to this theme more forcefully in his (1965) *Economic Journal* review article of Friedman and Schwartz's *Monetary History* (1963), arguing that Friedman had deliberately downplayed the interest sensitivity of velocity because, among other things, "to admit interest rates into the demand function for money is to accept the Keynesian Revolution and Keynes' attack on the quantity theory" (Johnson 1965, p. 396). In terms of Harry's conception of the nature of Keynes's contribution to economics he was surely right. The liquidity trap doctrine played a minimal role in that conception both because "speculation will take the form of movements between securities of different types rather than between securities and cash" (1961, pp. 8–9), and because the available empirical evidence had reduced the existence of a liquidity trap in the demand for money function to a purely semantic issue (see 1962, p. 38).

Though Harry was not the only reviewer to raise the issue of the interest elasticity of the demand for money—Meltzer (1965) and Tobin (1965a) also made much of it—it was Harry's attack that provoked Friedman (1966) into clarifying his views both on the role of interest rates in the velocity function—they did have a role to play—and on what he believed to be the essential characteristic of Keynesian mone-

---

[9] See Johnson (1962) as reprinted in *Essays in Monetary Economics* (*EME*), p. 41. The only way that I can make sense of the first paragraph on this page is to think that Harry was confused between the effects on the transmission mechanism of monetary policy of perfect interest elasticity and perfect interest inelasticity of the demand for money function. The Friedman-Meiselman study (1963) was not of course in its final form when Harry wrote this 1962 survey article. As I recall it, the first draft of that study did not contain an account of the transmission mechanism—though Harry urged the authors to include one—so it is perhaps understandable that he was somewhat muddled on this particular issue at that time.

tary theory—the liquidity trap. Thus Friedman declined the invitation to embrace the Keynesian revolution, but in doing so he clarified the issues in such a way that those who had regarded him as an anti-Keynesian, but did not regard the liquidity trap as an important ingredient of Keynesian economics, were able to come to a far better appreciation of the significance of his contribution to the subject than they had before.[10]

Even so, critical though he often was of it, Harry always took Chicago empirical work seriously and learned from it. The study of Canadian monetary policy that he and Winder undertook in 1962 was strongly influenced by Friedman and Meiselman (1963), though some aspects of it followed Ando et al.'s (1963) lead. The conclusion he drew from that work (Johnson and Winder 1962), that the effect of monetary policy in the Canadian economy is imprecise, slow, and variable, led him to argue that monetary policy should be used, not for short-run stabilization policy, but for "creating and maintaining a stable long-run monetary environment" (1963a, p. 217). This was the conclusion of Friedman on the one hand and of the Radcliffe Committee on the other, and in 1963 he was not willing to commit himself either to the Friedman view that stability in the rate of growth of the quantity of money should be the policy target or to the Radcliffe view that stability of interest rates was the key.[11] By the next year he noted evidence produced by Friedman showing that the slackening of U.S. aggregate demand in late 1962 was associated with the previous behavior of the money stock, and he was "inclined to attach a greater importance to monetary policy in . . . sustaining the [subsequent] expansion than the Council [of Economic Advisers] does" (1964, p. 251). Moreover, the effects in question had been the "unintended consequence of a policy intended to be modestly restrictive in the sense of raising the level of interest rates . . . that . . . turned out to be quite expansionary in its effects on the money supply" (p. 251). And for all his criticisms of it, he nevertheless argued that the *Monetary History of the United States* documented "quite conclusively" the

---

[10] Friedman's reply to criticism on this score was published in the *Journal of Law and Economics* (1966). His subsequent exchange with Tobin (see Gordon 1974) essentially goes over all this ground again without advancing matters any further. In fairness to Friedman, it should be noted that there is much in the literature on Keynesian economics to justify his view of the central role of the liquidity trap doctrine, particularly the British literature (see, e.g., Hicks 1957 or Kaldor 1970).

[11] This matter is discussed in (1963a). On pp. 217–18 of the *EME* reprint, the reader will find a perfect statement of what would now be called the "Poole problem" (cf. Poole 1970). The contribution of Alvin Marty to this paragraph is acknowledged, but it still stands as a particularly good example of the way in which Harry would put highly original formulations of problems into his survey papers and policy writings but not systematically follow them up.

presupposition that "the stock of money is the dominant monetary variable in the economy" (1965, p. 389).

Neither in the papers just cited nor in any other that I have been able to find did Harry come close to arguing that the quantity of money was *all* that matters. He thought that money was more important than did the Council but not "to the point of denying that fiscal policy was an important influence on income and employment" (1964, p. 251); and of course what he regarded as an underemphasis of the importance of real shocks, stemming from downplaying the interest elasticity of velocity, was a key element of his criticism of the *Monetary History*. In 1965 Harry was still by his own lights a Keynesian. Though he was critical of the underlying methodology of the Friedman-Meiselman study (and of the *Monetary History* as well), particularly of the insistence that one simple theory could explain a long run of historical data—"Occam's Razor is a useful principle, but there is no need to cut the throat of empirical research with it" (1965, p. 395)—he accepted its results and did not find anything in them to disturb him: "Any Keynesian can well argue that the 1930's was the period for which the Keynesian theory was designed . . . and that in showing that the Keynesian theory works better for that period Friedman and Meiselman have vindicated the Keynesian Revolution" (1963d, pp. 102–3). Nor did he find it difficult to accept the empirical evidence on a stable, albeit interest-sensitive, demand for money function. As he later put it, reiterating a view that he had by then long held, "There is . . . nothing to prevent the absorption of the empirical evidence of a stable demand function for money into the corpus of the Keynesian general equilibrium model . . . other than the conditioned Keynesian reflex against the 'quantity theory' label and the conditioned Keynesian belief that 'money does not matter' (or, at least, 'does not matter much')" (1970, pp. 91–92).

IV. Money, Inflation, and the Monetarist Label

Though very few people would have called Harry a "monetarist" in the mid-1960s (had the label then been in use), he was widely regarded as such in the 1970s and, indeed, often found it useful to pin the label on himself. However, I believe the evidence of his written work shows that he had gone as far towards monetarism by the mid-1960s as he was ever to go. A further shift towards monetarism after 1965 is an illusion, but why it is such a widely believed-in illusion needs to be explained. Part of the explanation lies in the fact that in 1966 Harry took up his chair at the London School of Economics (LSE) and "conditioned Keynesian reflexes" were more prevalent in Britain than the United States. Kaldor's (1970) celebrated attack on

JOURNAL OF POLITICAL ECONOMY

"The New Monetarism" amounted to a denial of the existence of a stable demand for money function and a reassertion of the unimportance of money; thus, in Britain, a Keynesian of Harry's type found himself labeled a monetarist whether he liked it or not. However, other factors were also important. The problems upon which he worked after 1965 required that he emphasize Friedman's specific contribution to monetary economics more than he had previously, although, as we have seen, he had much earlier recognized and absorbed Friedman's contribution into his own thinking.

As early as his 1961 anniversary lecture, Harry singled out the failure of Keynes to take account of the influence of inflation expectations and systematically to incorporate the distinction between real and nominal interest rates into his work as an important shortcoming of the *General Theory.* He called attention to the importance of Friedman's analysis of this problem in terms of a capital theoretic approach to the demand for money, and a recurring theme of his commentaries on monetary economics thereafter was the weakness of those branches of neo-Keynesian monetary theory that neglected this factor.[12] But of course the influence of inflation expectations is important as a practical matter only if inflation itself is important as a practical matter. As Harry himself remarked, "It is no accident that the appearance of monetarism as a strong intellectual movement has had to wait until the [inflationary] aftermath of the escalation of the war in Viet Nam in 1965" (1971a). Nor is it an accident that the aspects of Harry's macroeconomics most readily identifiable as having been learned from Friedman came into prominence in his own work at the same time; the mid-1960s was precisely the time when the analysis of price-level movements began to occupy an increasing amount of his attention. Even so, it should be noted now that one characteristic monetarist belief—that the absence of a long-run inflation/unemployment trade-off is an *empirically* important matter—does not, as far as I have been able to discover, and to my considerable surprise, appear in his writings.

Like any other macroeconomist, Harry was compelled by the circumstances of the late 1960s and early 1970s to pay attention to inflation as a policy problem, but he also at that time carried out important original work in monetary theory. Characteristically, there was a substantial spillover from this work on pure theory into his policy writings, and though the theoretical literature to which he contributed has become unfashionable, his work there still retains inter-

[12] In particular, the work of Tobin and the Yale School on portfolio behavior is systematically criticized for this (see, e.g., Johnson 1970, 1974); but note that Tobin's work on money and economic growth is immune to this criticism.

est if only because of this spillover. The literature in question is epitomized in such phrases as "money in a growth model" and "money and welfare."

Harry had long been dissatisfied with the literature on the classical dichotomy and neutral money, not only because it was not dealing with the problem in the context of the uncertain world which he regarded as fundamental to Keynesian economics, but also because it abstracted from economic growth. The literature on money and growth meets the second of these objections, but only by completely ignoring the first: that is one reason why it has now fallen out of fashion. Harry's particular contribution to it (1966), in contrast to Tobin's initial work (1965*b*), "stressed the necessity of allowing money a function in a monetary economy, and therefore of attributing to the presence of money an increase in economic welfare" (1970, p. 109). In short, this paper incorporated Friedman's analysis of money "as if" a consumer durable; it showed that because the rate of inflation influenced holdings of real balances it would also influence "real income" and hence the savings rate, the details depending on the way in which savings behavior was modeled. The conclusion established by this literature—and Harry's contribution sets out all the essential results while managing also to be the most readable paper on the subject—is that the full-employment equilibrium properties of a monetary economy are extremely unlikely to be independent of monetary factors (specifically the rate of change of the nominal money supply). This conclusion holds even if all Keynesian problems about uncertainty are assumed away by making inflation, and everything else for that matter, "fully anticipated."[13] Since one of the properties of "full-employment" equilibrium that fully anticipated inflation might affect is presumably the "natural" unemployment rate, the literature in question may be relevant to important policy issues. But such relevance is still open to doubt.[14] In my view based on Harry's judgment of the upshot of the closely related money-and-economic-welfare literature, it is likely to remain so.

As is well known, Pesek and Saving (1967) showed that the "inside-outside money" distinction of Gurley and Shaw—to which Harry devoted considerable space in his early 1960s surveys—stemmed from endowing accounting conventions with spurious economic content. Once we leave a commodity money world, the key distinction—and this only became clear after a somewhat convoluted discussion to which Harry made an important contribution (see 1969*b*, 1969*c*)—is

---

[13] See Johnson (1966). Some of the analysis there presented is further developed in the latter half of "Inside Money, Outside Money" (1969*b*).

[14] I am indebted to Douglas Purvis for some discussions on this point.

between money that bears interest at competitive rates and that which does not because its issue is monopolized. But all the results of the money in growth-models literature and the "schizophrenic policy proposals" that emerged from Friedman's "Optimum Quantity of Money" (1969) essay hinge upon variations in the rate of nominal monetary expansion influencing the opportunity cost of holding money. Thus, as Harry was quicker than anyone else to stress (see 1968*b*), they depend on the assumption of a particular institutional anomaly—namely, that the monetary system is not competitive. Only if "the practical point that the payment of interest on currency holdings is infeasible . . . is taken as being of predominating importance" (1970, pp. 106–7) does the rate of nominal monetary expansion have any long-run significance, and Harry was sufficiently unimpressed with its importance to be willing to abstract from it entirely in his most extensive discussion of these very issues (1968*b*). Otherwise, as far as he was concerned, the welfare analysis of money was significant in two respects: first, as a component of the case for more competition in the banking system, this was an important policy issue in Britain in the late 1960s; and, second, inasmuch as it dealt with the transition from commodity to fiat and credit money systems, it yielded insights into the problems of reforming the international monetary system.[15]

The notion of a fully anticipated inflation rate is fundamental to the literature on money in a growth-model or money-and-welfare literature. The recognition that if agents allow for inflation expectations in their portfolio behavior they are also going to allow for them in their behavior toward money wages and prices underlies the literature on the expectations-augmented Phillips curve. The "accelerationist hypothesis" follows from the proposition that, in the long run, inflation is indeed fully anticipated—that is, it is expected to occur and behavior is completely adapted to the expectation in question. Like everyone else in the 1960s, Harry was slow indeed to incorporate expectations into his treatment of the Phillips curve, and once he had, though he immediately grasped the logic of the accelerationist hypothesis as a piece of economic theory, he never embraced it as a hypothesis relevant to the practical conduct of monetary policy in an inflationary environment.

In his article "A Survey of Theories of Inflation" (1963*e*) Harry provides as good an example as one could find of a man who knows something without knowing that he knows it. He criticized "Keynesian models" that analyze inflation in terms of competition between various social groups for greater shares in national income because, unlike the "quantity theory approach," which he identified with the

---

[15] On the international monetary system see Johnson (1968*a*). On competition in banking see Johnson (1967*b*).

Cagan-Bailey analysis of the inflation tax, they failed to recognize "that the processes of determining wages and prices are fundamentally real processes." Protection against inflationary redistributions "is available to all groups in a freely competitive system, through negotiation of contracts to take account of expected inflation, and is increasingly resorted to as the fact of inflation is recognized" (1963e, p. 122). He even pointed out that "there are some serious doubts about the applicability of the Phillips curve to the formulation of economic policy. . . . it may reasonably be doubted whether the curve would continue to hold its shape if an attempt were made by economic policy to pin the economy down to a point on it" (pp. 132–33). Nevertheless, "the Phillips curve appears to be far the most reliable of [the] relationships" describing statistical trade-offs between policy goals (p. 133). It formed the basis for his subsequent discussion of policy trade-offs; and Reuber's pioneering (1964) attempt to quantify, in dollars and cents terms, the trade-off between inflation and unemployment was held up as an example of the type of work which must be further developed so that the curve could be used as a basis "for intelligent policy-making" (1963e, p. 141).

It is not difficult to understand why Harry fell into this particular inconsistency. His writings over the years make it clear that he thought the rapid inflations experienced by underdeveloped countries presented a very different set of problems from the mild inflations of the pre-1970s in the developed world (see 1967a). The Phillips curve was a potentially interesting tool for analyzing the latter, while the quantity theory approach had proved its worth empirically in dealing with the former. "For the mild type of inflation typical of the United States and other advanced countries . . . the [quantity theory] approach has not proved nearly so useful . . . the expected rate of price change has not appeared as a significant determinant of the quantity of money demanded" (1963e, p. 126). Because the empirical evidence suggested to him that the expected inflation rate was unimportant in such a context, there was no reason for Harry to incorporate it systematically into his thinking about the Phillips curve. Thus even when, in the Introduction to the second edition of *Essays in Monetary Economics* (1969a), he noted the inconsistency in question, he argued that it was of more theoretical than practical significance. The importance of incorporating inflation expectations into the Phillips curve ". . . for the theory of macro-economic policy . . . depends on the length of time it takes for changes in expectations generated by experience to begin to affect behaviour significantly; and the empirical evidence is that the lags in adjustment of expectations are sufficiently long for contemporary policy makers safely to disregard them—even though the cumulative effect may be substantial" (p. x).

I have already said that I have found no statement in any of Harry's writings of a belief in the empirical, as opposed to theoretical, relevance of a vertical long-run Phillips curve. However, in his later work he certainly did pay increasing attention to the role of expectations in determining the economy's response to stabilization policy and expressed increasing doubts about the theoretical foundations of the Phillips curve itself. Thus, he argued (1968*b*) that "stabilization operations [themselves might disturb] expectations derived from previous experience" by way of "mechanisms [that] cannot be . . . satisfactorily dealt with by compressing them into the distributed lag structure of the economy." (p. 301). By 1972 he had come to the view that "contrary to the standard assumptions of economic theory, the economic public does not simply respond mechanically . . . to signals reaching it through the blind and impersonal operations of . . . competitive markets. Instead [it] engages in two kinds of political transactions with . . . policy-makers. . . . First, one of its major concerns is to guess how determined the government is about implementing its announced economic policies. . . . Second, the relevant economic public, aware of the sensitivity of government to political pressures, has an incentive to generate such pressures in its own favour" (1972, pp. 14–15).[16] As to the Phillips curve itself, new work "broadening the microeconomic foundations of the relationship in terms of the influence of information and adjustment costs and other real factors" (1972, p. 66) was required, a theme which he reiterated at greater length (1974).

Although he regarded neither the theoretical nor the empirical basis of the relationship to be well established, as an empirical matter he seems nevertheless to have believed in the existence of a long-run trade-off between inflation and unemployment, basing that belief on his reading of the empirical evidence—particularly that of Solow, whose work is cited in a survey (1970), lecture notes (1971*b*), and the DeVries lectures (1972).[17] On the empirical nature of the Phillips

[16] In the first of these quotations the reader will recognize the germ of the "rational expectations" idea. The second quotation represents a substantial extension of the notion, one that has not yet been taken up in the analytic literature. Harry's only explicit comments on the hypothesis in question occur in the introduction to his *Selected Essays* (1978), which are notable for his caution over the implications of a thoroughgoing application of the hypothesis to problems of short-run stabilization policy.

[17] Of course he should not have taken Solow's results seriously, because those tests were flawed (see Laidler 1970). However, it is easy to forget that in 1971 virtually all the available empirical evidence seemed to show that there was a long-run inflation/unemployment trade-off. It has only been with the growing sophistication of the modeling of expectations that results favorable to the long-run vertical Phillips curve have been generated. By the time that work was produced, Harry was mainly working on other matters, and only in the introduction to his *Selected Essays* (1978) does there appear any hint that such work might have persuaded him to change his views. However, there is no definite statement to this effect.

curve, Harry's position was thus closer to Tobin's than to Friedman's. It is worth noting that Harry's major reason for predicting the ultimate failure of the monetarist counterrevolution (1971a) was rooted in his perception of monetarism's inability to provide a satisfactory theory of unemployment to complement its theory of inflation.[18] However, in Britain in the early 1970s the belief that the excess demand for labor could exert any influence on the inflation rate was enough to get its adherent classified as a monetarist, regardless of his views about the role that inflation expectations, information costs, and such might play in the process, particularly if that view was combined, as it was in Harry's case, with opposition to wage and price controls.

Opposition to direct controls on wages and prices was a constant characteristic of Harry's writings on inflation from his very earliest papers in the 1950s to his last ones. He consistently argued that wage and price controls would make the effects of inflation worse without contributing anything to curing the disease. As he put it (1963e, pp. 134–35): "Does inflation necessarily lead to monetary collapse? The answer is no, provided that the price system is uncontrolled and prices are allowed to rise freely. . . . Where monetary breakdowns do occur is where rapid inflation is combined with general price control, so that money ceases to be usable for making transactions. . . . This is the explanation, for example, of the breakdown of the German currency after World War II. . . . Does inflation cause economic inefficiency? . . . The evidence seems to indicate that inflation does not reduce economic efficiency, at least when the inflation is mild and reasonably steady and prices and wages are not controlled." Harry's contribution to Parkin and Sumner (1972) and his preface to the 1977 edition of *The Canadian Quandary* reiterate much the same views, albeit with extra vehemence, born of the fact that he was then discussing controls as a current policy issue rather than from a purely academic point of view. But let it be noted again that, if opposition to such controls is cited as evidence of "monetarist leanings" on Harry's part, then he had acquired those leanings long before going to Chicago (see 1956b).

Harry's role in developing the monetary approach to balance-of-payments theory is beyond the scope of this paper. Some mention must be made of it at this point, however: a misunderstanding of

---

[18] The Ely Lecture to which I refer caused quite a stir when it was delivered, containing as it did attacks on both Keynes's and Friedman's means of propagating their ideas. If anything, that lecture is a contribution to the sociology of knowledge rather than to macroeconomics, and that is why I do not pay more attention to it here. It is ironical that Harry himself was subsequently criticized along identical lines in connection with his work on the monetary approach to balance of payments theory (see Hahn 1977; Coppock 1978).

Harry's own view of that theoretical development has contributed also to the opinion that he was a "monetarist." In 1974 he accepted that "criticisms directed at this approach for its neglect of dynamic disequilibrium behaviour, [and] the processes of international transmission of monetary impulses . . . are certainly justified by the published literature of the approach as it now stands" (1974, p. 224). However he argued that "some at least . . . recognize that reality occupies the area between the closed and the open economy theoretical assumptions, very much as the problem of how the effects of monetary impulses are divided between price and quantity responses defines the grey area requiring intensive empirical research in contemporary closed-economy monetary economics" (p. 224). His own research program at the LSE was "intended to pursue this matter in depth." In short, Harry's published writings on the monetary approach, "monetarist" though their characteristics undoubtedly were, particularly in their reliance on the assumption of full employment and the hypothesis of a stable demand for money function, were meant to set out a theoretical basis for organizing empirical work, not to state his beliefs about the nature of the world.

V. Conclusions

There is no neat and tidy ending to the story of the development of Harry Johnson's macroeconomics. He had always paid more attention than did the majority of contributors to the area to open-economy problems, and by 1969 he concluded, "Perhaps the greatest disservice that Keynes rendered to the development of economics [in Britain] was to develop the theory of macro-economics and money on the assumption of a closed economy. The extension of Keynesian theory to an open economy . . . has been built on the manifestly unsatisfactory assumption of money illusion on the part of wage-earners. . . . Much work remains to be done in developing a monetary economics appropriate to the analytical and policy problems of the British economy" (1970, p. 114). Thereafter the development of what has come to be called "the monetary approach to balance-of-payments theory" occupied an increasing proportion of his time, so that the 1970s saw very little from him that falls within the traditional boundaries of macroeconomics.

His survey article for *Oxford Economic Papers* (1974), already alluded to, and a *Journal of Economic Literature* paper written with Bob Nobay (Johnson and Nobay 1977) are the only major pieces of work. The latter, extending ideas originally set out first briefly in the DeVries lectures and later in a note in *Kredit und Kapital* (1976), is interesting for the parallels that it draws between the pre-Keynesian analysis of short-run monetary equilibrium and recent developments in American monetarism, especially those associated with the work of Lucas, Sargent, and Wallace on rational expectations. However, it lies outside the mainstream of his later work. That, to repeat, concerned the macroeconomics of the open economy; to deal with it would take me beyond the assigned scope of this paper. Let it be stressed, though, that Harry never regarded that work as dealing with a separate field. He viewed it as a natural development of his work on macroeconomics and money in which he integrated Friedman's notion of a stable demand for money function with his own, much earlier, attempts at generalizing balance-of-payments theory (1958*b*). Thus the reader of this essay should weigh his work on the monetary approach to balance-of-payments theory along with the contributions with which this essay has dealt when he assesses Harry's importance as a macroeconomist.

Of course, it is far too early to carry out such an assessment in any final way. What can be done, though, is to sum up the salient features of Harry's macroeconomics as it emerges from the work which has been surveyed in this essay. First and foremost, of course, it is remarkable for its breadth, but it is remarkable also for the consistency of its approach. In particular, at every stage we can see that Harry paid particular attention to empirical evidence in forming his views. It was the inflation of the 1950s that persuaded him to pay more attention to monetary factors; it was his own empirical work and that of Brown and of Friedman and his associates that persuaded him of the particular importance of the quantity of money and of the futility of using monetary policy for short-run stabilization policies; it was empirical evidence drawn from underdeveloped countries that persuaded him of the importance of the peculiarly "Chicago" contribution to monetary economics (namely, the role of inflation expectations in influencing the demand for money); and it was empirical evidence that led him to his views on the importance of inflation expectations in the context of the policy problems of developed countries. Closely related to his respect for empirical evidence is the consistency with which he searched for policy relevance in his macroeconomics. Debates about the Pigou effect, neutrality, and the classical dichotomy were examined for such relevance and found wanting; the literature on money, welfare, and growth provided him with tools to analyze the reform of domestic banking and the international monetary system; he always regarded unemployment as a more important policy problem for developed countries than inflation, so Friedman's contributions were to him a complement to Keynes's economics, not a substitute; and his LSE research program was designed to investigate the empirical content and policy relevance of the monetary approach to balance of payments analysis.

For Harry Johnson "the purpose of economics as a social science is to arrive at a set of principles for understanding and interpreting the economy that are both scientifically 'robust' and sufficiently simple to be communicable to successive generations of students and policy-makers and the general public" (1974, p. 214). No one worked more diligently and consistently to further that purpose than he did.

References

Ando, Albert; Brown, E. Carey; Solow, Robert M.; and Kareken, John. "Lags in Fiscal and Monetary Policy." In *Stabilization Policies*, by the Commission on Money and Credit. Englewood Cliffs, N.J.: Prentice-Hall, 1963.

Bhagwati, Jagdish N. "Harry G. Johnson." *J. Internat. Econ.* 7 (August 1977): 221–29.

Brown, Arthur J. *The Great Inflation, 1939–1951.* London: Oxford Univ. Press, 1955.

Coppock, Dennis J. "The Monetary Theory of the Balance of Payments: A Commentary." Mimeographed. Manchester: Univ. Manchester, 1978.

Friedman, Milton, ed. *Studies in the Quantity Theory of Money.* Chicago: Univ. Chicago Press, 1957.

———. "The Demand for Money: Some Theoretical and Empirical Results." *J.P.E.* 67, no. 4 (August 1959): 327–51.

———. "Interest Rates and the Demand for Money." *J. Law and Econ.* 9 (October 1966): 71–85.

———. "The Optimum Quantity of Money." In *The Optimum Quantity of Money, and Other Essays.* London: Macmillan, 1969.

Friedman, Milton, and Meiselman, David. "The Relative Stability of Monetary Velocity and the Investment Multiplier in the United States, 1898–1958." In *Stabilization Policies*, by the Commission on Money and Credit. Englewood Cliffs, N.J.: Prentice-Hall, 1963.

Friedman, Milton, and Schwartz, Anna J. *A Monetary History of the United States, 1867–1960.* Princeton, N.J.: Princeton Univ. Press (for N.B.E.R.), 1963.

Gordon, Robert J., ed. *Milton Friedman's Monetary Framework: A Debate with His Critics.* Chicago: Univ. Chicago Press, 1974.

Gurley, John G., and Shaw, Edward S. *Money in a Theory of Finance.* Washington: Brookings Inst., 1960.

Hahn, F. H. "The Monetary Approach to the Balance of Payments." *J. Internat. Econ.* 7 (August 1977): 231–49.

Hicks, John R. "A Rehabilitation of 'Classical' Economics?" *Econ. J.* 67 (June 1957): 278–89.

Hutchison, Terence W. *Economics and Economic Policy in Britain, 1946–1966: Some Aspects of Their Interrelations.* London: Allen & Unwin, 1968.

Johnson, Harry G. "Some Implications of Secular Changes in Bank Assets and Liabilities in Great Britain." *Econ. J.* 61 (September 1951): 544–61. (*a*)

———. "The Taxonomic Approach to Economic Policy." *Econ. J.* 61 (December 1951): 812–32. (*b*)

———. "Some Cambridge Controversies in Monetary Theory." *Rev. Econ. Studies* 19, no. 2 (1951–52): 90–104.

———. "The New Monetary Policy and the Problem of Credit Control." *Bull. Oxford Univ. Inst. Statis.* 14 (April/May 1952): 117–31.

———. "Recent Developments in British Monetary Policy." *A.E.R. Papers and Proc.* 43 (May 1953): 19–26.

HARRY G. JOHNSON   613

————. Review of *The Great Inflation, 1939–1951,* by Arthur J. Brown. *Econ. J.*
66 (March 1956): 121–23. (*a*)
————. "The Revival of Monetary Policy in Britain." *Three Banks Rev.* 30 (June
1956): 3–20. (*b*)
————. "Bank Rate Reform and the Improvement of Monetary Statistics."
Bull. Oxford Univ. Inst. Statis. 19 (November 1957): 341–45. (*a*)
————. "The Determination of the General Level of Wage Rates." In *The
Theory of Wage Determination,* edited by John T. Dunlop. London: Macmil-
lan, 1957. (*b*)
————. "Monetary Theory and Keynesian Economics." Lecture no. 5 of series
delivered to Pakistan Economics Association. *Pakistan Econ. J.* 8 (June
1958): 56–70. Reprinted in *Monetary Theory: Selected Readings,* edited by
Robert Clower. Baltimore: Penguin, 1969. (*a*)
————. "Towards a General Theory of the Balance of Payments." In *Interna-
tional Trade and Economic Growth: Studies in Pure Theory.* London: Allen &
Unwin, 1958. (*b*)
————. "Two Schools of Thought on Wage Inflation." *Scottish J. Polit. Econ.* 5
(June 1958): 149–53. (*c*)
————. "British Monetary Statistics." *Economica* 26 (February 1959): 1–17.
————. "Memorandum of Evidence." In *Principal Memoranda of Evidence,* vol.
3, by the Committee on the Working of the Monetary System. London: Her
Majesty's Stationery Office, 1960.
————. "The *General Theory* after Twenty-five Years." *A.E.R. Papers and Proc.*
51 (May 1961): 1–17.
————. "Monetary Theory and Policy." *A.E.R.* 52 (June 1962): 335–84. Re-
printed in *EME,* 1969*b.*
————. *Alternative Guiding Principles for the Use of Monetary Policy in Canada.*
Essays in International Finance no. 44. Princeton, N.J.: Princeton Univ.
Press, 1963. Reprinted in *EME,* 1969*a.* (*a*)
————. *The Canadian Quandary: Economic Problems and Policies.* Toronto:
McGraw-Hill, 1963. Carleton Library ed., Toronto: McClelland & Stewart,
1977. (*b*)
————. "Objectives, Monetary Standards and Potentialities." *Rev. Econ. and
Statis.* 45 (October 1963): 137–47. (*c*)
————. "Recent Developments in Monetary Theory." *Indian Econ. Rev.* 6
(August 1963): 1–28. Reprinted in *EME,* 1969*a.* (*d*)
————. "A Survey of Theories of Inflation." *Indian Econ. Rev.* 6 (August
1963): 29–69. Reprinted in *EME,* 1969*a.* (*e*)
————. "Major Issues in Monetary and Fiscal Policies." *Federal Reserve Bull.* 50
(November 1964): 1400–1413. Reprinted in *EME,* 1969*a.*
————. "A Quantity Theorist's Monetary History of the United States." *Econ.
J.* 75 (June 1965): 388–96.
————. "The Neo-Classical One-Sector Growth Model: A Geometrical Expo-
sition and Extension to a Monetary Economy." *Economica* 33 (August 1966):
265–87. Reprinted in *EME,* 1969*a.*
————. "Is Inflation the Inevitable Price of Rapid Development or a Retard-
ing Factor in Economic Growth?" In *Fiscal and Monetary Problems in Devel-
oping States,* edited by David Krivine. New York: Praeger, 1967. Reprinted
in *EME,* 1969*a.* (*a*)
————. "The Report on Bank Charges. II." *Bankers Magazine* 204 (August
1967): 64–68. Reprinted in *Readings in British Monetary Economics,* edited by
Harry G. Johnson. Oxford: Clarendon, 1972. (*b*)
————. "A Note on Seigniorage and the Social Saving from Substituting
Credit for Commodity Money." *Univ. Punjab Economist* 6 (June 1968): 1–8.

Reprinted in *Monetary Problems of the International Economy*, edited by Robert A. Mundell and Alexander K. Swoboda. Chicago: Univ. Chicago Press, 1969. (*a*)

———. "Problems of Efficiency in Monetary Management." *J.P.E.* 76, no. 5 (September/October 1968): 971–90. Reprinted in *Readings in British Monetary Economics*, edited by Harry G. Johnson. Oxford: Clarendon, 1972. (*b*)

———. *Essays in Monetary Economics*. 2d ed. London: Allen & Unwin, 1969. (*a*)

———. "Inside Money, Outside Money, Income, Wealth, and Welfare in Monetary Theory." *J. Money, Credit and Banking* 1 (February 1969): 30–45. (*b*)

———. "Pesek and Saving's Theory of Money and Wealth: A Comment." *J. Money, Credit and Banking* 1 (August 1969): 535–37. (*c*)

———. "Recent Developments in Monetary Theory: A Commentary." In *Money in Britain, 1959–69: The Papers of the Radcliffe Report Ten Years After*, edited by David R. Croome and Harry G. Johnson. London: Oxford Univ. Press, 1970.

———. "The Keynesian Revolution and the Monetarist Counter-Revolution." *A.E.R. Papers and Proc.* 61 (May 1971): 1–14. Reprinted in *Further Essays in Monetary Economics*. London: Allen & Unwin, 1972. (*a*)

———. *Macroeconomics and Monetary Theory*. London: Gray-Mills, 1971. (*b*)

———. *Inflation and the Monetarist Controversy*. DeVries Lectures. Amsterdam: North-Holland, 1972.

———. "Major Issues in Monetary Economics." *Oxford Econ. Papers* 26 (July 1974): 212–25.

———. "Comment on Mayer on Monetarism." *Kredit und Kapital* 9, no. 2 (1976): 145–53.

———. *Selected Essays in Monetary Economics*. London: Allen & Unwin, 1978.

Johnson, Harry G., and Nobay, A. Robert. "Monetarism: A Historic-Theoretic Perspective." *J. Econ. Literature* 15 (June 1977): 470–85.

Johnson, Harry G., and Winder, John W. L. *Lags in the Effects of Monetary Policy in Canada*. Ottawa: Queen's Printer (for Royal Commission on Banking and Finance), 1962.

Kaldor, Nicholas. "The New Monetarism." *Lloyds Bank Rev.* (July 1970), pp. 1–18.

Laidler, David. "Recent Developments in Monetary Theory: Discussion." In *Money in Britain, 1959–69: The Papers of the Radcliffe Report Ten Years After*, edited by David R. Croome and Harry G. Johnson. London: Oxford Univ. Press, 1970.

Leijonhufvud, Axel. *On Keynesian Economics and the Economics of Keynes*. London: Oxford Univ. Press, 1968.

McKinnon, Ronald I., ed. *Money and Finance in Economic Growth and Development: Essays in Honor of Edward Shaw*. New York and Basel: Dekker, 1976.

Meltzer, Allan H. "Monetary Theory and Monetary History." *Schweizerische Zeitschrift fur Volkwirtschaft und Statistik* 101 (December 1965): 404–22.

Modigliani, Franco. "Liquidity Preference and the Theory of Interest and Money." *Econometrica* 12 (January 1944): 45–88.

Parkin, Michael, and Sumner, Michael T., eds. *Incomes Policy and Inflation*. Manchester: Manchester Univ. Press, 1972.

Pesek, Boris P., and Saving, Thomas R. *Money, Wealth, and Economic Theory*. New York: Macmillan, 1967.

Poole, William. "Optimal Choice of Monetary Policy Instruments in a Simple Stochastic Macro Model." *Q.J.E.* 84 (May 1970): 197–216.

Reuber, Grant L. "The Objectives of Canadian Monetary Policy, 1949–61:

HARRY G. JOHNSON   615

Empirical 'Trade-Offs' and the Reaction Function of the Authorities."
J.P.E. 72, no. 2 (April 1964): 109–32.
Tobin, James. "The Monetary Interpretation of History." *A.E.R.* 55 (June
1965): 464–85. (*a*)
———. "Money and Economic Growth." *Econometrica* 33 (October 1965):
671–84. (*b*)
Welham, P. J. *Monetary Circulation of the United Kingdom: A Statistical Study.*
Oxford: Blackwell, 1969.

[7]

Harry G. Johnson as a Development Economist

Arnold C. Harberger

University of Chicago

David Wall

University of Sussex

I. Introduction

In making an assessment of Harry Johnson's work in the area of development economics one must recognize (*a*) that as an individual he belongs first and foremost to the whole discipline of economics rather than to any particular branch or field thereof and (*b*) that, certainly in his own view, economic development is not itself a separate field of economics in the same sense as, say, international trade or monetary economics (the areas in which his roots were deepest, his interests strongest, and his contributions most numerous and powerful). That he belongs to all of economics is reflected in the enormous scope and range of his work. His denial of separate "field" status to economic development (a position we also share) had as its counterpart a firm conviction that the discipline of economics had great relevance for all countries, regardless of their stage of development. He preferred the term "development economics" to "economic development," because he found it more compatible with his views that there is really only one science or discipline of economics and that most important policy problems have to be faced by economies at all levels of wealth (or stages of development).

The main task of development economics was, in Johnson's view, simply to apply good economics to the analysis of the economic situa-

We are grateful to Nancy Wall for her help in the preparation of this paper.

[*Journal of Political Economy*, 1984, vol. 92, no. 4]

tions of one or more of the less developed countries (LDCs) and to the study of particular policy problems facing them. Sometimes his applications were quite straightforward, entailing only modest adaptations (if any) from the way the same task would be done in a typical advanced economy. In this vein, much of Johnson's "advice" to the LDCs took the form of trying to convince them that they were not (either individually or collectively) "special cases" of one or another particular problem. Sometimes, however, without being subject to a different kind of economics, a less developed country could have certain characteristics (e.g., one-crop export agriculture) that led to problems different from those of more advanced countries. At other times questions arose, usually in international forums, concerning the relationship of the LDCs as a group to the principal industrial centers. Dealing with these questions, too, was in Johnson's view a legitimate part of development economics.

We are not interested even in attempting to set what would in any event be arbitrary boundaries to "development economics," nor indeed was Johnson. The main point is quite the opposite—development economics is often just ordinary economics applied to less developed countries, and where it is different the differences are so varied and often so subtle that the idea of a clear borderline is itself absurd. This in turn makes it difficult to say just which of Johnson's many works should or should not be considered as falling within the scope of this review. In spite of the difficulty, we have done our best to cull from his vast bibliography a list of works that seem to us to fit reasonably comfortably under the rubric of development economics as described above.

Apart from a single entry in 1950, "The De-stabilising Effect of International Commodity Agreements on the Prices of Primary Products," no other met the test until the article "Notes on Economic Development and the Maximum Rate of Growth" (1957) appeared in the *Malayan Economic Review.* This was but one of what became a long series of papers published in that journal, the *Pakistan Economic Review,* the *Pakistan Development Review,* the *Philippine Economic Journal,* and a few other similar outlets; in such cases we took the outlet itself to create a presumption (in what might otherwise be a doubtful case) for including the paper in our "development economics" list.

Despite all of the difficulties of classification, we consider our selected list to be revealing in the dimensions both of time and of subject matter. On the time scale, after one article in 1950, there was one in 1957, two in 1958, and one in 1959. There were three each in 1960 and 1961, followed by a hiatus of sorts (one article in 1963), after which Johnson's productivity in the development economics field really burgeoned, with 20 articles in 1964–66 and another 10 in

1967–68. The pace fell off to three or fewer per year from 1969 through 1973, followed by a spate of 18 articles in 1974–77. Clearly, the mid-1960s formed the first major period of concentration, and during this time there were also four books (1965c, 1967b, 1967c, 1968) that we felt merited being classified as dealing with development economics. The second major period was the mid-1970s; here there were an additional three books (1975, 1976a, 1977b) bearing on this field.

Subject matter shows a significant shift of emphasis through time. Articles that we would classify as dealing principally with customs unions and with tariffs and trade restrictions are significantly concentrated in the 1950–61 period (five articles) and 1963–68 period (six articles). The policies of the developed countries (most particularly the United States) vis-à-vis the Third World enter strongly (seven articles) in the 1963–68 period, while the themes of UNCTAD and the so-called link between international aid and the international monetary system (six articles) come to the fore during the 1970s. Papers dealing with the general area of economic development (10 articles), on the other hand, are scattered quite evenly along the time dimension.

In the sections that follow, we try to convey both the content and the "flavor" of Johnson's work in development economics. Wherever possible we use his own words, for in most cases it was possible to find, among his various writings, one or more versions in which a given argument or line of thought was quite elegantly distilled.

The organization of the remainder of this review is as follows. In Section II we present Johnson's view of the development process. Subsequently, we deal with his writings, first (in Sec. III) concerning economic policy within the developing countries and then (in Sec. IV) concerning policies of the advanced countries that had particular bearing on the LDCs. Section V deals with Johnson's thoughts on the mobility across national boundaries of factors of production (labor and capital) and of technology, while Section VI goes into the whole complex of problems encompassing international arrangements, including both developing and advanced economies. These include international commodity agreements, trade preferences for the products of LDCs, and institutional arrangements such as UNCTAD and the "link" (between the creation of international liquidity on the one hand and the distribution of foreign aid to the LDCs on the other).

Our final section treats the more human aspects of Harry Johnson's connection with development economics—his incessant travels to and labors in developing countries, his personal ties to scores of former students, and his efforts to aid young representatives of modern economics in their struggles to improve the teaching, the application, and the diffusion of economic science throughout the developing world.

II. The Development Process

Starting at least with some early postwar writings, much of the literature on economic development has been characterized by mechanistic assumptions of various types. Johnson was at pains to distance himself from those. Nowhere is this more apparent than in one of his last papers (1977a). In his own words:

> The Keynesian idea that capitalism typically produced mass unemployment . . . expressed itself in the belief that less developed countries were characterized by large-scale "disguised unemployment," an assumption that incidentally justified all sorts of import-substituting and protectionist policies by its implication that labor for domestic production had a zero social alternative-opportunity cost. Its more important implication, however, was that development planning could safely and should necessarily concentrate on the accumulation of capital, in the narrow sense of physical productive equipment, structures, and "infrastructures." In this connection, . . . the Harrod-Domar equation ($g = s/k$, where g is the growth rate, s the savings ratio, and k the capital-output ratio) provided the essential skeleton of a model for development planning. The growth rate could be maximized by maximizing the marginal saving from output growth and minimizing, through choice of techniques and expanding sectors, the "incremental capital-output ratio." . . .
>
> . . . The "Mahalanobis model," derived from Soviet planning and the Marxist model of development . . . focused on the choice between investing in machines to make consumption goods and in machines to make machines to make consumption goods . . . and demonstrated that a shift toward "heavy" as against "light" industry investment would [ultimately] result in a . . . faster growth rate of consumption. . . . The apparently startling nature of this result was largely due to the fact that the concentration on the choice between . . . "heavy" and "light" industry successfully concealed the fact that the real choice at issue was between a higher and a lower savings ratio, that is, between more consumption later and more consumption now.
>
> The inapplicability of the Keynesian assumption of the availability of masses of unemployed, appropriately skilled labor was gradually recognized as a lesson of hard experience. Its positive consequence was an emphasis on "manpower planning" and manpower-requirement forecasting as a supplement to savings-investment planning and forecasting—a vogue which later encountered increasing criticism

on the same grounds as the savings-investment planning approach had already encountered, namely, the assumption of fixed coefficients between "capital" ("physical" in the earlier case, "human" in the later) and output. Its negative consequence was a continuing effort to provide theoretical support for the concept of "disguised unemployment" in the face of criticism of it on grounds of inconsistency with economic rationality and utility maximization. [Pp. 363–64]

The Harrod-Domar model['s] . . . successor was the Chenery-Strout "two-gap" model for analyzing and projecting development assistance needs and investigating the question of if and when development aid would cease to be necessary. The model envisaged two "constraints" on development investment, domestic savings and foreign exchange expenditure needs, the tighter constraint being binding. The model, aside from its assumption of rigid coefficients to the neglect of substitution possibilities, is logically inconsistent since it confuses two different sources of foreign exchange—earnings, which absorb domestic resources in production, and gifts, which add resources to domestic savings. [P. 368]

The preceding direct quotations leave no doubt as to Harry Johnson's position with respect to the various mechanistic approaches to the analysis of economic growth. It is less easy to get an equally succinct statement, in his own words, of his own position. This is understandable, since his style, both of writing and of thinking about problems, tended to be interwoven like a fabric rather than linear and aimed at a single point.

Nonetheless, one can construct a fairly clear picture of where Johnson stood. His starting point was the neoclassical one-sector growth model with technical advance, about which he wrote a nice article (1966a) expounding the basic model and extending it to include the monetary as well as the real side. The essence of this model is that economic growth comes from additions to the stock of basic resources and from changes in technique. He emphasized that the role of physical capital accumulation had been grossly exaggerated in the literature and spoke favorably of the tendency for economic research to attempt to break down "the residual factor in economic growth" into components such as economies of scale, improvements in the quality of productive factors (through education in the case of labor and through improved efficiency in the case of machines), and shifts from a less efficient to a more efficient allocation of resources.

As his ideas evolved in this area, his vision of the process became richer and more detailed, with excursions into the relevance to the growth process of migration, of patents and other incentives to innovation, and of educational policy choices. The general tenor of his thinking on the process of growth can be gleaned from the following quotations taken from his 1963 lecture, "Economic Growth and Economic Policy" (1963*a*), which aimed at presenting "the main outlines of a policy aimed at promoting economic growth in a free enterprise economy":

> Such a policy would involve reform of the tax system to eliminate elements that inhibit growth and promote inefficiency. [Appropriate reforms] would entail replacing income by expenditure as the basis for personal taxation [so as to] eliminate the double taxation of saving; [integrating corporate and personal taxes with] corporate earnings being attributed to stock-holders and taxed as personal income; and finally [eliminating] the tariff, [using] subsidies . . . from the regular government budget if certain industries are deemed of special national importance. [Pp. 61–62]

> A second . . . series of measures would . . . increase the efficiency of the market system, particularly by improving the mobility of labour between regions and between occupations, [reforming] the educational system [and initiating] programmes for the retraining and relocation of labour. [P. 62]

> Tax concessions for industrial investment and research [are not advisable because they] introduce a new set of distortions into the functioning of the market system, and substitute the judgments of the legislators [for] the calculation of the competitive system. . . . To the best of my knowledge [evidence] has not . . . substantiated [the existence of] external economies [whereby such investments] yield social benefits that do not accrue to the enterprises undertaking them. [P. 63]

III. Economic Policy in the Developing Countries

Harry Johnson's thoughts on economic policy in the LDCs can be approached either through his contributions to the general literature of economics or through those that focus specifically on the LDCs. His general contributions reveal him as virtually embodying the neoclassical tradition in economics; his more specific comments on the LDCs show him as an acute and astute observer, wise though at times sharp and acerbic in his judgments.

Good examples representing the neoclassical tradition are his related papers on "Tariffs and Economic Development" (1964) and "Optimal Trade Intervention in the Presence of Domestic Distortions" (1965*a*). Some of his key conclusions in these treatments are:

> The economic analysis of the various arguments for protection . . . can be summarized in two central principles: (1) Only the optimum tariff argument provides an economic justification for tariffs: all other arguments for protection are arguments for subsidies. (2) The use of the tariff on the basis of any of the other arguments may make matters worse rather than better. . . . whether . . . the tariff increases or decreases real income depends on . . . various [parameters] . . . and cannot be determined by *a priori* reasoning. [1964, p. 8]

> Welfare maximization requires a correction of [a] domestic distortion by an appropriate tax or subsidy on production, consumption, or factor use, and not a tax or subsidy on international trade; [moreover], given the presence of a domestic distortion, protection designed to offset it may decrease welfare rather than increase it. [1965*a*, p. 31]

> For the [infant industry] argument to be valid, . . . it must be demonstrated . . . that the social rate of return exceeds the private. . . . [One reason why this might occur stems from] the fact that . . . once knowledge of production technique is acquired, it can be applied by others than those who have assumed the cost of acquiring it. . . . The other reason why the social benefit may exceed private hinges on the . . . technique of production [being] embodied in the skill of the labor force [in which the workers have] property rights [even when they were] acquire[d] at the employer's expense. . . . [Whichever of these reasons might apply], it is apparent from the general principles governing optimal governmental intervention . . . that . . . some sort of subsidy to the infant industries, rather than protection [is indicated]. [1965*a*, pp. 27–29]

> The recommendation of a uniform tariff rate on commodities whose production it is desired to protect . . . has no theoretical validity. . . . For consistency, [a uniform rate rule]

must comprise all imports. [When it does so, such a rule makes sense] . . . for a . . . policy aimed at increasing self-sufficiency, [for a] uniform tariff rate applied to all importable goods will . . . minimize the total excess cost of import-saving. [1964, pp. 18–19]

The preceding excerpts illustrate very well the flavor of that part of Johnson's theorizing that most directly bore on the policies of less developed countries. But they are unquestionably pieces of theory. There follow a few excerpts reflecting Johnson as an observer of and commentator on the policy behavior of the LDCs, taken from his (1967*b*) Brookings book, *Economic Policies toward Less Developed Countries.*

Economic planning, implemented by controls of all kinds over the allocation of investment resources, commodities, and foreign exchange, is characteristic of less developed countries, . . . [and] in practice . . . give[s] rise to all sorts of inefficiencies and wastes of resources. . . . Licensing systems inevitably favor the established enterprise against the new competitor and hamper the ability of the more efficient firm to [expand]. . . . Fair distribution of scarce licenses may [require] producing far below capacity . . . ; discriminatory distribution . . . may protect the inefficient. . . . [But] the main impediment . . . imposed by licensing . . . is its displacement of the market mechanism [by an] administrative mechanism of detailed quantitative decisions by civil servants. [P. 69]

Development plans typically steer a disproportionate share of the available . . . resources toward industry. . . . Further, development policy . . . depresses [agricultural] incentives [by raising] the prices of industrial inputs for agriculture [and by holding] down the prices received by agricultural producers. . . . [Where] an export surplus of agricultural products [exists], it is generally deliberate policy to tax their producers heavily, [reducing] export earnings [and encouraging] the development of alternative supplies from elsewhere. [Pp. 70–71]

[On industrialization via import substitution], it is particularly necessary to stress the importance of the input-output relations in a modern industrial structure and the effects of protection of inputs in raising the cost of production of the user industries, rendering them unable to compete in the world market. [The establishment of] a "new international division of labor" [requires] the abandonment of the effort [by LDCs] to achieve self-sufficiency. [Instead they should] favor . . . specialization on a few processes or products, allowing the producers to take full advantage of the availability of materials, components, and equipment in the world market.

   . . . The problems [above] of inefficiency and noncompetitiveness [are often exacerbated by] inflationary monetary and fiscal policies in combination with unwillingness to devalue the currency. [This unwillingness causes import restrictions to be] guided by political expediency and particularly by the priority accorded to investment goods and materials over consumer goods (especially "luxuries"). . . . the resulting protectionist system is extremely inefficient. [P. 74]

[Apart from their influence on protectionism] inflationary fiscal and monetary policies have a variety of deleterious effects on economic development and efficiency. The most serious are, first, the distortions . . . caused by effort to protect certain segments of the population from the effects of inflation, for example by holding down the domestic price of food or of urban transport to shield the industrial worker, or by holding down interest rates to channel real income to manufacturing firms; and second, the disturbance of the normal processes of investment decision by extreme uncertainty about the short-run rate of inflation to be expected. These effects of inflation are harmful both to economic development . . . and [particularly] to . . . development [based] on industrial exporting. [Pp. 75–76]

[Of course], endemic inflation . . . almost invariably [stems from] political inability to agree either on the taxation required . . . or . . . on the division of the national income among the claimants to it. . . . The insistence of outside advisers on conservative monetary and fiscal policies [often] amounts in reality to a demand for political stabilization and generally a demand for resolution of political conflict in favor of one of the disputants. [P. 76]

IV. Economic Policy in the Developed Countries

In this section we deal with how, in Johnson's view, the policies of the developed countries with respect to trade in goods and services impinge on the economies and in various senses the welfare of the

LDCs. The discussion is restricted to issues concerning trade in goods and services, because those concerning movements in factors and technology will be dealt with in the next section. The treatment of multinational "solutions" of various kinds (commodity agreements, preferences, etc.) is similarly deferred.

Within the purview of this section there are two main points: (*a*) the various mechanisms by which the policies of the industrial countries make the passage of the LDCs to higher levels of development more difficult; and (*b*) the costly extra burdens that the foreign assistance has typically placed on the recipient countries, or, put another way, the apparently endemic (yet unnecessary) inefficiencies that characterized the foreign aid process as Johnson observed it.

On tariff structures he had this to say:

> In the general case, failing concrete evidence to the contrary, it is reasonable to assume that the escalation of tariff rates with stage of production typical of modern tariff structures implies a corresponding but steeper escalation of effective rates of protection with stage of production. . . . So far as the pattern of world trade is concerned, [escalation induces a] bias [of] trade toward raw materials, fuels, and semi-fabricates; towards producers' goods (capital goods) rather than consumers' goods; towards goods of a luxury nature capable of bearing high tariffs; and towards . . . goods distinguished by technical superiority sufficient to overcome the competitive disadvantage imposed by tariffs. [1965*b*, pp. 20–21]

> The escalated tariff structures of the advanced countries obviously create serious barriers to the development of the underdeveloped countries on the basis of their resources of relatively cheap labour, and instead bias [their] opportunities for development . . . towards dependence on the exploitation of natural resources. [P. 21]

> The escalated tariff structures of the advanced countries are therefore a potentially powerful inhibitor of economic growth in the underdeveloped countries. This may be especially so with respect to industrial products that demand a mass market to permit efficient exploitation of economies of scale, a market not available within the underdeveloped countries themselves. [P. 23]

But if the escalated tariff structures bear against the healthy industrial development of the LDCs, the use by the industrial countries of various devices to protect their own agricultural sectors tends to drive down the world prices of similar products produced by the developing countries. Johnson cites in various places (1967*b*, p. 86) D. Gale Johnson's calculations of agricultural prices received by farmers in different advanced countries over the prices that would have had to be paid for the corresponding goods if imported. Harry Johnson's own work in this area consists of calculating the effects of reducing sugar protectionism of various types. In one of his very few excursions into substantive work with actual empirical data, Johnson calculates the estimated consumption cost of sugar protection (cum excise taxes) in a number of countries, together with the production cost of such protection for some of the leading industrial countries. He summarizes:

> In the major (Western) protectionist countries, substitution of imports for protected domestic production, allowing for the effects on sugar prices of world free trade in sugar, would have saved the expenditure of real resources worth $318.7 million [at 1959 prices]. The additional export earnings of the exporting countries due to this substitution would have been worth $675 million . . . and the estimated net benefit from this additional trade would have been worth in the neighbourhood of $120 million. Altogether, with respect to substitution in production alone, and entirely ignoring the effects of the expansion of consumption that would have ensued on the adoption of free trade in sugar, $438 million of additional resources could have been freed for development purposes from these seven countries alone through the abandonment of protection. . . . A part, and in some cases more than the whole, of this saving would be automatically transferred to the exporting [LDC] countries through the assumed increase in the prices of existing [sugar] imports. [1966*b*, pp. 39–41]

> [Without doubt] the prevalence of sugar protection has substantial effects both in wasting resources and in reducing the earnings of the less developed countries that have a comparative advantage in sugar production. [1966*b*, pp. 41–42]

On the matter of foreign aid, particularly bilateral aid, Johnson was extremely disturbed by the economic inefficiencies it entailed—the more so because he saw these inefficiencies as utterly unnecessary and unwarranted, as counterproductive from the standpoint of the ostensible purposes of foreign assistance, and as self-serving on the part of the donor countries.

[A] serious set of problems arises from the interaction of a number of elements in the present system of supplying aid: the predominance of bilateral aid, the predominance of project over program aid, and the practice of tying aid to purchases in the donor country. . . . The chief sources of [the resulting] inefficiency . . . are as follows.

First, less developed countries may be able to obtain aid for projects of a "display" or "monument" type because some country likes to finance that type of project, but not for other projects that have more . . . value because no donor is interested. . . .

Second, less developed countries may have to pay substantially more than the competitive world market price for equipment [financed by aid]. Consequently an element of inefficiency (artificially high capital costs) . . . is built into the project. . . . Moreover . . . [because of these excess costs] repayment of the loan will involve returning more real value than was received, and this may far more than offset any elements of "softness" in the loan. . . .

[Third, in addition to paying more for aid-financed goods], less developed countries may have to be content with less expert advisers than are available in the world market and, perhaps more important, accept a technology that is not well adapted to their economic conditions and especially their relative factor-scarcities. [1967b, pp. 81–82]

V. Factor Mobility and Economic Development

When Johnson advised developed countries on foreign assistance matters, he would urge them to introduce more liberal trade policies, to relax restrictions on immigration, and to remove controls over the free movement of capital. The tighter were a country's immigration laws and the stricter its controls on capital movements, the more liberal it should be toward accepting imports from developing countries and toward providing aid in the form of capital assistance. He felt that restrictions on factor movements lay at the core of many policy problems of international economic relations. His view was internationalist, humanitarian, and cosmopolitan. Opposed to it was the chauvinistic nationalism of the self-seeking elites of the nation states (large and small), into which he saw the world as having been accidently and arbitrarily split. He wrote extensively on three aspects of this debate: the brain drain—or labor mobility; the role of multinational corporations; and technology transfer.

Labor Mobility

Johnson's position on labor mobility, or the "brain drain," as it manifested itself in the development debate in the 1960s, is reflected in the following quotations.

> My objection to the [concept of the gap between rich and poor countries] as the focus of analysis is not merely that the use of statistical averages can produce unnecessary paradoxes or nonsense results, but that it assumes the nation as the unit of analysis rather than the people that are born and live in a world divided into national states, and hence biases thinking towards a nationalist rather than a cosmopolitan view of the nature of the problem and solutions to it, and towards a neglect of the welfare of the individuals who better themselves by moving. No one seriously disputes the economic benefits, in the form of both improved allocative efficiency and competitive pressures for increasing productivity, that result from the mobility of labour within the nation; in fact nations typically seek to increase labour mobility by public policy. But the same type of movement of labour in search of better opportunities, but between rather than within nations, is widely regarded as a serious problem, damaging to the economic development of the poor nations.
>
> If one takes a cosmopolitan point of view, there can be no doubt that efficiency, growth and the relief of world poverty would be very effectively promoted by unlimited freedom of migration. . . . The prevalence of poverty among the nations, and the need for transfers of capital and knowledge to help remedy it, can be attributed to an important extent to the barriers to immigration imposed by the advanced countries, coupled with tariff and other barriers to trade that restrict "indirect immigration" from poor to rich countries via the export of goods and services. [1972, pp. 381–82]

Replying to criticism of the "gap" paper, to the effect that being in favor of free migration meant that he supported an unequal distribution of world income, he said that, on the contrary, "in believing that emigration was a good thing, he was trying to improve income distribution. Migration laws were contrary to improving income distribution. They prevented people emigrating and were often accompanied by barriers to removing such differences by trade" (1972, p. 408). In the body of the paper (pp. 389–91) he dubbed as "bad economics" the argument that alleged market failures (with human capital not being paid its full social value) justified some form of restriction of the free

HARRY G. JOHNSON   629

emigration of educated citizens out of poor countries. He accepted
that

> the ease of migration of educated people from underde-
> veloped countries, especially those in which English is the
> language of instruction, to advanced countries is a serious
> limitation on the potentialities of achieving economic devel-
> opment by educational investment and suggests the social
> desirability of devising means of obliging either the emi-
> grants themselves or the countries receiving them to repay
> the social capital invested in them to their countries of origin.
> [1963*b*, p. 233, n. 6]

But he insisted that "compulsion should be confined to the subgroup
of students . . . whose education is paid for by their own or an advanced-country government as a social investment in the promotion
of economic development" (1972, p. 390).

The one qualification to his advocacy of freedom of migration arose
from his Malthusian fear that the populations of some developing
countries might breed to the subsistence level, quickly replacing the
emigrants. Indeed, emigrant remittances (which on the whole he considered to be a much overlooked benefit of migration) could in an
extreme Malthusian case produce a population multiplier effect.
Since optimal family size is a function of expected income, which in
turn is a function of education, he believed that developed countries
could make "a constructive response to less-developed-country demands in the indirect forms of substantial support for population
control policies and for programs of mass elementary education with
an emphasis on vocational training" (1976*b*, p. 333).

Multinational Corporations

In the analysis of international economic policy issues Johnson placed
a great deal of importance on the increasing conflict among the state
as a political entity, the various forms of private enterprise as economic entities, and the economic welfare of the individual (see his
papers in *Economic Nationalism in Old and New States,* 1967*a*). He recognized that serious conflicts can arise "in the relations between the
nation-state as a powerful political entity with a bordered geographical domain and the multinational corporation as a powerful economic
entity with an unbordered world market domain" (1970, p. 28). But
he felt that private enterprise in the form of the multinational corporation could, while seeking its own private profits, contribute significantly to the economies of the less developed countries. He thought
that the planning approach to development had failed and that offi-

cial aid, designed to support this approach, would decline. The following quotations indicate how, in his view, multinational corporations could contribute to development:

> While the multinational firm has an incentive to invest in the transformation of the local economy only to the extent that such investment promises greater profits, the incentive may nevertheless be sufficient to induce a substantial contribution to development. Two particular incentives are especially important in this connection. First, labor skills imported from the developed countries are extremely expensive in comparison with the cost of training local labor, especially as the cost of training is largely either the labor-time of teachers or the labor-time of students, both of which are infinitely cheaper in poor countries than in rich ones. The foreign company will thus have a large profit incentive to train a local staff rather than import foreign labor.
>
> Second, given the complex input-output relations characteristic of modern industry and the dependence of profitable utilization of the product on the knowledge of the user, the firm may have a substantial incentive to invest in the diffusion of productive knowledge in two directions: to the local suppliers of the inputs needed in its production process and for which it demands quality standards superior to the customary standards of those industries and to local customers who have to be taught the technology of using the firm's products effectively. [1970, pp. 26–27]

> Any more general influence in promoting development will have to stem, on the one hand, from the exemplary value for local enterprises of the existence of efficient, well-managed, science-based subsidiary firms and their production of skilled local workers and executives who can be attracted into local enterprises and, on the other hand, from the ability of the state to use corporate and individual income taxes levied on foreign firms and their employees to finance education and other developmental expenditures. [1970, p. 27]

He believed that "the limitations on the potentialities of foreign direct investment as an agent of economic growth derive in part from social considerations that are generally accepted as just by well-intentioned people but in fact serve to inhibit the development process" (1970, p. 27). Pressure for wages and working conditions comparable to those in the home country of the company comes in this category. Other limitations come from a variety of other pressures: to use local inputs, to hire nationals beyond the point the company itself considers efficient, to meet export targets, and to conduct research and development locally. All these can misallocate the resources involved and raise production costs—sometimes to the point of dissuading potential investment or even provoking disinvestment.

Johnson considered that some of the problems encountered by multinational corporations represent LDC reactions to the practice (in some countries outside the United States) of influencing the activities of large businesses "covertly by conspiracy and backscratching among specialized members of a recognized and homogeneous political, economic and cultural national elite" (1970, p. 29), rather than through the law. He also recognized that competition among developing countries for the investments of multinational corporations could eat away at the potential development contribution that those investments could make.

Technology and Economic Development

Johnson's views on technology are easy to identify once his fundamental positions are understood:

a) "[Optimal output in the competitive model requires] that everyone has access one way or another to comparable technology—through competition in the supply of goods embodying such technology, or through migration of either capital or labor or both, or through the free availability of knowledge in written form or in the 'oral tradition' " (1973*b*, p. 44).

b) "Technology is a form of capital, and its availability alterable by investment" (1977*c*, p. 322).

Against this background he argued that

> society is faced with a dilemma—that the production of new knowledge costs resources, and investment in it must be paid for somehow, but that optimization of its use requires that it be freely available to all potential users. The uneasy compromise society has chosen, at least for most commercially useful knowledge, is to grant a limited monopoly to the inventors of new knowledge, protected either by patents or by commercial secrecy, and trust to time and competition gradually to erode the monopoly. The result is both an alliance of technological superiority with the ownership of capital, especially in the large national and multinational corporation, which generates political and social tensions, particularly in less developed countries playing "host" to direct foreign investment in

order to acquire better technology; the persistence of long technological lags among the more and the less advanced countries both reflects the slowing down of the diffusion of new technology by monopoly, and preserves inequalities of factor prices. One should observe, however, that such technological lags among nations may reflect the existence of barriers to the free movement of goods, capital and labor, rather than anything inherent in the nature of technology itself. If, for example, there were no barriers to the free movement of goods, one would expect production with a new technology to locate itself in regions with the lowest cost of factors of production; and if capital were free to move, these would be the regions with the lowest labor costs. But with barriers to trade on both sides, the transplantation of technology for production for export back to the home market is impeded; production for sale in the market of the "host" country becomes profitable only when factor prices, tariffs, or income levels make it profitable—and the transplant can easily be uneconomically premature. [1973*b*, pp. 44–45]

Johnson did not regard such restrictions on the development of new technology–based trade as necessarily involving a welfare loss for developing countries. For example, he argued that

competition within and between . . . countries with surplus or elastic populations tends to drive prices down to subsistence, on classical unlimited-labour-supply lines; and this is likely to be the result of unlimited competitive expansion of exports, initially made highly profitable by the diffusion of technology to and among the developing countries.

The fundamental solution to this problem obviously lies in the control of population growth in the less developed countries, pending ultimate arrival of the stage of development at which procreation is controlled by voluntary choice of the number of children the parents can afford to feed, house and educate to their own or better standards of productive contribution. In the meantime, control over the speed of development of trade based on technological diffusion may, intentionally or unintentionally, have the effect of contributing more to the raising of living standards and the strengthening of automatic economic pressures for development than cut-throat competition among developing countries in exporting technologically-advanced products to the developed countries. [1975, p. 159]

HARRY G. JOHNSON   633

He did, however, feel that "where labour is prevented from moving to [an] advanced country by restrictive immigration laws, the transmission of technical knowledge can be regarded as a form of compensation for damages" (1961, p. 12, n. 21).

VI. Institutional Aspects of International Economic Relations

Johnson had strong feelings about the international economic relations issues covered in the North/South debate, feelings that he made no attempt to hide and that crop up frequently in his writings. His position rested on three convictions. First, he accepted that a moral case can be made for transferring resources from the developed to the developing countries. This case could be either based on humanitarian concern or justified as compensation for the injuries inflicted on the LDCs because past and present interventions in the market by developed countries had been and were biased against the trade and investment interests of developing countries. Second, he believed that many of the biased and injurious interventions resulted from the fact that policymaking in both developed and developing countries was often in the hands of elites that were at best nationalistically chauvinistic and at worst, but all too frequently, self-serving and self-preserving. The policies of such elites only rarely promoted the best interests of the citizens of developing countries on whose plight the rhetoric of development focuses attention. And third, as he demonstrated so frequently and so conclusively, many of the reforms proposed for the new international economic order were misconceived and analytically unsound. And many such proposals emanated from the secretariats of the international organizations (in particular UNCTAD); these he saw as deriving largely from the national elites, and carrying their predominant attitudes, while constituting a new self-serving international supra-elite. Three areas of reform about which Johnson felt particularly strongly were international commodity agreements, trade preferences, and the link between the creation of international liquidity and aid.

International Commodity Agreements

Johnson had strong views on international commodity agreements. He considered them to be "[one of the] ideas of Raùl Prebisch, especially as institutionalized and vulgarized through UNCTAD, [which] have become an increasingly powerful obstacle to co-operation in the promotion of the development of the developing countries, in the specific sense that sympathy with aspirations for development has to be demonstrated by the acceptance of economic nonsense and the endorsement of proposals that . . . maximize the prospective costs and minimize the prospective return" (1976*b*, pp. 329–30). He believed that economic theory and experience teach us that commodity agreements "aside from the difficulty of devising and operating them—are an exceedingly doubtful instrument for promoting economic development" (1976*b*, p. 327) and that

> economically, such agreements . . . amount to an extremely
> cumbersome method of transferring income from consum-
> ers to producers, a method that entails considerable eco-
> nomic waste through the distortion of consumption and pro-
> duction decisions by arbitrary high prices, and through the
> probable necessity of production restrictions and surplus dis-
> posal. In addition . . . there are not many commodities for
> which the long-run demand is sufficiently inelastic for price-
> increasing measures to increase total revenue; and . . . price-
> fixing is a very inefficient method of providing equitable
> incomes for agricultural producers. It would be econom-
> ically far more rational to provide income transfers directly
> from the rich to the poor countries, rather than to seek the
> same effect through the cumbersome and probably ineffec-
> tive route of international commodity agreements.

Although he allowed that in a few cases increased transfers could under very special circumstances be effected by some forms of agreement, by the mid-seventies he was increasingly disillusioned with attempts to "disguise" transfers. He had come to the conclusion that "the successor governments of the independent developing countries have . . . become much more sophisticated, in the sense of appreciating that there is no reason why high prices for commodity exports should be passed along to the stupid farmers, instead of being creamed off for spending on and by the educated government bureaucracy in the name of promoting economic development, social justice, or what have you" (1976*b*, p. 320). Apart from this, he believed that the continued popularity of international commodity agreements is a matter of faith which "as is usually the case, . . . rests either on ignorance of past history or the obstinate belief that what went wrong last time was attributable either to lack of will or cleverness, or unwillingness to commit sufficient financial resources to the enterprise—but never to inherent difficulties that could be understood in terms of elementary economic analysis" (1976*b*, p. 322).

Trade Preferences

Johnson's initial position on preferences was fairly straightforward. He felt that "the clear implication of the theoretical considerations

and empirical evidence is that, despite impressions to the contrary
derived from contemplation of nominal tariff levels, preferences in
developed-country markets for exports of manufactures and semi-
manufactures might well exercise a powerful influence in expanding
the export earnings and promoting the industrialization of the less
developed countries" (1967*b*, p. 173). This position was based partly
on the assumption that the "formation and policies of the European
Common Market will block further progress after the Kennedy
Round toward trade liberalization along traditional GATT lines"
(1967*b*, p. 205) and partly on the assumption that any preference
scheme negotiated would be fairly liberal in terms of country and
product coverage and in the extent of the preferential margin extended.

Johnson was wrong on both counts. In fact, the Europeans did not
stop the process of liberalization in GATT. Moreover, the preference
schemes that did emerge were ill designed and were regarded by
Johnson as at best third- or fourth-best policy instruments, or at
worst—in the form adopted by the EEC for the African/Caribbean/
Pacific Group of States (ACP)—as a calculated move by the Europeans designed to keep their ex-colonies in a "neo-neo-colonialist"
dependent relationship. He felt that the developed countries should
not be encouraged to bend the rules of international trade in order to
establish such schemes.

> The less developed countries would be better advised to in-
> sist, so far as they can, that the developed countries should
> accept and live by the principle of comparative advantage,
> than to tolerate rich country violations of the principle and
> attempt to counteract these violations by violations of their
> own, coupled with demands for compensation in the form of
> foreign aid and trade preferences . . . [and their objective
> should be] to get the rules changed into something constitut-
> ing a closer approximation to honesty. Specifically, the less
> developed countries should have a strong concern with the
> promotion of freer world trade on a global basis, and espe-
> cially with respect to agricultural products, and should not
> allow themselves to be diverted into pursuit of such gim-
> micks as special trade preferences. [1973*a*, p. 34]

In addition, he became more and more convinced that his original
position, that the potential benefits of trade preferences might not be
realized because of self-imposed supply constraints, was correct and
in fact the case. In the Brookings volume he had said:

> It is necessary to determine what factors account for the
> inability of less developed countries, and specifically of the

"developing" countries that already produce manufactures
for the home market, to export in competition with the developed countries in spite of their comparative advantages
. . . of materials and low-wage labor, and how significant
these factors are empirically. . . . [In Johnson's view, the
culprits were] the import-substitution and currency-over-
valuation policies typically pursued by the governments of
less developed countries. . . . [To his mind the cost disadvan-
tages resulting from such policies were] frequently . . . far
greater than the competitive advantage that could be conferred by preferences from the developed countries
[implying that] neither preferences nor nondiscriminatory
tariff reduction would help the less developed countries unless they were prepared to make major changes in their tariff
and exchange-rate policies. [1967*b*, p. 206]

The "Link"

The various proposals to link the growth of some new form of international liquidity to the provision of aid to developing countries
elicited a strong response from Johnson. He recognized that the developing countries could benefit from a reform of the international
monetary system but did not feel that the various proposals for a link
between the growth of liquidity and aid were a sensible move. He
criticized them initially on the grounds that "there is no obvious advantage, and much evident and avoidable complexity, in attempting
to solve two different and incommensurable problems with one and
the same institutional change" (1967*b*, p. 223). He argued that most
of the proposals were simply hoping surreptitiously to increase the
total flow of aid to developing countries and did not think them likely
to succeed. "[This] assumes that the aid policies of the developed
countries are independent of international monetary operations, so
that whatever aid would be channelled by a world central bank to the
less developed countries would be a net addition to their aid receipts.
Since in the real world the left hand usually knows full well what the
right hand is doing (though it may not admit it publicly), this is an
unrealistic assumption" (1967*b*, p. 228).

Johnson's second criticism—that the proposals saddled one instrument with two potentially conflicting objectives—was two pronged.
On the one hand, the amount of new international liquidity required
in any period by the international economy might have no relation to
the requirements of developing countries for aid in that period. On
the other hand, there was no way of ensuring that a distribution of
funds to less developed countries according to their estimated liquid-

ity needs would correspond either with their capacity to absorb capital in economically sound projects or with the objectives of the donor countries. Making the aid objective paramount could result (through excessive global monetary expansion) in an unstable international economy. This, of course, would conflict with the long-run interests of the developing as well as the developed countries. He felt that the international monetary system as it was in the mid-1960s fragmented the international economy by pushing developed countries that faced (or were frightened at the prospect of) balance-of-payments problems into adopting policy measures that restricted the inflow of imports and the outflow of capital. He regarded both of these as being inimical to the interests of developing countries. He argued that

> the less developed countries would benefit . . . from the establishment of an international monetary system that provided a more adequate combination of liquidity and adjustment mechanisms. The most important contributions of such a system would be to remove the inhibitions to expansion of aid generated by fear of consequent balance-of-payments difficulties and to facilitate the untying of aid, thus increasing its efficiency. In addition, less developed countries would benefit significantly from the removal of restrictions dictated by balance-of-payments difficulties, whose effect is frequently to protect production in the developed countries and to aggravate uncertainty in international trade.
>
> The less developed countries have, however, a far more important interest in the establishment of an international monetary system that would promote the growth of world production and trade at high levels of employment and activity by providing an adequate secular expansion of international liquidity. [1967*b*, p. 215]

In the Brookings book he went farther than this, asserting that the developing countries "have a particular interest in the establishment of a system that will expand international liquidity at a rate great enough to impart an inflationary bias to world economic development" (1967*b*, pp. 216–17). Ten years later, however, he was more worried by inflation. He felt that the "favorable climate for economic development [in which] . . . the developing countries [have] the advantage of trading with an advanced-country world characterized by fairly steady sustained economic growth at fairly stable (more accurately, slowly rising) prices . . . has been destroyed, at least temporarily, by world inflation" (1976*b*, p. 321). This world inflation was to some extent the result of the International Monetary Fund's effectively introducing a disguised and limited form of "link" as a result of its attempts to

> strengthen its political support and acceptability by catering to the special interests of politically powerful groups of constituents. Specifically, the Fund has been cultivating support . . . by potentially extremely inflationary devices. . . . It has been steadily enlarging its role as a lender of international liquidity on concessionary terms to developing countries in balance-of-payments difficulties. . . . The danger is that the developing-country group will be so fascinated with . . . the age-old fallacy that the creation of money is a way of getting something for nothing—something real for something paper—that they will provide indirect support for international . . . monetary policies that [perpetuate] world inflation. [1976*b*, pp. 334–35]

VII. The Human Side

Harry Johnson's introduction to the world of developing countries came in 1956, when he was invited by the International Economic Association to teach refresher courses in Karachi and Singapore. This opened the door to a series of visits to Asian countries and to a great many abiding personal connections with Asian economists. (He later traveled to Ghana and made several trips to Latin America, lecturing in Argentina, Chile, Mexico, Panama, and Uruguay; nonetheless his deepest and firmest roots in the developing world were and remained in the Asian countries.)

Over the years he inspired many Ph.D.s from the developing nations, but he also had enormous influence on many who never studied directly under him. Few if any in our profession even came close to Harry Johnson in terms of willingness to read and comment on the papers of younger economists. This he did simply in his several roles as journal editor, but even beyond what he did "officially," he conscientiously read and commented on the work handed to him by younger economists at just about every institution he visited. A great many beneficiaries of his generosity in this respect were members of the post–World War II generation of professional economists from the LDCs.

Part of the human side of Johnson's links with the developing world lay in his selfless dedication of time, energy, and ideas to individuals and institutions there. Another part lay in the profound moral messages that permeate his writings concerning the developing countries. In his observations he was never naive, always realistic, never pusil-

HARRY G. JOHNSON   639

lanimous, always forthright. No one who reads his writings can fail to
sense that here was a man who cared deeply about improving the
physical well-being and the human dignity of the millions upon millions of individuals born into poverty and misery. Like other seers
throughout history, he recognized the fallibility and corruptibility of
men and institutions. His deep understanding of the human condition and his willingness to look unpalatable truths squarely in the face
helped to give his judgments a special force and power. He was no
simple preacher, but a seasoned, sage, and sound observer of the real
world who saw, through many and inevitable obstacles, a path to
bettering the lot of humankind.

His views on foreign aid reveal the interplay of realism and moral
tone that characterizes much of his work. On the one hand he felt that
foreign aid was a good thing because it increases the availability of
real resources to societies with many needy people. On the other, it
goes from government to government through fiscal systems that are
often corrupt; sometimes it even ends up going from the poor (in
donor countries) to the rich (in the receiving societies). The resulting
waste, together with the stridency of demands by some representatives of the developing countries, leads to disillusionment within the
donor societies and to a decline in the flow of aid. Therefore the
"useful life" of foreign aid is limited—one must use it well to induce
developing countries to reform their economic policies so that they
will be able to take fuller advantage of the opportunities for long-run
development that can follow from an intelligent application of economic principles.

Just as he did not mince words in talking about corruption, he was
forthright on the interactions of economic, political, and social forces.
This was partly reflected by his role as a founding member of the
Committee on New Nations at the University of Chicago. In his writings it came through in many places, perhaps nowhere more concisely
and characteristically than in the following statement: "To my mind,
economic development is an integral part of the process of social
development and social development consists of democratization and
increased personal freedom, which means destroying the powers of
the *élites* and not merely switching the party or social class label of the
élite that commands the power [of] the State" (1974, p. 9).

References

Johnson, Harry G. "The De-stabilising Effect of International Commodity
    Agreements on the Prices of Primary Products." *Econ. J.* 60 (September
    1950): 626–29.
———. "Notes on Economic Development and the Maximum Rate of
    Growth." *Malayan Econ. Rev.* 2 (April 1957): 16–22.

————. "Effects of Changes in Comparative Costs as Influenced by Technical Change." *Malayan Econ. Rev.* 6 (October 1961): 1–13.

————. "Economic Growth and Economic Policy." In *The Canadian Quandary: Economic Problems and Policies.* Toronto: McGraw-Hill, 1963. (*a*)

————. "Towards a Generalized Capital Accumulation Approach to Economic Development." In *The Canadian Quandary: Economic Problems and Policies.* Toronto: McGraw-Hill, 1963. (*b*)

————. "Tariffs and Economic Development: Some Theoretical Issues." *J. Development Studies* 1 (October 1964): 3–30.

————. "Optimal Trade Intervention in the Presence of Domestic Distortion." In *Trade, Growth, and the Balance of Payments: Essays in Honor of Gottfried Haberler,* by Robert E. Baldwin et al. Amsterdam: North-Holland, 1965. (*a*)

————. "The Theory of Tariff Structure, with Special Reference to World Trade and Development." In *Trade and Development* (with Peter B. Kenen). Geneva: Librairie Droz, 1965. (*b*)

————. *Trade and Development* (with Peter B. Kenen). Geneva: Librairie Droz, 1965. (*c*)

————. "The Neo-Classical One-Sector Growth Model: A Geometrical Exposition and Extension to a Monetary Economy." *Economica* 33 (August 1966): 265–87. (*a*)

————. "Sugar Protectionism and the Export Earning of Less Developed Countries: Variations on a Theme by R. H. Snape." *Economica* 33 (February 1966): 34–42. (*b*)

————. *Economic Nationalism in Old and New States.* Chicago: Univ. Chicago Press, 1967. (*a*)

————. *Economic Policies toward Less Developed Countries.* Washington: Brookings Inst., 1967. (*b*)

————. *Trade and Aid Policies: The UNCTAD Alternatives.* Washington: Brookings Inst., 1967. (*c*)

————. *Comparative Cost and Commercial Policy Theory for a Developing World Economy.* Stockholm: Almqvist & Wiksell, 1968.

————. "Thrust and Response: The Multinational Corporation as a Development Agent." *Columbia J. World Bus.* 5 (May/June 1970): 25–30.

————. "Labour Mobility and the Brain Drain." In *The Gap between Rich and Poor Nations,* edited by Gustav Ranis. London: Macmillan, 1972.

————. "International Trade and Economic Development." In *Trade Strategies for Development,* edited by Paul Streeten. London: Macmillan, 1973. (*a*)

————. "Trade, Investment and Labor, and the Changing International Division of Production." In *Prospects for Partnership: Industrialization and Trade Policies in the 1970's,* edited by Helen Hughes. Baltimore: Johns Hopkins Univ. Press (for World Bank), 1973. (*b*)

————. "The Western Model of Economic Development." *World Development* 2 (February 1974): 9–10.

————. *Technology and Economic Interdependence.* London: Macmillan (for Trade Policy Res. Centre), 1975.

————. *Trade Negotiations and the New International Monetary System.* Geneva: Graduate Inst. Internat. Studies, 1976. (*a*)

————. "World Inflation, the Developing Countries, and 'An Integrated Programme for Commodities.'" *Banca Naz. del Lavoro Q.,* no. 119 (December 1976), pp. 309–35. (*b*)

————. "Changing Views on Trade and Development: Some Reflections." In

HARRY G. JOHNSON 641

Essays on Economic Development and Cultural Change in Honor of Bert F. Hoselitz, edited by Manning Nash. *Econ. Development and Cultural Change* 25 (suppl.; 1977): S363–S375. (*a*)

———. *Money, Balance-of-Payments Theory, and the International Monetary Problem.* Essays in International Finance no. 124. Princeton, N.J.: Princeton Univ. Press, 1977. (*b*)

———. "Technology, Technical Progress and the International Allocation of Economic Activity." In *The International Allocation of Economic Activity: Proceedings of a Nobel Symposium,* edited by Bertil Ohlin, Per-Ove Hesselborn, and Per Magnus Wijkman. London: Macmillan, 1977. (*c*)

[8]

Harry Johnson as a Social Scientist

Richard E. Caves

Harvard University

"One of the penalties—or privileges, as the case may be—of advancing age and professional maturation in an academic career in the social sciences is that one is forced to think in terms of progressively broadening frames of institutional and cultural reference." So Harry Johnson (1975*b*, p. ix) prefaced his principal collection of essays on the social frontiers of economics. The widening sweep of his intellectual searchlight illuminated its targets not so much with originality of insight or breadth of social and cultural perception as with the penetrating power of his critical and analytical intellect. Johnson thought that the world revolved not from love but from individual utility maximization. These writings gain their unifying distinction from the remorseless application of its logic to interpreting economic and social behavior and criticizing economic policies. Although Johnson did not accord to the competitive market unlimited power to maximize human welfare, he did heap scorn on policies that took less than the full measure of rational behavior by the affected individuals and groups.

Another feature distinguishing many of these writings is their grasp of a large system of intersecting social and political forces. One reads with some surprise of Johnson's early fascination with Marxian analysis (Reuber and Scott 1977, p. 671). The Marxian postulates and analytical concepts were discarded long ago, but there survived a disposition to place social and political institutions on their foundations of the technology of production (and consumption, Johnson added) and the associated distribution of ownership claims and, in particular, to view political behavior as the outcome of economic interest groups.[1]

---

[1] Johnson (1974, p. 5) branded "clearly inadequate" the Marxian view that "the social, political, and ideological superstructure is determined by the technological and eco-

[*Journal of Political Economy*, 1984, vol. 92, no. 4]

HARRY G. JOHNSON   643

This essay attempts to draw together Johnson's ideas on three subjects: changing social phenomena and their foundations in rational individual behavior, the operation of political systems and their effect on the substance of economic policy, and the working of the university and the intellectual marketplace.

I. Social Phenomena and Rational Individual Behavior

Many of Johnson's thoughts about the economic characteristics of modern society grew from his reflections on John Kenneth Galbraith's *The Affluent Society* (1958). Although Johnson felt no sympathy for Galbraith's central conclusions, he was intrigued by the book's central question: What are the economically distinctive features of a society that has reached unprecedented high levels of income per capita? It offers to individuals greater personal freedom and broader opportunities for self-fulfillment, interesting careers, and more satisfying rewards for the development of personal talents. For most people it changes the basis for participation in production, so that it comes to rest on "personal knowledge, training, and education rather than on property ownership or the supply of labor time." The ascending importance of managerial ability and human capital in production processes makes every man a capitalist and contributes to social stability. The rising value of labor time also increases the capital intensity of household consumption. Even military technology had responded to the rising economic and social value of human life, with the United States leading the effort to substitute the sacrifice of material inputs for human lives as the cost of military conflict (Johnson 1975*b*, pp. 4–5).

Against these gains, Johnson felt that the affluent society imposes a series of hazards on its members. The household unit finds that most of its important choices are investment decisions with long pay-out periods, which demand complex calculations requiring elaborate information. These investments are often highly specialized, so that a bad forecast can produce results much worse than the decision maker expected. Smaller family units and looser ties mean less self-insurance within the family. As a result, noncapable decision makers are in most risk-exposed positions. Long periods of education (investment in human capital) reduce the individual's sense of control over his life. Affluence promotes and to some degree requires economic growth

---

nomic substructure, and specifically by the distribution of property rights associated with the system of production," because the "allegedly determinate superstructures react back on and change the economic substructure," and the technical substructure itself changes in response to human efforts to change and improve it.

and agglomeration; these bring a welter of externalities, with their potential for social conflict and market failure. These perceived social problems of affluence, Johnson felt, could be much clarified by application of such modern economic concepts as human capital, externality, and permanent income (1975*b*, chaps. 1–4).[2]

Human Capital

Johnson felt that the concept of human capital had "tremendous integrative power" to unify our understanding both of the labor market and of the household's decision problems. In the workplace the classical dichotomy between produced and original factors of production becomes increasingly meaningless. All factor inputs are best regarded as capital, their rewards consisting of a wage (interest and depreciation) plus a rent associated with the factor's ultimate scarcity (1975*b*, p. 43). The restrictive practices of professional organizations and trade unions are investments in the protection of quasi rents,[3] and "even the commitment of labor to the nationalization of certain industries can be interpreted as reflecting the desire to bring additional coercive power over the rest of society to bear in defense of the return to investment in . . . human capital" (1975*b*, pp. 20–21).

Johnson's concern with the acquisition of human capital dealt more sympathetically with the uncertainty and vulnerability of the investment than with the problems of income distribution that it poses. The ideology of a liberal democratic society supposes that the individual can be adequately equipped to cope, once provided with minimum education and socialized pensions. However, the complex knowledge required for prudent human-capital investments and the risks imposed by dynamic change call this into question. Personal risks are insurable in principle, but economic risks are unpredictable and hence uninsurable. The small size of the family unit condemns it to an undiversified portfolio of human capital, so that it is exposed to risks of illness, accident, and death, economic risks, and risks associated with inept policy choices. The family needs information and geographic and occupational mobility to make the most of its opportunities, but these are costly. Human capital in hand has some collateral value (consumer credit), but Johnson (1975*b*, pp. 47–49) felt that the inability to borrow on binding contracts against future quasi rents to human capital condemns this market to underinvestment in the ab-

---

[2] The earliest of these essays appeared in 1960. Papers discussed in this essay often made their first appearance in hard-to-find sources; citations will therefore be made to convenient reprinted versions.

[3] Krueger (1974) was later to develop this notion.

sence of public intervention. Family pride in education and the opportunity to make intergenerational transfers without inheritance tax, however, cut the other way.

Human-capital investments (on-the-job training excepted) cannot be financed like other investments, and Johnson wrote about various difficulties with the second-best procedures used instead. The provision of "free" university education has been undertaken by public authorities who often lose sight of the substantial remaining cost to the student of forgone income, and Johnson (1968) blamed some of the troubles of British universities in the 1960s on dissonant views of students and politicians about how much gratitude was due the latter from the former. An issue of more analytical substance arose in the "brain drain." Most countries underprice education and implicitly recoup the cost through progressive income taxes. Human capital is internationally mobile, however, and so it pays the individual once educated to migrate to a country offering higher pay or merely imposing a less progressive income tax. The country of emigration can lose because it then fails to collect tax revenue from the educated person equal to the cost of education supplied. An intergenerational transfer occurs if the current working generation pays to educate the next generation in the unfulfilled hope of being supported in retirement. A loss to society at large occurs, however, only if the incentive to migrate rests on differences in tax systems or if any externalities of educated people are greater in their birthplace than in the land to which they migrate (Johnson 1967b; 1975b, pp. 26–27).[4] Johnson felt that the national costs associated with the brain drain were generally overstated but that nonetheless they argue for loading more of the cost of education on the student.

Income Distribution and Poverty

Johnson (1975b, chap. 14) regarded a preference for equality in the income distribution as an ethical choice lying outside of economic analysis and the definition of poverty as economically arbitrary. Nonetheless, he felt that economic reasoning could do much to clarify the assessment of and prescription for each problem. To evaluate the maldistribution of income sensibly, one must apply the concept of permanent income. Different choices about early investments in human capital imply large differences in individuals' lifetime income profiles and, hence, some of the appearance of poverty in the distri-

---

[4]Johnson noted that the tendency to international equalization of the wages of educated people implied a widening of their scarcity rents in most countries (especially less-developed), with ensuing economic and social conflict.

bution of current income. Consumption needs also vary over the life cycle, to the same effect. The cross-section distribution of income reflects households' differing voluntary choices about their rates of saving and family formation, preferences regarding the balance of work and leisure and the regularity of the work pattern, and attitudes toward the riskiness of various possible jobs. One source of poverty in the affluent society is bad luck in the choice of specialized investments by individuals in skills or geographic location, a clear case for insurance through social assistance transfers (1975*b*, pp. 29–30).

The definition of poverty and policies toward it similarly need the application of economic analysis, Johnson (1975*b*, chap. 15) believed. Poverty is normally defined not by an absolute standard but by a moving one that maintains a fairly stable relation to average income. Economic growth tends to eliminate poverty only if it raises the share of productive assets owned by groups with initially lower incomes— not a likely outcome. The incidence of poverty also reflects utility-maximizing choices. Members of a multigenerational family group choosing to live under one roof might enjoy incomes on average above the poverty line, whereas some statistical poverty would appear if each generation maintains its own dwelling (1975*b*, pp. 28–29). Johnson was more concerned about poverty due to cultural restrictions on rational family planning and "weaknesses in the legal system governing the economic claims of mothers on the fathers of their children." If we are to make comparisons of current income, Johnson (1975*a*, pp. 12–15) warns that complex adjustments are necessary: labor income becomes current wages minus both interest on past investments in human capital and the costs of supporting the worker in retirement and raising children as replacements. Similarly, comparisons of the distribution of wealth ought to go beyond easily marketable assets to include, for example, the capital value of rights to the acquisition and maintenance of human capital provided free by the public sector. Poverty also results from discrimination, and Johnson (1975*b*, pp. 227–28) gave particular emphasis to discrimination against women. "In advanced industrial society, where reasonably good health and trained intelligence rather than muscular strength constitute the foundation of productive contribution, the traditional assignment of women to household management and child rearing is an anachronism." He held that society should choose between making women really equal, redesigning the family to relieve the differential burden it places on women, and acknowledging that the role of the household manager in maintaining the household is as exacting as the "breadwinner's."

The economist's preference for relieving poverty by outright income transfers clashes with the humanitarian's fondness for giving benefits in kind, and Johnson (1975*b*, pp. 232–35) sought to explain how the humanitarians come by their choice. The familiar paternalistic arguments assert that the poor should be induced to consume goods and services of which their humanitarian donors approve, so that "under the guise of improving the poor they are really seeking to create a society more deferential to people like themselves." Redistribution in kind thus serves to combat a negative externality for the middle-class majority from witnessing the behavior of people with preference functions different from their own. Better arguments for redistribution in kind, Johnson noted, are that they can partially correct for other market failures (food stamps as an offset to agricultural price supports, education countering imperfect markets in human capital). Also, they may help to avert the transference of poverty-prone attitudes from parents to children and the equipping of children with insufficient productive capacities.

Johnson (1975*b*, pp. 233–34) also noted that many poverty programs preferred by noneconomists presume that the poverty results from some social disequilibrium, so that those fallen into poverty could be restored with a relatively small social expenditure. Different conclusions tend to flow from economists' view of poverty as an equilibrium of choice and opportunity based on myopia, leisure preference, aversion to industrial discipline, or limited talents and capabilities.

Clear thinking about unemployment, he held, also requires recognition of the elements of individual choice lying behind it. The socially optimal value of any single index of unemployment depends not just on labor-market frictions and many economic policies but also on elements of voluntary choice. The leisure-labor trade-off is affected by unemployment benefits and social security but also by such factors as increased education, which eases the financing of voluntary unemployment. Differences in leisure preference may be implicit in higher long-run levels of unemployment in some regions. The leisure-labor preference itself is changed by the trappings of the affluent society. Technological change has predominantly raised the preference for leisure by lowering the relative cost of equipment used in leisure-time activities, but Johnson (1975*b*, pp. 22–23) was also intrigued by the possibility that some technological innovations in consumption might substitute material inputs for time in the creation of utility from leisure, thus raising labor supply. He was unimpressed by one economic influence asserted to affect the work-leisure choice—that of social security and the taxes to finance it (1975*b*, pp. 57–58); educated people are driven by the challenge of accomplishment, not the fear of hunger, and "work best when they have the security to concentrate on the job they are qualified to do." Also, the issue is a less urgent one in the affluent society with its revealed preference for increased leisure-time activities.

Externality and Property Rights

Johnson (1975*b*, pp. 5, 13) counted an increase in the perceived incidence of external diseconomies (pollution, congestion) as a market failure of the affluent society, because affluence is closely allied with overall economic growth and urbanization. But he relied heavily on the improved definition of property rights as the solution, with government interventions appropriate only where transaction costs frustrated a market solution. He heaped scorn (1975*b*, pp. 332–36) on people who would renounce present-day affluence because it allows too many others to compete with them for the private enjoyment of what we treat as public goods, yet he recognized (p. 13) a growing tension with the "common democratic presumption that every citizen regardless of income has a right to share in the original beauties of the natural environment, and that it is one of the functions of government to maintain and preserve that right." He emphasized once again the unifying role of capital theory for dealing with environmental problems. The environment provides a set of capital assets that can be either augmented or impaired by social progress, and their optimal exploitation or restoration can be managed only through investment decisions that properly value present and future benefits and costs.

II. Behavior of Political Decision Systems

In his technical writings, Johnson (1965, p. 256) expressed skepticism rather early about the traditional liberal posture of assuming that an identifiable way exists to maximize real income along social welfare lines and that the government wants to follow this course but needs only the analytical talents of an economist to tell it how to proceed. He thereafter showed recurrent interest in the behavioral approach to governmental decisions built with economic tools by Downs (1957) and others. Elected governments or political parties maximize votes in pursuit of various tangible rewards. The efficient development of their policy stances is hampered, however, by high costs of information, and so much information on voter preferences is injected by interest groups and lobbyists (and also the communication media). Likewise, the voters' investments in information about the policy stances of political parties are sharply limited, because the individual ballot has negligible power to influence political outcomes. Low-cost communication is provided by ideology, which reduces the detail that a party needs to relay to its potential adherents. Johnson (1967*a*, chap. 1) stressed ideology's role in shaping the political systems of less developed countries. Where voters' preferences for ideology are unimodal, as seems common in industrial countries, a two-party system tends to evolve with a good deal of imitation between the parties and jostling for the central position. Where democracy is less well established, however, the party in power has a strong incentive to forge a comprehensive and preclusive ideology in order to retain exclusive control of the government. The party's incentive for this strategy is greater in an LDC because the alternative job opportunities for office holders tend to be less good than in a developed country, where a larger cadre of administrative jobs can be found in the private sector.

Johnson used these ideas to explain many patterns of public policy, but perhaps nowhere more successfully than with the economic policy of nationalism. He encountered nationalist ideologies frequently in both LDCs and his native Canada and saw behind many economic policies the intersecting forces of nationalist ideology and interest-group pressures. Nationalism in the LDCs serves as an integrative force and the chief propellant of collective efforts to accelerate economic development, but Johnson (1967a, chap. 1) found it to exact serious costs by imposing policies that are probably inappropriate. One conspicuous component of LDCs' ideologies (and not just theirs) is a preference for industrial production over other forms of economic activity, which can express itself in policies to expand the industrial sector and depress the marginal return to the resources it employs below their best alternative uses. He showed formally (1965) how a preference for industrial output could affect the level of tariff protection chosen by a country, its participation in negotiations leading to reciprocal tariff reductions, and its choice of partners for a customs union. Reviewing actual patterns of output preference, he suggested that specific industrial preferences are likely to vary somewhat with a country's level of development, reflecting differences in both its comparative advantage and its aspirations—poor countries seeking steel industries, more developed ones automobile assembly, and rather advanced ones the high-technology industries. His economic explanation of output preferences and related policies (1967a, pp. 6–9) drew upon the interest-group mechanism. Producer groups are the winners when the nationalistic ideology fosters a preference for placing status-giving jobs or property in the hands of nationals (see Breton 1964). This goal can be sought either by shifting the composition of output to create the preferred jobs or property (e.g., the preference for industrial output) or by removing these things from the hands of foreigners (restricting employment of foreign nationals or restricting the ownership of subsidiaries by foreign companies in order to place equity shares in domestic hands). These transfers serve both the collective consumption of nationalism and the domestic producer interests that benefit directly. They could also raise national economic welfare as conventionally measured if nationals were formerly discriminated against; but if less competent nationals get the same salaries as more competent foreigners, income is redistributed within the country.[5]

Johnson's thoughts on LDC nationalism probably grew from earlier bouts with the phenomenon in Canada. He had traced (1967a, chap. 6) a vicious circle in Canadian macroeconomic policies that began in the late 1950s, in which the key errors of commission and omission resulted from attempts to pursue nationalistic objectives with macroeconomic policy instruments. And he had attacked (1963, chap. 1) a Canadian proposal to curb the independence of foreign subsidiaries in Canada by promoting the sale of minority shareholdings to Canadian capitalists. Because the foreigners would still retain control of the companies, Johnson saw this proposal purely as service to local financial interest groups.

Other applications of behavioral theories of the political process yielded interesting if less sharp-edged results. The overall level of public-sector spending, he suggested (1975b, p. 25), might be inflated if majority coalitions succeed in loading part of the cost on unwilling minorities. But it might be suboptimal if the voters shun taxes to finance public goods. He concluded that some public-sector activities are probably overprovided (those "justified by a vague but persuasive national purpose"), others undersupplied. Johnson (1975b, chap. 13) found the political acquiescence in inflation somewhat resistant to an explanation from rational political behavior. A commitment by the government to maintain full employment locks it into asymmetrical situations that on balance generate inflation. But then why does the public vote a commitment to full employment that takes this form? Why does it give an election-bound government reason to think that a short-term bout of inflationary policy is likely on balance to win votes? An interest-group explanation did not satisfy Johnson; although the short-run losers from inflation (e.g., pensioners) may be politically weak, the general voter's contemplation of his permanent income and ultimate pensioner status cannot lead him indefinitely to support inflationary policies. Johnson held that informed public opinion under-

---

[5] Nationalism also supports a preference for regulation of the economic activity carried on by alien entrepreneurs, even if it does not indicate exactly how the market outcome should be changed. Johnson wrote on several occasions about the clash between the nation-state, with this built-in procedural preference for control, and the multinational company able to pursue options outside of any given country (see Johnson 1967a, pp. 13–14; 1975c, chap. 5).

stands the consequences of macroeconomic policy and indeed anticipates them, and he evidently could not countenance the suggestion
that the public votes on the basis of a short time horizon or a biased
valuation of the long-run potential relation between inflation and
unemployment.[6]

Occasionally Johnson's efforts to explain policies that fail to maximize real income led him to hint that voters' expressed preferences
might give significant weight to objectives not counted in the economist's conventional view of utility maximization. Policies for assisting
distressed regions tend to sustain factors of production in their traditional locations turning out marginal products smaller than they
could in other regions. This might be the preference, stressed by
Scitovsky (1976), for continuity rather than maximum income.[7] Also,
the upsurge of concern for poverty in the 1960s, as in the 1930s,
followed a period of sustained unemployment and could well reflect
the feeling of the middle class that the poor might be doing badly
relative to their own reasonable expectations, even if no worse off
relative to the average income recipient (Johnson 1975*b*, pp. 5, 29–
30, 220).

But if voters may violate the axioms of welfare economics, they can
also act in the long run to avert the force of ill-conceived macroeconomic policies of central governments, or simply react to the
differing regional incidence of these policies. Either consequence of
national policy leads voters to appeal to lower and more politically
sensitive levels of government, promoting the decentralization of federal systems and regional nationalism in countries with centralized
political organs. This trend of voters' preferences is supported by an
affluent society's increasing concern with externalities that are local in
their incidence and, hence, more the province of local governments
(Johnson 1975*b*, pp. 177–78).

Scattered through Johnson's writings are references to governmental behavior patterns in international economic negotiations. These
are too much of their time to warrant review in detail, but we can note
an emphasis that runs through them—the economic cost of confusing
national prestige with national interest (e.g., 1972*b*; 1975*b*, chap. 17).
International monetary relations then become "merely one sphere for
the contention of national rivalries." Because the pursuit of national

---

[6]He did flirt with the suggestion that the household division of labor involves an
imperfect contract that motivates the husband to vote for full employment, the wife for
lower prices.

[7]Even here, voters' choices may be rational, according to Johnson (1975*a*, p. 9). The
voter knows that political decisions are based on short time horizons and are always
reversible; hence the preferences registered at the ballot box rationally reflect maximization over a short time horizon.

power and prestige is a zero-sum game, its confusion with the pursuit of agreement on international economic relations (with their potential for positive-sum outcomes) is fundamentally divisive. Nations may negotiate institutional arrangements such as the Bretton Woods agreement that impose a politically agreeable but fictitious equality on members of the system, only to find (with the subsequent emergence of the dollar standard) that real differences in countries' economic situations determine what arrangements are actually viable. When national economic rationality does prevail in international economic relations, however, it tends to reach outcomes similar to those reached in individual bargaining. For example (1975c, p. 9), the free-rider problem explains governments' efforts to obtain for their citizens use of the modern technology without paying for the research that created it.

III. The University and the Production of Knowledge

Johnson's eye turned frequently to social influences on the development of economic analysis and the quirks of the institutions that house its practitioners. A lifetime commuter among three countries, a compulsive guest at many houses of intellect, and a connoisseur of the swordplay of professional debate, he was well placed to spot the secrets of personal and institutional effectiveness in the processes of research and scholarship.

He set down one major statement about the university as a socioeconomic institution (1975b, chap. 11) and touched on several passing issues related to how many of society's resources it should command. The university he saw as a multiproduct firm, with some of its outputs public goods and most of them inappropriately priced. It has traditionally been under little pressure to maximize or even contemplate the productivity of its resource use. It provides public goods "by either setting standards of taste for the rest of the population or enabling the rest of the population to increase its productivity, command over consumption goods, or both" (1975b, p. 153). Qualitatively, this public-good problem is correctly being solved by public support and cost-free availability of the public goods (notably research), but the quantity is not necessarily optimized. Outputs of the university with increasingly less public character are the storage, organization, and synthesis of information, provision of general undergraduate education, and provision of professional education.

Johnson suggested a series of hypotheses about the economic function of general university education: (1) that it chiefly fosters the maturation of its students (it does not matter what you study, so long as it is rigorous and conveys cultural ambience); (2) that it filters out those best qualified for the "good jobs" that society has to offer (in which case the resources wasted educating those who pass through the filter pose a major question of efficiency); and (3) that its economic function is to create human capital with a discernible market value (so that it should attract not necessarily the best students but rather the most educable). The relative explanatory power of these hypotheses evidently has major implications for both the commitment of resources to universities and the character of training that they provide. Several factors discourage rational thinking about these problems of allocating resources in the university. The human-capital hypothesis faces a strong ideological opposition to the postulate that a university functions to whittle round pegs for society's round holes. And the attitude that universities should redistribute income to the young and intellectually ambitious beclouds the rational pricing of university education. University teachers, wrapped in the banner of the self-governing community of scholars, have dealt themselves terms of compensation that adduce an activity pattern poorly aligned with maximizing the value of the university's social product. Government finance of universities is blighted by information constraints that misallocate resources toward the more measurable inputs and outputs and occasionally distort the total amount on suspiciously transitory grounds (the faith in universities as progenitors of economic growth during the 1950s and 1960s). University administrations have little incentive to fight the faculty's misallocation of effort because the waste is not perceived in the outside world and because in most times opportunities for the administrators to pursue the bureaucratic quiet life are abundantly present.

Johnson's thoughts about a university's relation to its students were mostly set down against the background of student protest in the 1960s. He was annoyed at university faculties' unwillingness to recognize that the current generation of students (understanding the university's "filter" function) had the incentive of transient customers to secure soft options and at their acquiescence in the fiction that the university is a sovereign state with "oppressed" and "oppressor" classes (1972a). But he recognized (1968) among the causes of protest the mutually disappointed expectations that had flowed from the great expansion of university education. Heavily expanded and democratized universities had diluted (through expansion) the quality of their teaching staffs, and by greatly increasing the supply of graduates, they could no longer guarantee them a clear track into prestige jobs. Neither outcome was necessarily bad if properly adjusted to, but both created a disequilibrium of expectations.

Science policy, an issue of intellectual resource use related to the organization of universities, also attracted Johnson (1972c; 1975c, chap. 2). He found a good deal of muddy thinking to criticize. Procedures for evaluating the funding of applied research were being inappropriately applied to basic research and thereby creating an inducement for proponents of science to make excessive claims for the immediate payout of basic research. Nations were falling into confusion between scientific inputs and outputs, not recognizing that the international communication of scientific results frays the input-output relation within the individual nation's borders. The United States' scientific leadership has rested on "the capacity to put science and technology to work in the service of raising the standard of living of the masses, and the capacity to mobilise science and technology on a massive scale in the development of superior armaments" (1975c, p. 16), but this success is not clearly connected to public support of basic research. Scientists may argue for the support of an evolving "science culture," but they thereby make science a consumption good that must establish its claim against other social consumption goods. In sum, although the private market alone would underinvest in research, it is not clear that the actual market (a mix of government, private, and charitable actors) does so. And it is clear that the competitive progress of science, with a scientist's reward due to acclaim by fellow scientists, bears no necessary connection to a test of social usefulness.

Oddly enough, Johnson—whose personal needs for research inputs did not extend beyond pads of yellow paper—never applied these thoughts to the allocation of research resources to and within the economics profession.[8] The nearest he came was to address the question how far to extend programs of graduate education in economics (1973). These had proliferated during the 1960s (at least in Canada) beyond the optimal level. The proliferation had been promoted on the proposition that teaching and research interact. But this does not mean, he held, that they need to be carried on either by the same individual or at the same institution. He clearly felt that the research elite of the profession should be allowed to collect at leading institutions of graduate instruction, undistracted by undergraduates and free to enjoy the fruits of intellectual agglomeration and scale economies in graduate instruction. This might seem unfair to those sent down to teach the principles course, but it was an efficient use of resources.

---

[8]He wrote (1975a, p. 6): "I myself am fairly phlegmatic about and not much concerned with the question of whether economics is immediately socially useful in solving the current problems of society as society itself conceives them. . . . The current demand for 'relevance' . . . invariably amounts to an effort to force economists to lend their voices . . . to propaganda in support of the demander's political program."

HARRY G. JOHNSON   655

Development of Economic Analysis

Johnson wrote about both the influence of environmental conditions
on the progress of economics and the forces governing the outcomes
of debates within the profession. His travels among Canada, Britain,
and the United States caused him to compare the effectiveness of
their ambient conditions for nurturing scholarship (1975*b*, chap. 9).
After World War II the United States had both the material resources
and the aura of confidence to provide economists with a supportive
environment. Also, scholars abroad reaching professorial status automatically become elite figures and score their points outside of intellectual endeavor, whereas the academic world of the United States is
more self-contained and competitive. A pragmatic interest in research, boosted by the Sputnik boom in science, helped to consolidate
and advance the American profession's lead. University tenure systems in the United States emphasize the requirement to "publish or
perish," which disimpacts knowledge and discourages scholars from
indulging in personal idiosyncrasy. The sheer size of the American
economics profession allows a number of institutions to assemble critical masses of qualified people with serious research interests. Also
(1975*b*, p. 151), it discourages scholars from "setting themselves up as
across-the-board personal adversaries expounding conflicting holistic
views of the subject" in favor of the modern economist's competition
with the faceless host of his professional colleagues.

Anglo-American differences in political systems are also important,
as is the general influence on economists' behavior of occasional work
for the government. Ventures into policymaking subvert economic
discourse into political rhetoric and cast economists in ill-suited roles
"as both interpreters of the political will and eager servants of their
own interpretation of it" (1974, p. 8; see also 1975*b*, chap. 10). But
Johnson recognized (1975*b*, pp. 177–79) that an expanding government demand for economists had allowed professional training to
attain economies of scale and enlarged the pool of talent from which
the future academic stars are drawn. The casual involvement of U.S.
economists in government he found to be rather more benign and
scientifically oriented than in Britain, where their public-sector work
is less likely to lead to scholarly publication and more likely to cater to
the current and prospective interests of one political party.

Johnson relied totally on the competition for esteem among highly
skilled economists as the best guide for scientific progress, against any
test that might be imposed from the outside. However, his faith in this
nonmarket allocation mechanism did not blind him to the effects of
the participants' finite human abilities and the moral hazard associated with scoring debating points. In various writings (1975*b*, chaps.

5–8) he reflected on the success of the Keynesian revolution and its challenge by the monetarist counterrevolution. In a scientific discipline an "orthodoxy" is necessary and desirable to facilitate communication in the profession and promote cumulative additions to knowledge, but it builds vested interests that resist any major overhaul (1975*b*, chap. 7). Both the Keynesian revolution and monetarist counterrevolution thus found their opportunities only when the prevailing orthodoxies had become unable to explain some facts of pressing importance. The would-be revolution then has to "attack the central proposition of conservative orthodoxy." It has to appear new and yet absorb enough of the valid elements of the prevailing orthodoxy to usurp the whole territory. It has to be hard enough to understand that young "comers" in the profession will invest in it in order to unseat more senior figures unable or unwilling to make the investment. It has to allow room for new or stylish methodologies of theoretical and empirical research. With evident glee Johnson analyzed how both Keynes and the monetarists had managed in their times to meet all these tests.

The challenge of radical economics also caught Johnson's eye (1977). Although intellectually unsympathetic, he took a detached view of what he saw as a failed attempt at an intellectual revolution. The interest of economists in social philosophy was driven undergound by McCarthyism, "the period of witch-hunting on behalf of cultural purity and loyalty that has twice followed involvement of an immigration-based new nation in a totalitarian-democratic foreign war" (1977, p. 99). The expansion of government employment for economists and the post-Sputnik faith of the public in science as panacea all maintained this suppression. And economics teaching, lacking a market test and drawn toward preprofessional subject matter, increasingly lost contact with the humanistic tradition. When the Vietnam War shifted the balance, the scientific cast of standard research and training in economics both weakened and strengthened the traditionalists' response to the radical challenge. It was strengthened because the Keynesian and post-Keynesian experience in debating emotionally charged issues had instilled the attitude that conflicting ideas should be turned into testable propositions. But it was weakened by a habitual assumption that the protesters "were scientifically rational and maturely sincere in their protest." In any case, the radicals did not meet the test for a successful intellectual revolution, and Johnson saw its members as being ingested into the profession as they sought out viable research options in economic history and the history of thought.

The great bulk of Johnson's writing in social science is positive or

HARRY G. JOHNSON   657

only tentatively normative, but he did not conceal his views about the appropriate conduct of economic research itself. He applauded the increasing acceptance of the competitive model and pragmatism in the treatment of values as yielding increased professional competence and confidence (1975*b*, pp. 19–20). Given a diverse scientific community that judges the value of research projects and the quality of research design and execution, there is no great need for concern that partisanship will influence the selection of projects or result from the findings of scientifically conceived research (1975*b*, pp. 140–42). "Much of the work of economists concerned with policy issues is devoted to sorting out the true ends of policy from the means intended to achieve these ends, and to assessing the relevance and relative efficiencies of the various means proposed—in short, to determining what the problem really is, and attempting to evaluate the various ways of solving it" (1975*b*, p. 18).

References

Breton, Albert. "The Economics of Nationalism." *J.P.E.* 72, no. 4 (August 1964): 376–86.

Downs, Anthony. *An Economic Theory of Democracy.* New York: Harper, 1957.

Galbraith, John Kenneth. *The Affluent Society.* Boston: Houghton Mifflin, 1958.

Johnson, Harry G. *The Canadian Quandary: Economic Problems and Policies.* Toronto: McGraw-Hill, 1963.

———. "An Economic Theory of Protectionism, Tariff Bargaining, and the Formation of Customs Unions." *J.P.E.* 73, no. 3 (June 1965): 256–83.

———, ed. *Economic Nationalism in Old and New States.* Chicago: Univ. Chicago Press, 1967. (*a*)

———. "Some Economic Aspects of Brain Drain." *Pakistan Development Rev.* 7 (Autumn 1967): 379–411. (*b*)

———. "The Economics of Student Protest." *New Soc.* 12 (November 7, 1968): 673–75.

———. "The Dilution of Academic Power in Canada." *Minerva* 10 (July 1972): 486–90. (*a*)

———. "The International Monetary System and the Rule of Law." *J. Law and Econ.* 15 (October 1972): 277–92. (*b*)

———. "Some Economic Aspects of Science." *Minerva* 10 (January 1972): 10–18. (*c*)

———. "The Uneasy Case for Universal Graduate Programmes in Economics." *Minerva* 11 (April 1973): 263–68.

———. "Individual and Collective Choice." In *Man and the Social Sciences,* edited by William A. Robson. Beverly Hills, Calif.: Sage, 1974.

———. "Equity and Economic Theory." *Nebraska J. Econ. and Bus.* 14 (Summer 1975): 3–17. (*a*)

———. *On Economics and Society.* Chicago: Univ. Chicago Press, 1975. (*b*)

———. *Technology and Economic Interdependence.* London: Macmillan (for Trade Policy Res. Centre), 1975. (*c*)

————. "Economics and the Radical Challenge: The Hard Social Science and the Soft Social Reality." In *Culture and Its Creators: Essays in Honor of Edward Shils*, edited by Joseph Ben-David and Terry N. Clark. Chicago: Univ. Chicago Press, 1977.

Krueger, Anne O. "The Political Economy of the Rent-seeking Society." *A.E.R.* 64 (June 1974): 291–303.

Reuber, Grant L'., and Scott, Anthony D. "Harry Gordon Johnson, 1923–1977." *Canadian J. Econ.* 10 (November 1977): 670–77.

Scitovsky, Tibor. *The Joyless Economy: An Inquiry into Human Satisfaction and Consumer Dissatisfaction.* New York: Oxford Univ. Press, 1976.

Name Index

Pioneers in Economics

Section I: The Forerunners of Classical Economics

1. The Historiography of Economics

2. Aristotle (384–322 B.C.)

3. St Thomas Aquinas (1225–1274)

4. The Early Mercantilists
   Thomas Mun (1571–1641), Edward Misselden (1608–1634), Gerard de Malynes (1586–1623)

5. The Later Mercantilists
   Josiah Child (1603–1699) and John Locke (1632–1704)

6. Pre-Classical Economists Volume I
   Charles Davenant (1656–1714) and William Petty (1623–1687)

7. Pre-Classical Economists Volume II
   Pierre le Pesant Boisguilbert (1645–1714), George Berkeley (1685–1753), Baron de Montesquieu (1689–1755), Ferdinando Galiani (1727–1787), James Anderson (1739–1808), Dugald Stewart (1753–1828)

8. Pre-Classical Economists Volume III
   John Law (1671–1729) and Bernard Mandeville (1660–1733)

9. Richard Cantillon (1680–1734) and Jacques Turgot (1727–1781)

10. François Quesnay (1694–1774) Volumes I and II

11. David Hume (1711–1776) and James Steuart (1712–1780)

Section II: The Golden Age of Classical Economics

12. Adam Smith (1723–1790) Volumes I and II

13. Henry Thornton (1760–1815), Jeremy Bentham (1748–1832), James Lauderdale (1759–1839), Simonde de Sismondi (1773–1842)

14. David Ricardo (1772–1823)

15. Jean-Baptiste Say (1776–1832)

16. Thomas Robert Malthus (1766–1834) and John Stuart Mill (1806–1873)

17. Ramsay McCulloch (1789–1864), Nassau Senior (1790–1864), Robert Torrens (1780–1864)

18. Thomas Tooke (1774–1858), Mountifort Longfield (1802–1884), Richard Jones (1790–1855)

19. William Whewell (1794–1866), Dionysius Lardner (1793–1859), Charles Babbage (1792–1871)

20. George Scrope (1797–1876), Thomas Attwood (1783–1856), Edwin Chadwick (1800–1890), John Cairnes (1823–1875)

21. James Mill (1773–1836), John Rae (1796–1872), Edward West (1782–1828), Thomas Joplin (1790–1847)

22. James Wilson (1805–1860), Issac Butt (1813–1879), T. E. Cliffe Leslie (1827–1882)

23. Karl Marx (1818–1883)

Section III: Neoclassical Economics and its Critics

24. Johann von Thünen (1783–1850), Augustin Cournot (1801–1877), Jules Dupuit (1804–1866)

25. Leon Walras (1834–1910)

26. Carl Menger (1840–1921)

27. Eugen von Böhm-Bawerk (1851–1914) and Friedrich von Wieser (1851–1926)

28. Knut Wicksell (1851–1926)

29. Alfred Marshall (1842–1924) and Francis Edgeworth (1845–1926)

30. Gustav Schmoller (1838–1917) and Werner Sombart (1863–1941)

31. Dissenters
Charles Fourier (1772–1837), Henri de St Simon (1760–1825), Pierre-Joseph Proudhon (1809–1865), John A. Hobson (1858–1940)

32. Thorstein Veblen (1857–1929)

33. Wesley Mitchell (1874–1948), John Commons (1862–1945), Clarence Ayres (1891–1972)

34. Henry George (1839–1897)

35. Vilfredo Pareto (1848–1923)

Section IV: Twentieth Century Economics

36. Arthur Pigou (1877–1959)

37. Frank Knight (1885–1972), Henry Simons (1899–1946), Joseph Schumpeter (1883–1950)

38. Edward Chamberlin (1899–1967)

39. Michal Kalecki (1899–1970)

40. Harold Hotelling (1895–1973), Lionel Robbins (1898–1984), Clark Warburton (1896–1979), John Bates Clark (1847–1938), Ludwig von Mises (1881–1973)

41. Irving Fisher (1867–1947), Arthur Hadley (1856–1930), Ragnar Frisch (1895–1973), Friedrich von Hayek (1899–1992), Allyn Young (1876–1929), Ugo Mazzola (1863–1899)

42. Harry Johnson (1923–1977)

43. Bertil Ohlin (1899–1979)

44. Piero Sraffa (1898–1983)

45. Joan Robinson (1903–1983) and George Shackle (1903–1992)

46. John Maynard Keynes (1883–1946) Volumes I and II